IN BLACK & WHITE

125 MOMENTS THAT MADE
COLLINGWOOD

MICHAEL ROBERTS & GLENN McFARLANE

NERO

Published by Nero,
an imprint of Schwartz Publishing Pty Ltd
Level 1, 221 Drummond Street
Carlton VIC 3053, Australia
enquiries@blackincbooks.com
www.nerobooks.com

National Library of Australia Cataloguing-in-Publication entry:
Roberts, Michael, 1961– author.
In black and white: 125 moments that made Collingwood /
Michael Roberts, Glenn MacFarlane.
9781863958905 (hardback)
9781925435399 (ebook)
Collingwood Football Club—History.
Australian football teams—Victoria—Collingwood—History.
Australian football—Victoria—Collingwood—History.
McFarlane, Glenn, author.
796.336099451

Cover design by Peter Long
Text design and typesetting by Tristan Main
Cover photograph by *The Age*/Fairfax Photos

FOREWORD

Collingwood is all about big moments. It always has been. That's something that has set the Magpies apart from their rivals, since the time the club came into existence right through to the current day.

I was lucky enough to be involved in one of those big moments, the 1990 Premiership, when we finally won the flag after 32 long years. After being a member of two losing Grand Final sides, and with all the talk about the 'Colliwobbles' – which I never believed – the relief we felt winning that flag was overwhelming.

But the thing that struck me that day, and in the weeks and months afterwards, was just how happy the Magpie supporters were. I had a number of people come up to me and say they could die happy now that Collingwood had finally won another Premiership. That sums up what this football club means to so many of the people who support it.

My association with the Collingwood Football Club goes back long before I pulled on a black-and-white jumper. I was one of six kids and we all barracked for the Magpies, even though our parents didn't. At the school we went to, you didn't dare barrack for another club. I remember getting the 'Red Rattler' from Reservoir to Victoria Park to watch games. We would stand out in the outer with our mates; for young kids like us, it was like going to the Colosseum. Everything always seemed bigger at Collingwood – both the good and the not-so-good – and the scrutiny on the players and the club was greater than at any other club. It still is.

It has been nearly 40 years since I first went to Collingwood as a player, and so many big moments stand out for me. Many were on the field, but there were plenty off it as well. In some ways we caused trouble for ourselves: there were issues with the board (just think back to the 'New Magpies'), dramas with coaches (who could forget Tom Hafey being sacked?) and of course the recruiting wars of the 1980s.

A number of the stories in this book relate to a great Collingwood tradition: the importance of family. Over the years, we've had the Colliers, the Coventrys, the Pannams/Richards, the Roses, the Twomeys, the Richardsons, the Shaws and many more. I was so lucky to play with my brothers, Ray and Neville. And it was great to see Ray's sons, Heath and Rhyce, play senior football for Collingwood too.

In many ways, being part of Collingwood, whether you're a player, a coach, an official, a member or a supporter, is like being part of a big family. That's something that always remains with you.

Collingwood gave me my chance, and I will forever be grateful to it. All these years later, I still say the club owes me nothing and I owe it everything. That's why it is an honour to be able to write the foreword to this book, *In Black & White*.

I hope you enjoy reading about the 125 biggest moments of this truly remarkable club as much as I did.

Tony Shaw
September 2016

INTRODUCTION

As Collingwood fans, we experience the unfolding of our club's history week to week, year after year. So many things happen over the course of a year, and most are significant only in the context of the next game or the current season. But others end up having a huge long-term impact on the club.

Some, such as a career-ending injury to a star player or the sacking of a coach, are immediately recognisable as important. Others sneak up on us, their significance only becoming apparent over time. When Bob Rose made his debut in 1946, for example, he didn't have a kick in the first half. Who could have known then the impact he would have on the Collingwood Football Club over more than 40 years? Ditto with the recruiting of Peter Eakins in 1969/1970. Who could have foreseen then the knock-on effects of what seemed, at the time, nothing more than some long-overdue aggressive recruiting?

To mark Collingwood's 125th anniversary, we have – with the glorious benefit of hindsight – identified 125 of the most significant events in Collingwood's history. We've picked one from each year, and through those events told the club's story, from 1892 to today.

The moments we've chosen aren't only about the magical things that happened on the field. There are also heartbreaking setbacks, sackings and resignations, bloody board coups, cruel injuries, wicked twists of fate, strokes of administrative genius, fateful decisions and appointments, and examples of the best-laid plans going awry.

Together, these are the moments that shaped the Collingwood Football Club and helped make it what it is today: the largest, most famous and most storied sporting club in the country.

Long may it remain so.

1892

THE FIRST GAME

Collingwood's first 'official' game as a senior team was the sporting, social and cultural highlight of the year for those who lived in the suburb. It was also the culmination of nearly three years of hard work by the 'true believers' – the political, business and community leaders who had taken the dream of a Collingwood Football Club and turned it into reality.

More than 16,000 people – a phenomenal number for the time – crowded into Victoria Park on a glorious day in May, all of them buzzing with excitement, anticipation and, above all else, pride.

For it was pride that had driven the push for the establishment of the Collingwood Football Club in the first place. And it was pride that kept the campaign going for the best part of three years. So it was a landmark day for the local community when 20 young men wearing black-and-white striped jumpers ran out onto Victoria Park on 7 May 1892 to play the club's first game in the Victorian Football Association (VFA). The people of Collingwood, the suburb described by historian Bernard Barrett as having been 'crippled from birth', finally had a football team of their own.

But even the club's most optimistic advocates were blown away by the size of the crowd that turned up that first day. It confirmed the momentum that had been building right through the lobbying campaign, and especially since February, when the club held a public meeting to gauge community interest in the new venture. The response that night was overwhelming: the lecture room at the Collingwood Town Hall was filled to overflowing; many were forced to follow proceedings through an open window.

Speaker after speaker talked passionately about what the club would mean to Collingwood, and there were lavish predictions of success. Local MP John Hancock best summed up the mood of the night and elicited the biggest roars when he told the crowd that soon 'the very name Collingwood would strike terror into the hearts of opposition players'. He also set the standard for all future Magpie fans when he called on them to be at the grounds supporting the team, giving 'such unearthly shrieks as would terrify' opposing players kicking for goal.

It was, in all, a riotous evening. And the buzz it generated carried over into that first game. There was a truly festive air among the crowd that day. The team went down to Carlton by three goals to two – a highly creditable performance against a vastly more experienced opponent. But nobody cared too much about the result: the team's impressive effort, the huge numbers present and the passion displayed confirmed that Collingwood would soon be a force to be reckoned with.

The Magpies' debut season turned out to be the tough grind most had expected (although the club's membership of 400 was already the biggest in the VFA). The team won only three times for the year, and finished equal last.

But for possibly the only time in the club's history, the team's ladder position at the end of the season counted for little. All that mattered was that – at last – Collingwood had its own senior football team. The Magpies had arrived. And football would never be the same again.

H&A P18, W3, L14, D1 • **Finished** 13th • **Captain** Joe Delahunty • **Leading goalkickers** George Anderson & Archie Smith (12)

1893

BILL STRICKLAND ARRIVES

As Collingwood began its second season, it was clear that the playing list needed some major support.

Very few of the 1892 squad had previous senior experience, and those who did were almost on their last legs. The first captain, Joe Delahunty, lasted only four games into the 1893 season. His 1892 deputy, Tasmanian George Watt, would retire and head home within a year. And the man initially given the captaincy for 1893, Ken Macpherson, followed Watt to the Apple Isle.

Collingwood had a young list that was full of spirit and determination but in dire need of leadership. As the newest club on the block, it also lacked the pulling power needed to attract big-name recruits. But all that changed when Bill Strickland came to Victoria Park four games into the 1893 season.

Strickland was an established star of the game, after a magnificent career with Carlton. When he fell out with the Blues in a dispute over the captaincy, many clubs made a play for the 28-year-old. Remarkably, given the choices before him, he opted for the Magpies.

Strickland's arrival had several immediate and lasting impacts. First, it helped establish Collingwood as a club that good players would want to join. Another highly regarded Carltonite, George Williams, crossed with Strickland in 1893 and went on to be a key member of the 1896 Premiership team. Others, such as Fitzroy's William Callaghan, would follow.

Second, the team improved simply by having such a good player join their ranks. Broad-shouldered and strong-limbed, 'Strick' usually played in the centre or as a follower, and had come to be regarded as one of the best players in the game. He was strong, consistent, aggressive, a good mark and a splendid kick. He was also a masterful midfield general.

And it turned out he was still in peak condition. If the club had awarded a best-and-fairest medal in those days, he would have won it in at least two and possibly three of his five seasons at Collingwood. And in 1896, a Premiership year, he would later be named the Champion of the Colony – as close to a Brownlow Medal as you could get then. He was also widely acclaimed as the best player on the ground on Grand Final Day.

Perhaps most importantly, Strickland provided the leadership the club so desperately needed. He was appointed captain soon after his arrival, and would fill that role for the rest of his time at Collingwood. This was a time, remember, when there were no coaches: captains played a far bigger role directing activities on match days, and also in setting standards around the club.

The Collingwood players now had a true great of the game to look up to and learn from, and they followed Strickland's every instruction without questioning. This made it easier for him to instil far greater discipline right through the club, and he made it a particular focus to get the players combining together as a team, rather than playing as individuals.

Strickland's initial on-field impact was modest but significant: the Pies won four extra games in 1893 and finished ninth. More importantly, they now possessed one of the game's best players and great leaders. A key building block for future success was now in place.

H&A P19, W7, L10, D2 • **Finished** 9th • **Captain** Bill Strickland • **Leading goalkicker** George Anderson (20)

1894

THE CLASS OF '94

Bill Strickland's arrival gave Collingwood its first true star player. But the overall playing list, while improved, was still lacking in top-end talent, and it was not immediately obvious where the next batch of stars was going to come from.

As has so often been the case in football down the years, the answer ended up being simple: the Magpies turned to youth.

In 1893 the club had taken a major step towards developing its own talent by establishing the Collingwood Juniors. This was effectively the old Clifton Football Club, which had been the strongest of the local junior clubs in 1892. Collingwood president William Beazley became the first president of the Collingwood Juniors, and the new club was allowed to use Victoria Park. There wasn't much in the way of financial support in the first couple of years, but the Collingwood Juniors effectively became a 'feeder' club for the senior team.

The Juniors had already furnished the Pies with one youngster who would go on to be a star, the mighty Jack Monohan having debuted in 1893. With ex-Britannia player Bill Proudfoot, he formed a key defensive pairing that would dominate the next decade.

But in 1894 the club introduced a bumper crop of debutants. The Juniors produced three absolute beauties in Dick Condon, Charlie Pannam Snr and Frank Hailwood, while Lardie Tulloch joined from Carlton Juniors. Those four players, together with Proudfoot and Monohan, would form the core of not just the club's first Premiership, in 1896, but also the back-to-back flags of 1902–03.

Three of the 1894 quartet would go on to captain the club, and two – Pannam and Condon – were often rated among the best players in the competition. Each of the four played at least 150 games, and between them they ended up playing 735 games, kicking 353 goals and winning a swag of Premiership medals and other accolades.

Condon was a freakishly talented footballer who played mostly as a rover or centreman, though he also possessed a volatile temperament that would come to cost both him and the club dearly. Pannam was a fleet-footed wingman who dazzled opponents with his speed, skills and trickery, while Hailwood was an indefatigable follower/forward who tirelessly carried many of the big-man duties. And Tulloch, also a follower/forward, ended up achieving as much fame for his outstanding leadership skills as for his undoubted football ability.

Pannam, of course, also started football's most remarkable dynasty. One of his brothers, Albert, also played for the club, as did two of his five sons, Charlie Jnr and Alby, both of whom turned out to be bona fide stars. One of his daughters also came to the party by producing two sons who became Magpie legends, Lou and Ron Richards.

Back in 1894, Pannam, Condon, Tulloch and Hailwood were all just youngsters finding their feet in senior football, so their impact that season wasn't huge; the team rose just one spot to finish eighth. But the good judges at Victoria Park could see that the Magpies were building a team that could become formidable – and soon.

H&A P18, W8, L9, D1 • **Finished** 8th • **Captain** Bill Strickland • **Leading goalkicker** Archie Smith (25)

1895

ERN COPELAND'S FINANCIAL RESCUE

By 1894 the euphoria surrounding Collingwood's entry to football's big time had started to wane: membership and crowd numbers were down, and the club's financial position was looking precarious. By the end of that season, Collingwood found itself mired in a full-blown crisis – one that left the club's very existence in doubt.

The main reason was that the football club had been born in the early stages of a major global depression, and by 1894 it was biting hard – especially in industrial suburbs like Collingwood. The local Magpie fans still followed the club passionately, but they simply couldn't afford to attend as many games, let alone take out full-season memberships. The hit to club revenues was exacerbated by significant borrowings it incurred to build a new grandstand, and by the end of 1894 the club was deep in debt and staring into the financial abyss.

Collingwood needed some drastic action to right the ship. And the most significant change the club made was to bring in a new club secretary, Ern 'Bud' Copeland.

Copeland had been a clerk at the Metropolitan Gas Company. Despite having no football background, he took over at Collingwood for the 1895 season. Copeland knew what he was getting into, for he had audited the club's 1894 accounts, and upon setting foot in Victoria Park he immediately began to overhaul the club's finances.

He borrowed from a local patron to repay some immediate debts, then moved to attract more members by allowing them to pay for their season tickets in instalments and encouraging a more family-friendly feel at games. He also organised a series of highly successful fundraising projects: in his first year alone he arranged a gala concert, a cycling carnival at Victoria Park and a fancy-dress ball. All had the dual benefits of not only raising significant funds but also bringing the club even closer to the community.

By the end of his first year, Copeland was able to report that the club's financial position 'had very much improved'. Debts had been slashed, membership had risen by about 75 per cent, and donations more than doubled.

Copeland's financial makeover continued after 1895, achieving remarkable results. Most of the club's debts were paid off in just three years, while membership soared beyond 800 – double the level of its first season. It's unlikely that too many other senior sporting clubs formed at such a calamitous financial time would have survived. But the Magpies, under Ern Copeland's astute guidance, first hung on, and then flourished.

Just as importantly, Copeland also became captain Bill Strickland's keenest off-field ally in changing the club's culture, building on and backing the skipper's belief in discipline, unity and the subservience of individual interests to those of the team.

Ern Copeland's financial rescue act was aided by improved on-field results, with the Pies finishing fourth on the ladder but equal second on points. The genial Copeland would remain as secretary until 1924, and the importance of his contribution would later be recognised when the club's best-and-fairest award was named in his honour.

H&A P18, W12, L4, D2 • **Finished** 4th • **Captain** Bill Strickland • **Leading goalkicker** Archie Smith (27)

1896

THE FIRST FLAG

Things were looking bleak for Collingwood at three-quarter-time of football's first ever 'Grand Final'. The Pies hadn't kicked a goal since the first quarter, and although they trailed South Melbourne by only a goal, South had kicked two in the third term and seemed to have the momentum. It was a stiflingly hot October day, and a comeback seemed out of the question.

But not to Bill Strickland. At the last change he convinced his players of their superior physical fitness, and urged them to take the game on with quicker ball movement. He then pulled his master-stroke, shifting gun centre half-back Jack Monohan to centre half-forward.

That move changed the game. Monohan took three towering marks in the first few minutes of the final term, unsettling the South defenders and prompting wave after wave of Collingwood attacks. The war cry throughout that final term was 'Faster – make it faster!' and Collingwood ran all over their more experienced opponents. Frank 'Charger' Hailwood levelled the scores midway through the quarter, and then, just as extra time was looking likely, a free kick to Danny Flaherty allowed him to kick the winning goal.

The sounding of the final bell sparked wild celebrations at the ground but also throughout the suburb of Collingwood. More than 2000 locals turned out to the victory celebration at the Town Hall, while the parties, smoke nights and banquets that followed lasted over a month. One such function at the City Hotel in Johnston Street featured more than 80 speeches!

Local politicians took particular pleasure in the victory, rubbing it in the faces of those who had mocked both the municipality and the team. Mayor William Cody said the footballers were a credit to the city and had done much 'to do away with the bad name Collingwood once enjoyed'. Another councillor said the win had 'done so much to lift Collingwood in the eyes of the world'. (Yes, the *world*!)

It is almost impossible to overstate the significance of Collingwood's first flag. It gave Melbourne's most downtrodden residents something to be proud about, and cemented the club's place at the centre of the suburb's existence. It also helped change external perceptions. Until the flag, many observers actually liked Collingwood: they were happy to see the new boys from the slums doing so well. But success quickly changed that. Nobody had expected Collingwood to be this good – or this popular – so quickly.

That popularity prompted one of football's first commercial endorsements, when the players put their names to an ad for MacRobertson's Pepsin chewing gum.

A more significant endorsement had already come from the Magpies' rivals. The game's biggest clubs had been pushing to leave the VFA and form their own breakaway competition, to be called the Victorian Football League. After two years of courting, Collingwood finally said yes and the VFL was formed.

Ironically, the meeting at which the new competition was formalised was held the night before the 1896 Grand Final. Collingwood's first VFA flag was also its last involvement in the competition. New adventures awaited.

H&A P19 (including Grand Final), W15, L3, D1 • **Finished** Premier • **Captain** Bill Strickland • **Leading goalkicker** Wal Gillard (13)

COLLINGWOOD IN THE VFL

Collingwood's biggest moment of the 1897 season passed with relatively little fanfare. It came in the opening round, when the Magpies outpointed St Kilda at Victoria Park, at the same time as Melbourne took on South Melbourne at the Lake Oval, Fitzroy defeated Carlton at the Brunswick Street Oval, and Essendon out-classed Geelong at Corio Oval.

This was the brave new world of the Victorian Football League (VFL) – now in direct opposition to the VFA, from which it had emerged. And while today it might seem that a breakaway 'super league' must have been big news, at the time it was reported in a very matter-of-fact way.

But that shouldn't disguise how extraordinary it was for Collingwood to be a part of the new league at all, given where it had come from and how new it was. The 1896 Premiership was definitive proof that Collingwood had arrived as an on-field force, but the club's involvement in the VFL was testament to its pulling power and increasing off-field clout. After just five years, Collingwood was legitimately considered to be a power club.

This was something the other clubs had recognised back in 1895, when they first began talking to the Pies about being part of a breakaway competition. Even then, other clubs were envious of Collingwood's membership and attendances, and the ferocity of its supporters. They knew any new competition that wanted to be successful would have to feature the Magpies.

But Collingwood stayed loyal to the VFA, even as the established power clubs of South Melbourne, Geelong, Essendon and

Melbourne grew increasingly frustrated with the Association's stewardship of the game. All that changed when Collingwood and South Melbourne finished the 1896 season dead level, not only on match points but also on goals scored for and against. This meant that a final play-off match was going to be needed to determine that season's premier team. This was football's first 'Grand Final'.

But the VFA had a problem: with 13 teams in the competition, the fixture had to allow for byes and staggered scheduling, so there were still four matches to be played. Incredibly, the Association forced Collingwood and South Melbourne to wait an extra week before they played their Grand Final, while the four meaningless matches were played.

The VFA was ridiculed for its stance and both clubs appealed. Collingwood's delegates were furious at the decision and warned that a failure to overturn it would see the club switch allegiances and support the new competition. But the Association's officials stuck to their decision, and the Magpies – as promised – threw in their lot with the VFL.

Unfortunately, the Woodsmen couldn't carry their VFA Premiership form into the VFL. The season started badly when the Premiership flag stubbornly failed to unfurl at the first game, and thereafter the team played consistently without ever hitting the heights of 1896. In the end, they finished fourth on the home-and-away ladder, and won only one of their three finals matches. Still, the thing that mattered most was that Collingwood was now – officially – one of the big boys.

H&A P14, W9, L5 • **Finished 4th** • **Finals** P3, W1, L2 • **Finished 3rd** • **Captain** Bill Strickland • **Leading goalkicker** Archie Smith (15)

1898

THE FIRST BIG RIVALRY

The Collingwood Football Club was born out of a sense of civic pride, and it thrived on the rivalries it developed with its inner-suburban neighbours. And without question, the team with which Collingwood enjoyed its fiercest rivalry in its first 25 years was the one from the other side of Smith Street: Fitzroy.

That angst dated back to the birth of the Magpies in 1892: it wasn't long before one of the local newspapers, the *Mercury*, claimed that, 'metaphorically, each city is thirsting for the gore of the other'. The *Argus* summed up the same attitude when it declared in 1897 that, in Collingwood–Fitzroy matches, 'If you don't get good football [at least] you're bound to have bloodshed.'

The depth of feeling between the barrackers, too, meant that these contests were almost always hard-fought, bruising encounters, no matter the scoreboard. And things could get just as heated on the terraces as on the field, if not more so. The enmity only intensified at times when both clubs were among the best in the competition.

In the 1890s the neighbouring suburbs were vying over Melbourne infrastructure, too. Collingwood, with the train station now known as Victoria Park, had hosted a railway link to Heidelberg since 1888, while Fitzroy had formed part of an inner-circle line that took in Carlton and North Fitzroy. Towards the end of the decade, the councils were jostling for the right to secure the direct rail link between the heart of Melbourne and the expanding northern suburbs.

In 1898 the Railway Standing Committee awarded the route to Collingwood. And even though the extension would not be opened for another three years, the decision delighted the Collingwood Council every bit as much as it angered the citizens of Fitzroy.

It was against this backdrop that the two clubs met in the 1898 VFL season. Ill-advisedly, the Collingwood Council decided to offer the Magpies a bonus of £10 if they defeated Fitzroy in Round 9 at Victoria Park.

It was intended as a simple incentive, but the offer was widely criticised. After all, football was meant to be an amateur game at this time, despite constant conjecture about the sport being hijacked by professionalism, illegal payments and gambling. There were also concerns that the incentive offer might incite the crowds and players to further violence.

In the end Collingwood won the game and the bonus was duly paid. Luckily, the match had not descended into anything more violent than usual. But it certainly added fuel to an already simmering local rivalry, and helped build up a sense of the two neighbours being at war – a stirring of trouble that would come back to bite Collingwood in 1899, during a game that sealed Victoria Park's reputation as a place for only the bravest – or most foolhardy – opposition fans.

The council's offer was never repeated. And Fitzroy had the last laugh anyway, ending Collingwood's season with a semi-final win, and going on to win the Premiership. Bragging rights seemed incentive enough for both Collingwood and Fitzroy in those volatile early days.

H&A P14, W10, L4 • **Finished** 2nd • **Finals** P4, W3, L1 • **Finished** 3rd • **Captain** Bill Proudfoot • **Leading goalkicker** Archie Smith (31)

1899

THE CAPTAIN QUITS

Collingwood captain Bill Proudfoot was unquestionably the most senior and respected player at Victoria Park when the 1899 season kicked off. He had been at the club since day one, and he was not just an outstanding defender on the field but also a huge presence around the clubrooms.

So it was a massive jolt when, in the middle of the season, he quit the captaincy. Proudfoot cited the difficulties of combining football with his career as a police constable at Kyneton: he expressed concern that his frequent absences were affecting the team. More cynical observers felt his move might also have been tied to his push for additional 'expense' money.

The short-term impact of Proudfoot's resignation was muted: the brilliant but troublesome Dick Condon took over as club captain, Proudfoot kept playing, the team's form improved and they eventually finished third on the ladder. But the longer-term shockwaves were significant.

Proudfoot retired from football at the end of 1899, prompting an emotional farewell at the club's annual meeting and special presentations to recognise a distinguished career. But by 1900 he was back playing with Collingwood again, albeit intermittently. Condon was still in charge, but his hot-headedness made him ill-suited to leadership – and *that* would come to cost the club dearly.

In 1899 the Pies headed into the finals in good shape. They won their first two 'sectional' games under a complex new system, and went into their third and final game, against Fitzroy at Victoria Park, knowing that a win would secure them a Grand Final berth.

Within minutes of the game starting, however, important defender Matt Fell wrenched his back and was unable to take any further part. This was a cruel – and crucial – blow. The VFL had only that year dropped the number of players from 20 to 18, and there were no reserves or interchange players. Collingwood had to play virtually the whole game one player short, and with Proudfoot limping throughout. The Pies battled manfully but ended up losing by 14 points.

Fell's injury fuelled a sense of injustice among Collingwood fans, who were also angered by a number of brutal hits dished out by Fitzroy players. The fans' frustration boiled over at the final siren, and Jack Monohan's mother struck Fitzroy's Pat Hickey with an umbrella as he was leaving the field. Later, a large mob of Magpie fans waited outside the ground for the Roys' players to emerge. Police were called to provide protection, stones were thrown and an altogether unsavoury scene ensued.

The post-match kerfuffle drew plenty of criticism the club's way and provided a sour end to the season. It also turned up the heat on Collingwood's already fierce rivalry with Fitzroy, and helped establish Victoria Park's reputation as a particularly inhospitable venue for opposition players and fans.

Fell's injury also prompted Collingwood's VFL delegates to call on the league for 'a substitute to be allowed to take the field in place of an injured player'. The league said the suggestion would be considered before the next season. It was eventually introduced in 1930.

H&A P14, W10, L4 • **Finished** 3rd • **Finals** P3, W2, L1 • **Finished** 4th • **Captains** Bill Proudfoot & Dick Condon • **Leading goalkicker** Archie Smith (17)

1900

DICK CONDON IMPLODES

Collingwood knew it was taking a risk when it appointed Dick Condon to replace Bill Proudfoot as captain midway through 1899. Condon was unquestionably the team's best player – he was a truly brilliant footballer, and one of the stars of the competition – but he had a highly combustible temperament that caused all kinds of headaches for those around him.

Still, the club's committee decided to take the punt. They did so not only because of his quality as a player, but also because of his highly regarded football nous, his tactical awareness and a fierce competitiveness that, while it frequently got him into trouble, just as often provided inspiration.

Unfortunately, the decision panned out just the way Condon's critics had predicted. It all ended in tears – and with the Magpie skipper suspended for life.

The players had initially responded well to Condon's leadership. They won their first eight games under him in 1899, and only lost the ninth because of the early injuries to Proudfoot and Matt Fell. But things were never as settled in 1900. The team won only three of its first nine matches, a situation not helped by the fact that Condon missed three of those games after being suspended for swearing at an umpire in the Round 2 match against Geelong at Corio Oval.

By July, the *Argus* was reporting 'a good deal of growling going on in the Magpies' nest', and Condon actually came to blows with ruckman Artie Robson at three-quarter-time of a game against Essendon at Victoria Park.

The team recovered to end the home-and-away season fourth on percentage, but Condon, in the second sectional finals game against Geelong – there must have been something about Corio Oval he did not like – lost the plot in his anger over the umpiring, stormed from the field late in the game and asked the committee to call the team from the ground. Thankfully, the committee refused, but Condon's fuse was clearly even shorter than usual.

A week later he went berserk at umpire Ivo Crapp, generally regarded as the finest of his time. Enraged at having a free kick awarded against him, Condon told Crapp, 'Your girl's a bloody whore.' He was reported, and once more had to face the VFL. Condon's recidivism had worn out the patience of both his club and the league: Collingwood did nothing to support him, and the VFL duly suspended him for life.

Condon's repeated brain fades, and especially his tirade at umpire Crapp, cost Collingwood the services of one of the best players in the game. He also seems to have been largely responsible for the divisive environment that permeated the club during the 1900 season. About the only good thing that came out of the whole sorry affair was that the club made it clear it no longer supported Condon or his behaviour. This reinforced to all players that there were standards of discipline and team-first ethics that had to be followed, no matter how good a player you were.

But in the short term, the Pies had lost their captain and best player. They'd also narrowly missed out on another Grand Final appearance. It was an awful end to a frustrating season.

H&A P14, W8, L6 • **Finished 4th** • **Finals** P3, W2, L1 • **Finished 4th** • **Captain** Dick Condon • **Leading goalkicker** Archie Smith (21)

1901

THE LOSS THE MAGPIES HAD TO HAVE

It's often said in football that you need to lose a Grand Final before you can win one. And while that's not always true, it was certainly the case with Collingwood in 1901.

This was the year in which the club at last made it back to the final game of the season. And though the Magpies were thumped in the Grand Final, all at Victoria Park took a degree of comfort from having at least made it. The loss also prompted some tactical rethinking that would bear fruit a year later.

It had been a crazy old season for the Pies. The VFL had not relented on Dick Condon's suspension, so the team was without arguably its best player. But the gap was at least partially filled by the equally brilliant, but hitherto more inconsistent, Fred Leach, who stepped up with a season that saw him voted by many as the best player in the competition.

There was widespread anger within black-and-white ranks when the Pies lost to Melbourne by a point in Round 11 after two glaring errors by the goal umpires. But the protests were more muffled two weeks later after a time-keeping error worked in the Magpies' favour: the game against Fitzroy was stopped five minutes early, when the Roys were five points down and charging home.

On balance, then, a third-place finish for Collingwood was about right – equal on points with Essendon, but two games behind Geelong. Nobody gave the Pies too much hope against Geelong in their cut-throat semi-final, but they produced their best performance of the year to win by 21 points, with Leach giving what was described as 'a perfect exhibition of all-round football'.

The less said about the Grand Final against Essendon, however, the better. The contest was over at half-time, with Collingwood having scraped together only three measly behinds in the first two quarters. The Pies managed a pathetic 2.4 for the entire game, and the 27-point final margin flattered them. Essendon's veteran champion Albert Thurgood dominated with three goals, including one scored with an 86-yard drop kick. About the only encouraging thing for the Magpies was the huge crowd of more than 30,000: Collingwood was back on the biggest stage and their fans turned out in droves.

At the time, the Magpies were disappointed but not crushed: there was no disgrace in being beaten by a team such as Essendon and a star like Thurgood, who is generally considered one of the greatest players of the time. The club's annual report was decidedly upbeat, noting that the team had brought 'gladness to your hearts and smiles to your countenances on many occasions'.

But even if it wasn't demoralising, the Grand Final loss still proved to be a turning point for Collingwood. The club's leaders realised that, should they face the 'Same Olds' again in 1902, they would need a better plan for keeping the mercurial Thurgood quiet. They must also have wondered how much Dick Condon would have improved their line-up, and what a difference he might have made on Grand Final Day.

What they didn't know was that, within a year, they would have developed a revolutionary game plan that would change the way football was played.

H&A P17, W12, L5 · **Finished** 3rd · **Finals** P2, W1, L1 · **Finished** 2nd · **Captain** Bill Proudfoot · **Leading goalkicker** Ted Rowell (31)

1902

COLLINGWOOD BRINGS SCIENCE TO FOOTBALL

By 1902, the Magpies had become used to mid-season jaunts to country locations such as Bendigo, Castlemaine and Bright. Collingwood was one of the first clubs to introduce such trips – partly for promotion and recruitment, partly to reward players and partly for team bonding. The players loved them.

In July of 1902 the Pies took their mid-season break to a new level: they headed to Tasmania on the SS *Coogee*. Former captain Dick Condon was among the touring party, the VFL having lifted his life suspension after Collingwood – perhaps pragmatically, in light of the previous season's results – finally decided to support his appeal.

The promotional games on these trips rarely provided a stern test; that wasn't the point. But in one game in Tasmania, Condon found the opposition so weak that he began toying with them, trying dinky little kicks that he would put just out of reach of opponents and into the arms of his teammates. He also experimented with passes that became lower and faster. Other highly skilled teammates such as Charlie Pannam, Fred Leach and Ted Rowell joined in, and – almost before they knew it – Collingwood had invented the stab pass. But it was mostly just a bit of fun at that stage, and nobody thought too much about it.

After a rough sea voyage delayed their return to Melbourne (the team headed straight to the Geelong train after getting off the boat), the players tried their new passing game at Corio and found it worked just as well against more qualified opponents. They thumped Geelong, and went through the rest of the home-and-away season undefeated.

The key wasn't just the stab pass itself: it was the game Collingwood built around it. Each time a player got the ball, a teammate would run to space to allow the ball to be passed to him, usually via a low, skimming stab kick. The Pies were able to move the ball systematically, quickly and with fewer turnovers. Once they had the ball, opposition teams struggled to get it back. And the speed of the movements and passing left opponents in their wake.

This might sound simple, but in 1902 it turned the game on its head. In effect, Collingwood became one of the first clubs to introduce its own game plan, and the newspapers excitedly reported that players had marked out planned moves on a chalkboard at Victoria Park. This was the famed 'Collingwood system': the Pies brought science and strategy to football.

The results were stunning, and the Pies lost only one game for the rest of the year, to Fitzroy in the first week of the finals. They again met Essendon in the Grand Final, and showed they had learned from 1901 by using Fred Leach to blanket Albert Thurgood. This was a courageous and unexpected move, for Leach was a brilliant centreman in his own right. But it worked perfectly, and Thurgood's influence was much dimished on the previous year. The Woods fought off an early challenge to prevail by 33 points.

Collingwood's dominance in the second half of the season left other clubs scrambling either to replicate this new style of play or to find ways of counteracting it. The Pies, meanwhile, could bask in the glory of their first VFL Premiership. They were confident there would be more to come.

H&A P17, W15, L2 • **Finished** 1st • **Finals** P2, W1, L1 • **Finished** Premier • **Captain** Lardie Tulloch • **Leading goalkicker** Ted Rowell (33)

1903

THE SYDNEY EXPERIMENT

Given Collingwood's position as reigning premier, and its standing as the best-supported club in the land, it was no surprise when the VFL decided to use the Magpies as a Trojan horse to spread the game into the New South Wales market. The result was Collingwood and arch rival Fitzroy facing off for Premiership points in an early-season clash at the Sydney Cricket Ground.

This was the first time a 'real' VFL match had been played outside of Victoria. It was also the first time players wore numbers on their jumpers, to help the Sydney crowds identify them. While the game drew good crowds and was a promotional success, Collingwood fans hated it. For a start, they had been deprived of the chance to watch what most felt would be the game of the season. But worse than that, the Pies lost.

The Sydney experiment confirmed Collingwood's position as the VFL's 'go-to' club for new initiatives – and that has remained the case pretty much ever since. In the shorter term, it elevated the Pies' rivalry with Fitzroy to a whole new level. The Roys had now unpicked Collingwood's famed system twice in successive matches, and the teams' ongoing battle would be the story of the season.

The Magpies stopped off for some R&R in Rutherglen on their way back from Sydney, and resolved that they would make up for their loss. They did so by embarking on a 14-match unbeaten run heading into the Grand Final. This included a much-savoured 20-point win over Fitzroy in an atmosphere even more febrile than usual. (This was the game in which Bill Proudfoot played under an alias, 'Wilson', because the police force had banned its members from playing football.)

Many of those 14 victories were close, but this was a team that knew how to win. It wasn't just the old enemy from Brunswick Street challenging the Magpies, either. Carlton was emerging as a serious threat, and other teams were also devising ways to combat Collingwood's style.

Almost inevitably, though, the Grand Final was against Fitzroy. It was a tight, tough, fiercely contested game played in humid conditions before a huge crowd that started the game at fever pitch and stayed that way until the very end. Collingwood led by 11 points deep into the game, but Fitzroy made a late charge, and when their skipper, Gerald Brosnan, marked just 30 yards from goal, only three points separated the teams.

The entire season came down to this final, gut-clenching moment. Brosnan was usually a beautiful kick, and this one initially looked to be heading straight through, but it died near the line and veered narrowly wide. Proudfoot, who was standing on the goal line, later claimed that the lace of the ball had actually touched one of the goal posts. Even as the crowd was still gasping, the bell rang. The 1903 flag was Collingwood's, and it had been decided on the very last kick of the season.

Collingwood's application of strategy over the previous two seasons had changed football. A team now needed a system, as well as talent, to succeed. But the rest of the competition was catching up, and the Pies knew it.

H&A P17, W15, L2 • **Finished** 1st • **Finals** P2, W2 • **Finished** Premier •
Captain Lardie Tulloch • **Leading goalkicker** Ted Lockwood (35)

1904

COLLINGWOOD APPOINTS ITS FIRST COACH

In 1903 Carlton became the first VFL club to appoint an official coach, giving the role to legendary former Fitzroy player John Worrall. The next year, never wanting to be left behind in the innovation stakes, Collingwood followed suit. It surprised nobody when the job went to former skipper Bill Strickland.

Strickland had been a brilliant on-field leader at Victoria Park during his playing days, and had played a pivotal role in the 1896 Premiership. After he hung up the boots at the end of the 1897 season, Strickland's role effectively became that of coach before it was given the name. He was regarded as a 'general adviser' or 'chief adviser' to the captains who succeeded him, and he frequently delivered stirring addresses. In 1898 'Markwell' in the *Australasian* wrote this about the team's improved form:

'The coaching of his old club's players is a real labour of love with Strickland, and he has succeeded in imbuing every man amongst them with the earnestness which characterised his own play in seasons past. Strickland it is who gauges the abilities of every Woodsman, senior and recruit, and allots to each his task upon the field. So long as Collingwood's executive and Collingwood's players have Strickland at their elbow, so long will the Collingwood Club continue to be a power in the land.'

Still, it was a landmark moment when Collingwood formalised Strickland's role as coach midway through 1904, after the team had found itself struggling in its attempt to win a third successive flag. The Pies regained both ground and momentum under his control, with newspaper reports noting in September how much both performances and morale had improved since he had taken over. 'Once more there is joy in the Magpies' nest,' wrote the *Age*, 'and confident hope of retaining the Premiership, which a few weeks ago seemed to have slipped away.'

The *Leader* went even further after the Magpies' last-round win over Melbourne: 'The happiest man on the ground, except the Collingwood men on the turf, was their old skipper, W. Strickland, who when the team recently looked like going to pieces, pulled them together and by personally supervising the practice completely restored the famous system which won the premiership for Collingwood last year. It might win it again, eh?'

Unfortunately, the *Leader* journalist was a little too optimistic, as the Pies' third-place finish condemned them to a sudden-death final against ladder leader Fitzroy, and they went down by 11 points. Even more gallingly, especially for the fans, Fitzroy went on to win the Premiership.

Strickland's time as Collingwood's officially appointed coach was brief. His role with the Australasian Football Council was growing, and he stepped down from the position at the end of the 1904 season. (He returned to the role again briefly in 1908, when the club was once more in trouble, but didn't have as big an impact.)

However fleeting, his appointment set Collingwood on the path of having official coaches, rather than 'advisers'. Interestingly, though, Strickland would be the only non-playing coach until Jock McHale eventually retired in 1920.

H&A P17, W10, L7 • **Finished** 3rd • **Finals** P1, L1 • **Finished** 3rd • **Captain** Lardie Tulloch • **Coach** Bill Strickland • **Leading goalkicker** Charlie Pannam (24)

1905

INJURIES KILL A FLAG

Collingwood was still smarting from its failure to win a third successive flag – with the added pain of having to watch Fitzroy triumph – when the 1905 season rolled around. The Pies appointed the temperamental Dick Condon as playing coach, a move every bit as courageous as it was surprising. The committee had judged that his astute football brain and inspirational qualities would outweigh the almost inevitable bust-ups that would happen along the way. And for 1905, they were right.

The team played brilliant football under Condon's guidance. The Woodsmen lost the first game of the season in a nail-biter, and then went on a 12-match unbeaten run, during which the press were calling Collingwood the greatest team of all time and a certainty for the Premiership. Condon himself seemed lifted by being made coach and was rated by many as the best player in the competition. His Magpies lost only two games for the season and finished it 10 points clear at the top of the ladder, indisputably the best team of the year. But it all fell apart in September.

First up, the Pies were smashed by Carlton in the second semi. The finals system allowed Collingwood, as the minor premier, to challenge the winner of the Carlton–Fitzroy final, setting up another Grand Final against the Roys.

The two teams went in at half-time with scores level at 1.3 apiece after a tight and torrid first half. But two key injuries had already cruelled Collingwood's chances. Dashing wingman Percy Gibb hurt his hand so badly that it was later found to be permanently disfigured. But worse still, the influential Condon, the key to Collingwood's hopes, had been forced off the field in the first quarter with a badly wrenched ankle.

It became clear at half-time that Condon would play no further part in the game, and in the third term Fitzroy pounced, kicking three goals to one. They then threw all their players onto the ball in the last quarter – an early version of flooding – in a successful bid to stifle Collingwood's scoring ability. The Roys went scoreless but the Woods added only a behind, and a Premiership that had seemed destined for Victoria Park went begging. It would not be the last time.

The injury to Condon not only killed the club's flag chances in 1905, but also foreshadowed the disastrous 1906 that would follow. He never quite recovered from the disappointment, and that seemed to affect his attitude and approach.

Off the field, the Collingwood Juniors Football Club folded, and Collingwood decided to anoint the Collingwood District Football Club as its feeder operation. But the year was dominated by a bitter and protracted wrangle with the Collingwood Council, which wanted a bigger say in the running of the ground and a greater share of the revenue the increasingly popular club was generating. Things got so bad that at one stage the club threatened to leave Victoria Park.

Ultimately, the dispute was resolved – both parties actually needed each other more than they realised – but it was a sign of the decades of squabbling to come.

H&A P17, W15, L2 • **Finished** 1st • **Finals** P2, L2 • **Finished** 2nd • **Captain** Charlie Pannam • **Coach** Dick Condon • **Leading goalkicker** Charlie Pannam (38)

1906
'GOOD OLD COLLINGWOOD FOREVER'

Collingwood has known few seasons so riven by internal conflicts as 1906. Which makes it all the more ironic that this was the year that saw the creation of one of the greatest and most enduring symbols of the club's unity and success: the anthem 'Good Old Collingwood Forever'.

The song was written during a late-season trip to Tasmania. A promising young Yarraville defender called Tommy Nelson had moved to Collingwood in the week leading up to the trip. Yarraville's officials were incensed, convinced that the Pies had used the incentive of the Tasmanian jaunt to lure away an important player just before the finals. Nelson ignored the controversy and joined his new teammates in the Apple Isle, where he performed well enough to be selected in three senior games for the Magpies upon his return to Melbourne. Those senior games passed largely without comment, and Nelson returned to Yarraville in 1907, where he went on to enjoy a fine career.

But Tommy Nelson had left Collingwood a huge legacy in his brief stint at Victoria Park. For Nelson was a highly talented singer and musical performer who regularly took to the stage at functions, meetings and concerts in and around Yarraville, including smoke nights, dinners and banquets for sporting clubs and other community bodies.

Nelson put his musical talents to good use while in Tasmania with his new teammates, taking a Boer War marching song called 'Goodbye Dolly Gray' (the song was actually written during the Spanish–American War but became popular during the Boer War) and adding his own words to it to make 'Good Old Collingwood Forever'. Singing songs was part and parcel of footballers' trips in those days, and at the time there was no club anthem. But that changed once people heard 'Good Old Collingwood Forever'.

The song was performed publicly for the first time on Saturday, 11 August 1906, as the players were being driven to play a game against a combined Southern Tasmania team outside Hobart. Nelson performed 'Good Old Collingwood Forever', accompanied by Ed Drohan on the accordion. The touring party's Tasmanian hosts apparently loved it.

Along with the earlier choices of colours, jumper and nickname, the creation of the song is one of the most significant events in the club's early history. Little else impacts as directly on the club or its fans today.

Yet it didn't draw much attention in 1906, as fans and media alike were preoccupied with the club's infighting. The 1905 captain, Charlie Pannam, was dumped, and the compromise choice to replace him, 'Rosie' Dummett, had to stand down mid-season due to poor form. There was much acrimony between warring factions, and talk of players refusing to pass to each other. Coach Dick Condon got involved and had to be stood down for several weeks 'for causing dissension in the team', as did vice-captain Jack Monohan. It was ugly, and no one was surprised when the Pies lost their only finals match.

Season 1906 had been an acrimonious, testy affair at Collingwood. But it unexpectedly left a glorious, uplifting gift that endures to this day.

H&A P17, W11, L6 • **Finished** 3rd • **Finals** P1, L1 • **Finished** 3rd • **Captains** Alf Dummett & Arthur Leach • **Coach** Dick Condon • **Leading goalkicker** Dick Lee (35)

1907

DICK LEE TOPS THE VFL GOALKICKING

Even in the VFL's earliest years, it wasn't unusual to find a Collingwood player at the top of the competition's goalkicking charts. Archie 'Snapper' Smith, Ted Rowell, Ted Lockwood and Charlie Pannam Snr all headed the goalkicking table at different times during the league's first decade. But none of those players was just a kid in his second season.

So when 18-year-old Dick Lee finished the 1907 home-and-away season 14 goals ahead of his nearest rival, everybody sat up and took notice. He'd kicked an impressive 35 goals in his first season to finish third on the VFL table, despite not making his debut until Round 7. In 1907 he fared even better, finishing with 45 goals, at that stage the equal highest regular season tally ever. He then added two more in his only final. Collingwood knew it had found a truly special talent.

And so it would prove to be. In a 17-year career, the son of legendary Collingwood trainer Wal Lee would set all kinds of goalscoring records, play in three Magpie Premierships and establish himself as not just the pre-eminent forward of his generation but also one of the greatest, and most thrilling, Collingwood footballers ever to pull on a boot.

Even in 1907, which was just his first full season of VFL football, it quickly became apparent that Lee was the kind of player around whom you could build a team. It was also clear – after a couple of sensational 'speccies' he took against South Melbourne and St Kilda – that he was an excitement machine crowds would flock to see.

Lee's impact on the team's fortunes wasn't immediate, as the Pies struggled into fourth spot and were dispatched in the first week by South Melbourne. But that wasn't entirely surprising, as Dick Condon had quit after 1906 and fellow stalwarts Charlie Pannam and Jack Monohan transferred to other clubs early in the season. Collingwood was rebuilding, and in young Dick Lee the club had found the centrepiece of its rebuild.

This was also a season in which the Magpies once again turned football on its head – this time by dispensing with the long knickerbockers hitherto in vogue, which they replaced with shorts that ended above the knee. This might not have had the same profound impact on the game as, say, the advent of scientific football in 1902, but it was big news nonetheless.

Indeed there was quite a buzz of excitement around the ground when the Collingwood players took to the field in their new attire for the first time. 'Observer' in the *Argus* reported that they 'looked smart and workmanlike – in all respects a team of thoroughbreds – and the new style gives the impression of increased height and weight'.

The other little-known contributing factor is that this was the only season in which the Magpie players wore something other than (mostly) plain black socks. In 1907 the socks had a solid white band at the top, which heightened the impact of the shorter shorts. The socks lasted only one season, but the shorts caught on very quickly and were being used by other clubs within weeks.

H&A P17, W9, L8 • **Finished** 4th • **Finals** P1, L1 • **Finished** 4th • **Captain** Arthur Leach • **Coach** Ted Rowell • **Leading goalkicker** Dick Lee (47)

1908

BOB RUSH BECOMES TREASURER

Bob Rush began the 1908 season as a valuable defender who helped out at an official level by acting as assistant secretary. He finished it as a former player who had added the title of Collingwood treasurer to his footballing CV.

Far from being a convenient way to look after a former player, this appointment proved a masterstroke. For a start, Rush turned out to be an outstanding treasurer. And in the bigger picture, his was the first of a number of key administrative appointments that would come to earn the Collingwood Football Club an envied reputation for off-field stability.

Bob Rush came to Collingwood in 1899 and quickly established himself as a fine running defender, usually off half-back. Even in his early days he showed he was interested in club affairs off the field, becoming a players' representative on the committee in 1902 and assistant secretary the next year. He impressed everyone with his quiet, measured approach in both roles.

When his playing career wound down in 1908, Bob was immediately appointed to the position of treasurer. It would be a staggering 42 years before the club would need to appoint another.

As treasurer, Rush soon established an enviable reputation for accuracy, thoroughness and attention to detail. When club auditors went through the books in 1950 they were stunned to find they were almost without blemish. He was methodical, genuine and straight as a die. As a player he'd enjoyed a reputation as one of the fairest in the game, and his work as treasurer carried similar qualities.

This was obviously of huge benefit to the club's financial management. But the added bonus was that Rush loved the footy club and loved his job – so he stayed. And stayed. Together with a small band of long-serving colleagues – coach Jock McHale, presidents Jim Sharp and Harry Curtis, and secretaries Ern Copeland and Frank Wraith – Rush provided a stable and solid base for the club's operations until well after the Second World War. It's no coincidence that this period of sustained administrative stability also delivered what proved to be Collingwood's glory years on the field.

That time of success seemed a long way away in 1908. Despite another record-breaking season from the wondrous Dick Lee, the year turned out to be much like the two that had gone before. Another fourth-placed finish, another first-week finals defeat. Once more there was a mid-season change of captain, Eddie Drohan making way for Bob Nash, and this time there was a change of coach as well, with Ted Rowell stepping down and Bill Strickland helping out late in the season.

But even Strick's magic couldn't help the team to any great heights, and Essendon more than doubled the Magpies' score in their semi-final. The club had now been through no fewer than five captains and three coaches in four seasons: it seemed to be lacking both on-field stability and off-field direction. Bob Rush's appointment turned out to be an important step forward, and others would soon follow.

But Collingwood fans were sick of just sneaking into the finals and making up the numbers. They wanted to be winning in September again.

H&A P18, W10, L8 • **Finished** 4th • **Finals** P1, L1 • **Finished** 4th • **Captains** Eddie Drohan & Bob Nash • **Coaches** Ted Rowell & Bill Strickland • **Leading goalkicker** Dick Lee (54)

1909

THE GLORY OF VICTORIA PARK

The culmination of a decade of upgrades and improvements to Victoria Park came on the opening day of the 1909 season, when the club unveiled a magnificent new grandstand at the western end of the ground. It confirmed Victoria Park as one of the finest grounds in the competition, and underlined just how popular and successful Collingwood had been. There always seemed to be a need to accommodate more spectators, more members, or both.

The program of improvements had started back in the late 1890s, with a succession of upgrades to the playing surface, the grandstand and surrounds. In 1900 a pavilion for the club's lady members was added on the wing (where the Ryder Stand would later be located). The next year the club announced a more substantial overhaul, adding seating and raising and widening the banks around the ground to accommodate up to 30,000 people in comfort. Eight automatic turnstiles were also installed to help prevent crowding at the entrances. Further improvements followed after the big blue with the local council in 1904–05.

But those improvements, while important in establishing Victoria Park as one of the finest playing reserves in Melbourne, made nowhere near the impact of the new stand that opened on the first day of the 1909 season.

Despite not having won a finals match since 1903, Collingwood continued to attract record-breaking crowds that were the envy of every other club in the competition. It soon became clear that Collingwood desperately needed more ways to accommodate those crowds, especially a larger, more modern stand. What they got was much more than that: it was a structure of grandeur and beauty that would remain the centrepiece of the ground for the next 60 years. The *Herald* called it 'a noble, substantial structure'; it was 'a stand of which the people of Collingwood ought to be proud, for it is the grandest of grandstands in Melbourne'.

Based on a grandstand a local councillor had seen in Maryborough, in western Victoria, the new structure housed two dressing rooms, committee rooms, a gymnasium, and bathrooms and toilets for both teams. There were also covered tunnels for the teams to use, which would protect them from unruly fans.

The introduction of the new 1500-seat grandstand led to other changes, too. The original stand was shifted to the south-west corner of the ground, where it became a public reserve stand. The women's pavilion became a smokers' pavilion. Most importantly, the reserve was extended to the south, in order to provide more space for the club's ever-growing army of fans.

The end result was a bigger, more modern and overall vastly improved Victoria Park. Its opening was the cause of great celebration in the local community; at the laying of the Foundation Stone, a man had been fired from a cannon! This was now a serious ground for a serious football club.

On the field, the team once again finished inside the top four but lost its only finals match. Collingwood now had a ground fit for a Premiership team; the only thing missing was a new flag to fly from the grandstand roof.

H&A P18, W12, L4, D2 • **Finished** 3rd • **Finals** P1, L1 • **Finished** 3rd • **Captain** Bob Nash • **Coach** George Angus • **Leading goalkicker** Dick Lee (58)

1910

THE BRAWL AND BEATING THE BLUES

Sometimes all it takes is a spark to catch alight, and the combustion can last a lifetime. That's the way it was for Collingwood and Carlton late one October afternoon at the MCG in 1910, when a relatively tranquil relationship was shattered during the course of one of the most violent Grand Finals ever staged.

Prior to that spark, the Magpies and the Blues had co-existed without too much angst, with Fitzroy being the main source of Collingwood's hostility. But that changed utterly in the 1910 Premiership playoff after a season marred by betting, bribery and brawls. Two Carlton players had been disqualified for 'playing dead' before the finals, which cast a shadow over the sport and had VFL officials desperate for a scandal-free Grand Final. Those hopes were dashed even before the teams took to the field, with umpire Jack Elder noting in the rooms before the game a 'sullen hostility' among the players.

There was tension early, though most of the attention was on the ball. But in the last quarter, after a relatively innocuous contest on the wing between Collingwood's Tom Baxter and Carlton's Jack Bacquie, the game degenerated into 'the most disgraceful scene witnessed on a Melbourne football field'. First, Bacquie threw an elbow at Baxter and the Magpie retaliated. Then Collingwood's Jim Shorten came in and floored Bacquie, and Magpie Les 'Flapper' Hughes was knocked out.

Almost every player was part of the mayhem, and the police threatened to become involved to restore order. Elder decided that the only course of action he could take to stop the melee was to bounce the ball and hope the players would remember that there was still a Premiership to be won. 'I feel certain if I failed to get the game going again that day,' he said later, 'the crowd would have swarmed onto the ground and rival camps of barrackers would have been at each other's throats.'

Elder's idea worked. Collingwood held on to a narrow lead throughout the final term, resolutely keeping Carlton at bay. The Magpies won by 14 points – their first flag in seven years, and the only one achieved against the Blues in a Grand Final.

Forward Dick Lee was outstanding, kicking four goals for the game – more than a quarter of the majors from either side. Jock McHale enhanced his reputation as one of the game's most reliable players, and captain-coach George Angus showed resilience to overcome injury and keep playing when others might not have. The *Australasian* recorded that 'the heroic efforts of Angus ... set his men a noble example of pluck and earnestness'.

For Collingwood, the ill-tempered finish paled into insignificance when compared to what the players had achieved. There was widespread condemnation of the fight, but the flag meant more to the Magpies than any criticism.

The bitterness between the two clubs spilled over into the postseason, when Collingwood's Baxter had his year-long suspension overturned after Richard Daykin, a teammate about to retire, took the blame, even though others swore he had no part in the incident.

The flag prompted club treasurer and former player Bob Rush to bestow the club with a Latin motto, *Floreat Pica*, which was meant to translate as 'May the Magpies prosper'. In 1910 they had prospered, and their Grand Final win over Carlton sowed the seeds for one of Australian sport's most bitter rivalries.

H&A P18, W13, L5 • **Finished** 2nd • **Finals** P3, W3 • **Finished** Premier • **Captain-coach** George Angus • **Leading goalkicker** Dick Lee (58)

1911
EQUAL PAY FOR PIES

The VFL had little choice but to permit the payment of players for the first time in 1911, following one of the most divisive and controversial seasons on record. Clubs had been clandestinely paying players for years; by removing the cloak of 'shamateurism' – as the under-the-table payment schemes were dubbed – at least the system would become more transparent.

It was a watershed moment for the competition, and particularly for Collingwood. Not everyone was in favour of the repealing of Rule 29, which specified that 'any player receiving payment directly or indirectly for his services as a footballer shall be disqualified for any period the League may think fit, and any club paying a player either directly or indirectly for his services as a footballer shall be dealt with as the League may think fit'. Indeed, one of the founding fathers of the game, H.C.A. Harrison, had argued strongly against it.

A meeting of 68 players at the Orient Hotel in Bourke Street before the start of the 1911 season resulted in a 63-to-five majority to take the matter further with the VFL. The players' motion stated: 'That its interests would be best served by open professionalism, leaving each club to its own management.' A committee of players, including Collingwood's Jock McHale, was set up to deal with the VFL on the issue.

The league was initially slow to react and unable to reach a consensus, but finally it approved a motion for player payments at a meeting on 12 May – the night before Collingwood's Round 3 game against Geelong. Anticipating the change, the Magpie club leaders had met with their players earlier that month to form the cornerstone of an egalitarian financial policy that would last for generations. Collingwood wanted all its players to receive the same reward, without exception.

The *Argus* detailed this in May 1911: 'The Collingwood executive, who has always been on the best of terms with its players, has formulated a definite scheme whereby the executive takes 25 per cent of the takings for administrative purposes, and the other 75 per cent is to be divided [equally] amongst the players … Whether a man lives 100 yards or 100 miles from the ground, he gets his allowance of one pound … They [the players] have decided that they will not have in their team, to share in the profits, any man who wants to live on the game. A man must have a trade or honest profession.'

McHale would ultimately see the policy as one of the key reasons for the club's extraordinary period of success, even if others believed the Magpies persisted with it for too long.

The Magpies defeated South Melbourne in a semi-final to bring on a Grand Final clash with Essendon. The 'Same Olds' had beaten the Magpies twice in the home-and-away season (once by 85 points), and were expected to do the same in the finals.

Injuries to Dick Lee and Dan Minogue hurt Collingwood in the Grand Final, though the result was in the balance until the dying moments. The Magpies fell six points short, with part of the blame centring on Tom Baxter, who missed several late chances. Baxter was accused by some of 'playing dead', though he did kick his team's only goal in the last term. While he never played for Collingwood again, most of his teammates believed there was no foundation to the allegations.

H&A P18, W12, L6 • **Finished** 4th • **Finals** P2, W1, L1 • **Finished** 2nd • **Captain-coach** George Angus • **Leading goalkicker** Tom Baxter (31)

1912

COLLINGWOOD APPOINTS McHALE AS COACH

Collingwood had a significant decision to make in the lead-up to the 1912 season: it had to find a new coach.

Four men had previously held what was still an evolving role for the Magpies, and for the game. None had been in the position for more than three seasons. Thirty-seven-year-old George Angus was stepping aside to coach Williamstown in the VFA, his physical prowess slowed by the passage of time and a number of injury concerns. Wearing a red rose in his coat, Angus told a hearing of VFL delegates in April 1912, 'I don't think I'd be of much further use to the [Collingwood] club.'

Collingwood hoped Angus's successor would be there for the long haul, but not even the wildest optimist could have envisaged just how long the club's fifth coach would survive in the role, or how much success he would have.

His name was Jim McHale, although those who knew him called him Jock. After being appointed just prior to the 1912 season, he would remain in the role for a staggering 38 seasons, 714 games and eight Premierships. In the process, he would become known as 'the King of Coaches', and he would help shape not only the course of coaching for two generations, but also the destiny of the Collingwood Football Club.

The son of Irish immigrants, McHale had been born in Sydney and spent some of his early years in country New South Wales. He had an inauspicious debut season as coach in 1912, losing his first three matches and overseeing the first Collingwood team to miss the finals in VFL history. The Magpies won nine of their

18 games, finishing in seventh position. The club's annual report called the year 'the most disastrous in the club's history'. There was even talk of a 'reform group' of supporters keen to blame the management – and the coach – for the unusual state of affairs at Victoria Park.

But the club's powerbrokers were steadfast, firmly believing McHale was the right man for the future. In time, he would develop a brand of football on the field and a series of values off it that helped establish Collingwood as the most successful, envied and, *yes*, hated team of the first half of the 20th century.

McHale took a systematic approach to management of the club's players. He recruited locally, and, believing the team was infinitely more important than any individual, saw that they were paid in an equal manner. He also had an uncanny sense of the fitness levels and mindsets of his men. Through it all, the successes kept coming: he coached Premierships in three separate decades, and was the man in charge of 'the Machine', the fabled side which won four flags in succession between 1927 and 1930.

McHale saw Australian football as a game that taught players to be unselfish and manly, saying, 'All this may be summed up in the one word – character – and if that is not worth developing, nothing is.'

After appointing McHale, the club would not need to seek a new coach for almost another four decades. When it did appoint the team's next coach, he would last only four days. McHale had been in the role for almost 14,000.

H&A P18, W9, L9 • **Finished** 7th • **Captain-coach** Jock McHale • **Leading goalkicker** Les Hughes (13)

1913

TAKING THE GAME TO THE PEOPLE

Almost since its birth, the Collingwood Football Club has taken the game and its players to all parts of the country to further the sport's cause. These trips helped forge the sort of camaraderie that can win Premierships, and played a significant role in making Collingwood the most supported club across Australia.

Jock McHale was a great believer in the importance of these trips, having been on one – to Sydney – in 1903, his first season as a player. In his second season as coach a decade later, he oversaw the club's trip to Stawell, Ararat, Hamilton and Ballarat. After the Magpies missed the finals the previous year, this mid-season trip proved an important step in building the relationships that would turn this team into a successful one.

The team played two matches – at Hamilton and Stawell – with the Magpies winning both. Both the coach and the players were more than satisfied with the outcome. According to the *Australasian*, 'Collingwood vote[d] their recent trip to the Western District one of the most enjoyable undertaken by the club'.

The players brought back many fond memories of their excursion, as well as two boomerangs decorated with black-and-white ribbons. These had been presented to the club at the match in Hamilton by a group of 15 Aboriginal men from the Lake Condah Mission. Their display of boomerang throwing at the half-time break gave an idea to the club's secretary, 'Bud' Copeland.

Copeland would introduce boomerang throwing as part of the half-time entertainment at Victoria Park in the coming years, and it became a popular fixture, especially when an Indigenous buck jumper and showman named Mulga Fred, from Lake Condah, showed off his considerable skill and expertise. It was said that he could 'whistle a boomerang over the crowd and they gasped as it returned to him'.

These country trips furthered the cause of Australian football in the country zones, and they were also a nice reward for the players. The trip in 1913 was no exception, as the club's annual report recorded: 'The able management of your worthy secretary [Copeland], the smoke nights, dance socials and pleasure drives arranged by the football enthusiasts at the places visited, all tended to make the trip a most pleasant reflection for those who participated.'

After missing the finals in McHale's first year, the team responded with a solid season in 1913, winning 13 of its first 15 games. But the Magpies lost the last three home-and-away games on their return from the country trip. Instead of pushing for top spot, they finished third at the end of the home-and-away season. And a season which had started so promisingly faded out in a one-sided semi-final loss to the eventual premier, Fitzroy.

The final margin stretched out to 37 points in the end. Somehow it seemed apt that rain swept across the MCG in the second half of the game as the Maroons took control. The bigger and stronger players from Fitzroy adapted to the conditions better, as the Magpies wallowed in the wet.

Some may have been tempted to blame the 'tour' for interrupting Collingwood's season – there were rumblings of discontent from outside the club – but McHale knew such trips would be worth it in the long run.

H&A P18, W13, L5 • **Finished 3rd** • **Finals** P1, L1 • **Finished 4th** •
Captain-coach Jock McHale • **Leading goalkicker** Les Hughes (22)

LEE'S LEAP AND RETURN

As the premier forward of his time, and one of Collingwood's favourite sons, Dick Lee had the freakish capacity to turn the impossible into the achievable almost on a weekly basis. Yet for all the goals he kicked, and the many marks he took, arguably Lee's greatest triumph was taking the field again after suffering what could have been a career-ending knee injury in 1911.

He missed all but one round in 1912, and managed to return from what is believed to be Australian football's first cartilage operation to play five games in the second half of the 1913 season. Lesser men might have given up. But Lee's resilience and persistence prevailed. He refused to give up on the game that he loved so much, or on the club that had been a part of his life since he was a kid.

Magpie fans were almost ecstatic to see their hero back in action once more, and there was great expectation surrounding his appearance in the Round 1 clash with Carlton at Victoria Park on 25 April 1914. Delight turned to delirium when Lee launched himself into the air – bung knee and all – to drag down one of the first 'hangers' captured by a newspaper photographer.

Thus the moment was immortalised on film: Lee almost hanging in the air, his knee buckled in flight and his teammate 'Doc' Seddon reaching up with a mix of awe and wonder. Through it all, Lee grasped the ball with absolute certainty.

He would explain later how he had 'a bigger spring or leap than most players … this was a great advantage in marking. But equally important was judgment – timing your leap to a split second, so as to snatch the ball out of the air just above the other fellow's fingers. I somehow seemed to have an uncanny knack of doing that.'

It wasn't just the spectacular mark, though. In that game – which brought about a dramatic draw, one of two on the same day in a remarkable opening round to 1914 – Lee also kicked four of Collingwood's eight goals.

There would be more highlights in Lee's second coming as a Magpie, a career that many in the Collingwood community feared might have ended prematurely. Fortunately for him, and for the Magpies, it would extend long into the future.

Later in 1914, in Round 14 – and just under three weeks before Australia declared war on Germany – Lee kicked 11 of his team's 15 goals against University, a remarkable feat. The *Leader* acknowledged that Lee 'was "fed" to a certain extent by his mates, but he made the most of his opportunities and was tricky and clever'.

The Magpies were left with a simple equation in the last round: defeat Geelong at Victoria Park and play finals, or lose and miss out. In a blow, captain Dan Minogue was laid low with influenza and could not play. Geelong proved too strong, winning by 24 points, and Collingwood's 1914 season was over.

The war in Europe was ominous. No one knew what impact it would have in far-off Australia. But at least Collingwood had its hero back in black and white, and while Lee continued to have issues with his knees for the remainder of his career, he went on to kick 707 goals across 230 games and 17 seasons, retiring at the end of 1922.

H&A P18, W10, L7, D1 • **Finished** 5th • **Captain** Dan Minogue • **Coach** Jock McHale • **Leading goalkicker** Dick Lee (57)

1915

A FALLEN MAGPIE

Alan Cordner played one of his best games for Collingwood in the Round 1 draw with Carlton in 1914. Exactly one year later, on 25 April 1915, the young defender was killed on the first day of the Gallipoli campaign.

Collingwood had initially been slow to embrace the war effort. But Cordner was one of the first VFL footballers to volunteer to fight. He pledged his allegiance on 22 August 1914, on the morning of his 11th and final game in black and white. The club held a special gathering in his honour and presented him with a gold wristlet watch as a farewell gift, but no one knew he was already living on borrowed time.

As Collingwood played its first game of the following season, Cordner was preparing for his greatest challenge. He and the 6th Battalion were ready to launch an attack on a stretch of the Gallipoli Peninsula which had hosted battles dating back through the millennia.

Cordner survived the landing itself, but not the day. One of his superiors detailed what took place: '[Cordner was] in the firing line about two miles from the beach. The informant was next to the casualty when he was shot. He tried to make the casualty speak, but could not move him from where he was. [The] informant really thought the casualty was dead, but admits he may have been mistaken.'

Sadly, the informant wasn't mistaken. The Magpie defender was one of at least six VFL footballers killed on the first day of the battle.

Given Cordner's body was never found, however, some cruel pieces of misinformation followed. There were unconfirmed reports he had been repatriated, or had been wounded and joined another battalion, or even more ridiculously that he had re-emerged as part of the August Offensive.

His desperate father, Isaiah, wrote in July 1915 that he had not 'heard from my son ... since his arrival at the Dardanelles'. When Collingwood played in the 1915 Grand Final against Carlton, Cordner had been missing for five months, and was presumed dead.

A few former teammates – including Dan Minogue and great mates 'Paddy Rowan' and 'Doc' Seddon – had enlisted after news of the Gallipoli battle had reached Australia. They kept playing for Collingwood through their initial training and were selected to play in the Premiership playoff against Carlton.

Rowan and Seddon were in camp on Grand Final morning, and took part in a 10-mile march. They were then fed Irish stew for lunch. Club secretary Bud Copeland drove the exhausted Magpie players back to Melbourne to play in the Grand Final. Like their club, Rowan and Seddon tired badly in the game, as Carlton proved too strong, winning by 33 points. Seddon suspected the adjutant who had ordered them on the march barracked for the Blues.

Cordner's fate wasn't confirmed until the following year, when a Court of Inquiry extinguished any last flicker of hope. He was the first Collingwood footballer killed in any war, but tragically, he would not be the last.

H&A P16, W14, L2 • **Finished** 1st • **Finals** P2, L2 • **Finished** 2nd • **Captain** Dan Minogue • **Coach** Jock McHale • **Leading goalkicker** Dick Lee (66)

1916
THE SHOW MUST GO ON

It was to be one of the bleakest years in Australia's history, and if it hadn't been for Collingwood, there would almost certainly have been no football played in the 1916 VFL season. As it was, only four teams agreed to play; significantly, the Magpies had argued that men and women on the home front needed a distraction from the dreadful war news happening abroad.

Collingwood president Jim Sharp said at the club's annual meeting that he could not see 'why, of all sports, football – the poor man's pastime – should be singled out while horse racing – the Sport of Kings – took place as usual'. Mind you, given the rise in enlistment numbers from club ranks, and the stretch on potential recruits, the Magpies were forced to issue a note for local footballers to join the club if they could not enlist.

The plea read: 'Many players are needed and a hearty invitation is extended to any married men who have not felt it their duty to enlist and youths who have been rejected or cannot receive parental authority. We feel there are numbers who love the game and will be willing to play to give enjoyment to thousands who must have a little pleasure on a Saturday afternoon, knowing at the same time their efforts result in hundreds of pounds being raised for the benefit of those who are risking their lives for their fellow men.'

Collingwood finished second at the end of an abbreviated home-and-away season, but the football paled against the backdrop of appalling casualty numbers and deaths on the Western Front, especially at the battlefields of Fromelles and Pozières.

The Magpies lost their semi-final against Fitzroy that season, and the Maroons progressed to win the Premiership, despite having finished last of the four teams in the regular season. The game was meant to be a celebration for Jock McHale, who had become the first VFL player to reach 250 games. Things had looked promising at half-time as the Magpies led by nine points. But their opponents were too strong in the second half, holding on to win by six points. For Collingwood, however, the pain of missing out on a flag was nothing compared with the loss the club would suffer off the field.

In the last month of that dreadful year, the lives of three Collingwood footballers were altered forever. Two died, while another suffered wounds that would ultimately cost him his life.

Paddy Rowan (whose real name was Percy Rowe) was critically wounded and died at the Somme on 4 December 1916. Three days later, Peter Martin, who had worn the Collingwood jumper more than a decade earlier, and who was already beyond his 40th birthday, suffered gunshot wounds to his head. He lost his right eye, and was permanently discharged from the army and returned home to Australia. He would be dead within 15 months. And then, as if the month could hardly have been any worse, on 12 December 1916 another popular former player, Tom Wright, was killed by a German shell in France.

Those who had wanted football to continue had their way, but the fighting overseas had continued to take a terrible toll.

H&A P12, W6, L5, D1 • **Finished** 2nd • **Finals** P1, L1 • **Finished** 3rd • **Captain** Dan Minogue • **Coach** Jock McHale • **Leading goalkicker** Dick Lee (48)

1917

A HORSESHOE FOR GOOD LUCK

A horseshoe fashioned out of a German shell, with a personal inscription, landed on the doorstep of the Collingwood Football Club in September 1917. It was both a salient reminder of the sacrifices soldiers were making on the other side of the world, and also a good-luck charm sent in the hope of delivering the Magpies another Premiership.

The soldier who sent it was Malcolm 'Doc' Seddon, who had sailed off to war with his Collingwood teammate and best friend, Paddy Rowan. By the time the horseshoe arrived, Rowan had been dead for nine months, and Seddon was still 'doing his bit' fighting on the Western Front, while never forgetting those back in Melbourne.

The inscription was simple but heartfelt. The banner on the top of the horseshoe read: 'Good Luck.' The message below it was: 'To CFC. From Doc, France, 1917.'

Seddon included a letter explaining how the horseshoe had been made by his company's blacksmith while under heavy fire, with the metal coming from a shell he had found near Bapaume. The nails added to it came from a German plane shot down by the Australians. 'I hope that this shoe will bring the boys to the top of the tree this year,' Seddon wrote.

Collingwood duly finished on top of the ladder during the 1917 home-and-away season, and won its semi-final against South Melbourne by 10 goals. Yet in the next match, against Fitzroy, the Magpies offered little resistance; it was only the *Argus* Challenge finals system – which allowed the minor premier a second chance – that kept the club's Premiership hopes alive.

This time coach Jock McHale had a plan, and his players followed it to the letter. In the wet conditions of the Grand Final, he instructed his men to play body-on-body in an effort to outmuscle Fitzroy, and it worked. The Magpies, too, had the best goalkicker in the competition, Dick Lee, who kicked four goals for the game, while fellow forward Harry Curtis chimed in with three.

By three-quarter-time the difference was out to 28 points. The *Australasian* noticed a steely determination in the Magpies at the last change. 'In their previous engagement,' it wrote, 'the great majority [of players] lay full length on the grass ... not on this occasion. With one exception, they were standing, ready for the fray.'

Fitzroy kicked the first two goals of the final term, but Lee's fourth goal steadied the Magpies. The final margin blew out to 35 points.

The Magpies celebrated wildly, and for a brief interlude the war was forgotten. McHale was proud of his men. He had won his first Premiership as a coach, and dared to dream of more. The players who had made it happen were presented with medals donated by some of the club's leading supporters, including benefactor and businessman John Wren.

Collingwood had won the 1917 Premiership, just as Seddon had hoped when he sent the horseshoe from the battlefields of the Western Front all the way to the suburb in which he was born. To this day that remarkable talisman survives. And, as a constant reminder of the sacrifices made by others, it forms a central part of Collingwood's commemorations each Anzac Day.

H&A P15, W10, L4, D1 • **Finished** 1st • **Finals** P3, W2, L1 • **Finished** Premier • **Captains** Percy Wilson & Jock McHale • **Coach** Jock McHale • **Leading goalkicker** Dick Lee (54)

1918

THE ONE THAT GOT AWAY

It was three-quarter-time in Collingwood's finals match against South Melbourne, and it looked as if the Magpies were about to produce an upset win and continue their season for another week.

The Southerners had been minor premier, having lost only one match through the home-and-away season. They had narrowly beaten the Magpies on the two previous occasions they had met that year. Now, under the *Argus* finals system, which had assisted Collingwood in 1917, it was the Magpies who had to beat South Melbourne twice if they were to win back-to-back Premierships.

Coach Jock McHale was under no illusions about how hard that would be, but knew his team was capable. Twelve of the previous year's Premiership side were back to chase another flag.

Optimism was in the air. The war was looking more promising for the Allies, with an end in sight, and that helped bring out the biggest football crowd since the start of the conflict – almost 40,000 fans.

Despite being underdogs, Collingwood controlled much of the final, leading by four points at the first change and dominating the second quarter, albeit with some inaccuracy. In that second stanza, the Magpies kicked a wasteful 1.6, while managing to keep their opponents scoreless.

The talented South Melbourne outfit scored 4.1 in the third quarter, and Collingwood 3.5, meaning the margin going into the last quarter was 12 points. McHale instructed his team that it only needed to bring the same intensity to the final stanza to force South Melbourne into a sudden-death Grand Final the following week.

But South Melbourne kicked the opening two goals of the final term, levelling the scores. Dick Lee had the chance to break the deadlock late in the game, but his kick fell short. Then Ernie 'Snowy' Lumsden, who was Lee's cousin, scored a point with three minutes to spare, and Magpie fans dared to believe they might hold on.

The Southerners charged forward in the dying moments. Deep into the final term there was a mad scramble in the goal square, and South's Chris Laird got his foot to the ball and soccered it through for the match-winning major. Thirty seconds later the final bell rang, sounding the death knell for Collingwood's hopes of a second consecutive Premiership.

The *Argus* acknowledged how unlucky the Magpies had been: 'On the day, the honours were with Collingwood … South Melbourne, however, by sheer doggedness, wore the opposition down and in the last minute just managed to get in front.'

There was to be no Grand Final the following week. South Melbourne had won the flag that so many thought they would. All that did was to make McHale even hungrier for success in 1919. But the end of the war two months and four days later put everything into perspective for the coach, and for the club. After more than four years of conflict, the guns fell silent on 11 November 1918, with the *Australasian* calling it 'the greatest day in history'.

H&A P14, W10, L4 • **Finished** 2nd • **Finals** P2, W1, L1 • **Finished** 2nd • **Captain** Percy Wilson • **Coach** Jock McHale • **Leading goalkicker** Tom Wraith (26)

1919

DAN'S DEFECTION

Collingwood was desperate to win the 1919 'Peace Premiership'. This time, according to coach Jock McHale, there would be no excuses and no near misses.

Part of this confidence stemmed from the fact that the club's pre-war captain, Dan Minogue, was expected back in the country by the middle stages of the season. The war had ended the previous November, and Minogue returned to Australia on the *Barambah* on 26 July 1919.

The club was preparing a parade for Minogue along Smith Street, as well as a 'Welcome Home' party for its returning hero, but those plans came to an abrupt halt when it emerged that, instead of returning to the black and white, Minogue intended to join Richmond. It was a bombshell in a time of peace, and a new bitter rivalry with Richmond was about to be born.

There were several reasons for Minogue's desire to defect. Firstly, he had his eyes on a coaching role, and knew McHale would hold the post at Collingwood for many years to come. He had also developed a strong relationship with Richmond's Hughie James in the war years. Another motivation was Minogue's belief that the Magpies had treated his good friend Jim Sadler poorly by overlooking him in the 1917 Grand Final.

Whatever the issue, Minogue wanted to be the captain-coach of Richmond. Collingwood was steadfast in opposing the move, and moreover refused to pay Minogue his entitlements from the retirement fund. 'Side by side' wasn't just a line drawn from the club's theme song; at Victoria Park, loyalty was paramount. The Magpies effectively blocked Minogue's pathway to Punt Road, forcing him to sit out the rest of the 1919 season.

Adding to the drama of the season, Richmond, *sans* Minogue, emerged as Collingwood's greatest threat for the Premiership. And when they produced one of the shocks of the year by beating Collingwood in a final, it set the scene for a Grand Final full of emotion and enmity.

The night before the game, local police had to break up a number of disturbances between rival supporters on the streets. That mood continued onto the field the following day, with one observer noting that 'fists were showing at various periods' in what was a hard-fought and sometimes fiery clash.

After a relatively even first term, Collingwood managed to get on top in the second and led by four points at the main break. The Magpies opened their lead out to 16 points at the last change after having the wind in the third quarter, but the big question was whether it would be enough to stop Richmond.

McHale produced a masterstroke in the final quarter. Instead of trying to shut down the game, as many of his contemporaries would have, the coach urged his men to play attacking football and put the result beyond doubt. That tactic rattled Richmond, and as a consequence Collingwood outscored the Tigers in the final term, with the Magpies taking the flag by 25 points.

Minogue, and Richmond, had been taught a lesson – or so it seemed. But it wouldn't be the last that the Magpies, or McHale, would hear of their newfound rivals.

H&A P16, W13, L3 • **Finished 1st** • **Finals** P3, W2, L1 • **Finished Premier** • **Captain** Con McCarthy • **Coach** Jock McHale • **Leading goalkicker** Dick Lee (56)

1920

COVENTRY STAYS

An irregular timetable on the Hurstbridge railway line may have been the difference between one of the greatest VFL careers flourishing and the loss of a future champion.

The silhouetted figure on the Victoria Park station platform, which almost bordered the grounds of the Collingwood Football Club, was waiting for a train to take him home to his family's orchard at Diamond Creek. Nerves had got the better of this shy 19-year-old, who made a snap decision to forego his invitation to train with the Magpies and instead take the next 'rattler' home.

But the longer he waited, the more frustrated he became. As each minute passed, he could not stop thinking about the ribbing he would receive from his brothers when he arrived home. Fortunately, before the next train arrived, he put his nerves aside and headed back across to Victoria Park for his date with destiny.

The young man's name was Gordon Coventry, and 17 years later he would retire from the game as its greatest goalkicker, with a record that would be unsurpassed for generations.

Coventry's family nickname was 'Nuts', which had its origins in the unusual size of his head when he was a child. But even though he showed good talent as a young sportsman, he could never have been accused of having a swollen head. He was as modest as any champion to play the game.

Coventry had played the 1920 season with the Diamond Creek senior team, and after its year ended in August, an offer came from Collingwood to join the club immediately. A delegation of Collingwood officials had traipsed out to the Coventry home and offered

Nuts the chance to play the following weekend, in the absence of long-time spearhead Dick Lee.

The young man accepted the invitation and arrived in Collingwood on a city-bound train. But he changed his mind, saying later he was 'rapidly becoming a nervous wreck'. After waiting the best part of 10 minutes for a train to take him home, he made the smartest decision of his football life. Many years later, Coventry told the *Sporting Globe*: 'I decided I would sooner face what was in store for me at Collingwood than go home and tell my brothers that I was too nervous to enter the dressing rooms.'

Nuts played his first VFL match the following weekend, kicking a goal for Collingwood against St Kilda. The Magpies won by 58 points, but the *Australasian* noted that the young recruit was 'a trifle stage-frightened, for he did not shine'.

Coventry agreed with this assessment: 'I saw hundreds of young lads having their first League games thereafter, but none was as inglorious as mine.' He was dropped the next week, but returned for the club's last four games of the 1920 season, kicking three goals in the losing Grand Final to Richmond, now captain-coached by Dan Minogue.

The *Sporting Globe* later linked Coventry's decision on the platform that night to his new club's future, noting: 'No decision ever affected the fortunes of a football club as did Gordon's determination to turn again and join the Magpies.' In time, he would go on to break almost every record in the game, kicking 1299 goals from 306 games.

H&A P16, W10, L6 • **Finished** 4th • **Finals** P3, W2, L1 • **Finished** 2nd • **Captain** Dick Lee • **Coach** Jock McHale • **Leading goalkicker** Ern Utting (23)

1921

SYD RENEGES ON THE SAINTS

At around the time Gordon Coventry was making his nervous debut for Collingwood in August 1920, his elder brother Syd was playing football for 'the Miners' in Queenstown, Tasmania, as well as working in the mines.

It was a long way from the family's Diamond Creek orchard, but Syd had always been anxious to explore new challenges. 'I was always a wanderer,' he said years later, 'keen to strike out for myself, anxious to see other places, and I was only a youngster when I went to Tasmania. I was living at Queenstown and joined the football club, and – well, they tell me I was a good player then.'

Coventry was a good player, all right, and fitted in perfectly with the rough-and-tumble nature of Tasmanian football. But once homesickness set in, he returned to Melbourne and was courted by several VFL clubs.

One was St Kilda, whose officials travelled to meet him. 'I wanted to play in [VFL] premiership matches,' he later said, 'so I returned to Diamond Creek. One night I had a visit from the secretary of the St Kilda club. That was in early 1921, and I was keen to get in some business. The end result was that after a chat, I signed on to play with St Kilda.'

But almost as soon as he put his signature on the agreement, he regretted it, knowing that he really wanted to play with Gordon, and with Collingwood. *Table Talk* detailed his dilemma: 'Syd Coventry originally had an idea of turning out in red, white and black, and to that end ... he signed a permit form from the seaside club. But blood will tell and talk persuasively.' Another factor was that

Victoria Park was much closer to the Coventry home than was St Kilda's base, the Junction Oval.

'I realised I had made a mistake,' Coventry told the *Argus* almost a decade later, 'for my ambition was to play with Collingwood, but they had not asked me, and I knew that was where I wanted to go.'

After much encouragement from his brother, and belatedly from the Magpies, Coventry applied for a permit to join Collingwood. It was instantly rejected by the Saints. 'I *could* not play for Collingwood, and I *would* not play for St Kilda … it was too far away for one thing,' he said. '[So] the Collingwood committee tried to have the case opened, but it was no use: I was settled for that year, and so I stood down at the pleasure of the league.'

In 1921 Syd Coventry was able to play for the Collingwood District side, and some matches with Diamond Creek. His patience was rewarded the following year, when his passage to Victoria Park was assured.

For Collingwood fans, it was worth the wait. Syd made his VFL debut in Round 1 of 1922, and adapted to the tempo more quickly than his brother. 'I found that the Collingwood fellows were really good sports,' Syd said. 'They wanted to see a young fellow coming along.'

By the end of the decade, Syd Coventry would be acknowledged as one of the club's greatest players, and undoubtedly its greatest captain.

H&A P16, W9, L7 • **Finished** 3rd • **Finals** P1, L1 • **Finished** 3rd • **Captain** Dick Lee • **Coach** Jock McHale • **Leading goalkicker** Dick Lee (64)

1922

STARS QUIT AS WAGES BITE

For the 1921 VFL season, pretty much every Collingwood footballer was on the standard pay rate of £2 a week, plus expenses. The Magpies had made it a point of honour that, with few exceptions, all players would be paid on the same level. This tended to make Collingwood players susceptible to more lucrative approaches from other clubs, but to this point it hadn't proved too damaging to the club's fortunes.

Con McCarthy was one of those who had been made an attractive offer (which he refused) by a VFA club in 1921. That was hardly surprising: he was the man who had stepped into the breach in 1919 after Dan Minogue's defection to Richmond. McCarthy, a ruckman/follower of similar style to Minogue, had proved himself a similarly inspirational captain, leading his boys to the 1919 flag.

Yet McCarthy didn't enjoy the captaincy, and asked to be relieved of it after his one successful season; it passed instead to Dick Lee. But he remained one of Collingwood's most important players, and one of the best followers in the competition. So it was a massive blow to the club when he decided to quit Collingwood and join Footscray for the 1922 season.

Things got even worse when brilliant young winger Bill Twomey Snr also quit, to move to Stawell to pursue his dream of winning a Stawell Gift. Most fans thought Twomey's decision a relatively noble one, and he even returned to play some games with the Magpies late in 1922, after Stawell's season ended. But McCarthy's decision was another matter.

The economics were simple enough: the Dogs had offered McCarthy a staggering £400 for two seasons as playing coach, and Collingwood couldn't go anywhere near matching that offer. The Pies were prepared to meet the costs of McCarthy's appendix operation and play around a little at the edges, but the club firmly believed in the level playing field of its pay structure and would not budge. So McCarthy walked.

His departure sparked a major public debate about the amounts involved, the morality of such behaviour and the likely impact offers to players by rival clubs would have on the game in the future. Many critics were less than impressed.

Collingwood was spooked. Minogue's defection had been, most believed, an exceptional circumstance. An ageing Percy Wilson had been allowed to cross to Melbourne. Twomey was driven by non-monetary factors. A couple of other, less credentialed players had left for better pay. But this was one of the first times a key Collingwood player, in his prime, had been lured to the VFA for big money. The warning bells started sounding.

The departures didn't have a major impact on the Pies in 1922. The team finished six points clear on top of the ladder, but lost both its finals and went down to Fitzroy by 11 points in the Grand Final, which turned out to be Dick Lee's final game. It was a disappointing end to his magnificent career, and to what had been a promising season. But at least the club had a solid list to work with for 1923 and beyond. Or so it thought.

H&A P16, W12, L4 • **Finished** 1st • **Finals** P2, L2 • **Finished** 2nd • **Captain** Tom Drummond • **Coach** Jock McHale • **Leading goalkicker** Gordon Coventry (42)

THE STRAW THAT BROKE THE CAMEL'S BACK

If Collingwood felt the loss of Con McCarthy to Footscray, it was nothing compared to the maelstrom that followed its loss to Fitzroy in the 1922 Grand Final. Five important players – Dick Lee, Charlie Pannam Jnr, Bill Twomey Snr, Tom Drummond and Maurie Sheehy – would not return as players in 1923 for varying reasons, and their collective absence hurt the club immeasurably.

Lee, at the age of 34, retired after what had been an extraordinary career. No one begrudged him a spell after his 230 games and 707 goals. Besides, he would go on to serve the club off the field in the future. Drummond, who had captained the Magpies in 1922, and Sheehy were appointed playing coaches of Benalla and Northcote, respectively. Twomey was now living in Stawell and aiming at a Stawell Gift. The departure that hurt Collingwood the most was the defection of Pannam, who had been offered the position of playing coach of South Melbourne.

Collingwood refused to release Pannam when it received his request for a transfer. He was, after all, an extremely important player, not to mention one who had family links to the club dating back to the third season of Collingwood's existence, through his father of the same name. So Pannam could coach South Melbourne, but Collingwood's resolve meant he could not play for them. Effectively, the Magpies' decision meant Pannam would be unable to play football for three seasons.

In the club's annual report for 1923, which was released ahead of the 1924 season, Collingwood was blunt: 'Last year, in the Metropolis and Country Associations, there were 12 former pupils instilling into others the precepts learned at Victoria Park. The action of a League club in enticing a leading player to leave his own club last year to act as coach and pretend to live in the new district in the hope of getting a clearance, is "the last straw that broke the camel's back". Your committee has, in consequence, decided that no clearances will be granted to players as coaches except for legitimate reasons.'

Collingwood was unwavering and Pannam was not granted a permit to play until 1926. A year earlier, in the *Emerald Hill Record*, the Magpies were said to have 'adopted a particularly stubborn attitude over this matter, which makes us wonder, for Collingwood in the past have generally shown themselves to be good sports'.

The mystique surrounding McHale's coaching meant that rival clubs were intrigued by the Collingwood system and style of play. A profile on the legendary coach years later explained: 'Players were besieged with coaching offers on retirement (and often before), and ex-Collingwood players were first choice wherever possible. It was a well-known fact that to appoint a "McHale-coached" applicant as coach, the country team was assured of success on the field.'

But the Magpies had had enough. A tough stance needed to be taken, and it would form part of the club's strategy in the coming years. An era had ended, but Collingwood was confident a new one wasn't far away, even though the 1923 season concluded unsatisfactorily. After being runners-up the year before, the Magpies had been around the mark for much of the home-and-away season, but a draw with Carlton late in the year proved costly. In the end, despite wins in the final two rounds, Collingwood finished half a game out of the finals.

H&A P16, W8, L7, D1 • **Finished** 5th • **Captain** Harry Curtis • **Coach** Jock McHale • **Leading goalkicker** Gordon Coventry (36)

1924

PIES TARGET A NEW RULE

It is doubtful that any club in the history of the game has adapted to a rule change as successfully as Collingwood when it capitalised on a contentious 'out of bounds' rule change in the mid-1920s.

Collingwood missed the finals for a second successive season in 1924, the first time that had happened to the club since the start of the VFL competition. But coach Jock McHale was confident his group of emerging young players and recruits could once more restore the club's laurels.

He took note of a new rule that was proposed – and accepted – at the Australian Football Council meeting in Hobart in August 1924, during the carnival series played in Tasmania. It would become an important part of his future strategy.

Collingwood's long-serving secretary, 'Bud' Copeland, had been instructed as a VFL delegate to vote against a new proposal which guaranteed a free kick against the team who touched the ball before it went out of bounds. But Copeland went against the wishes of the league when it came time to vote, saying that he would 'like to give the suggestion a fly'. Copeland believed the new rule would reduce congestion and speed the game up, especially in the ruck scrimmages around the boundary line, which brought about repeated throw-ins.

With Copeland's vote crucial, the motion was carried, much to the chagrin of many football officials in Victoria. Even the Victorian coach at that carnival, Rod McGregor, expressed his disappointment, stating that 'as Copeland was given a definite instruction by the Victorian Football League to vote against the proposal and as Victoria is against it, Mr Copeland's vote should not stand'.

It did stand, however, and Copeland made no apology, saying that 'to pass the rule has been my last and best action in football ... the new rule may revolutionise football'. The VFL had little choice but to adopt the rule for the 1925 season.

McHale believed the new rule would provide a better look for the game. But he had self-interest at heart, too. He quickly adopted a game plan of direct, long football up the middle, with the aim of getting the ball from point to point as quickly as possible. 'Listen to the cheers of the crowd,' the coach said, 'and you will hear the deep-throated roar when the ball is moving quickly ... my desire is to see the game kept fast and open, and unduly rough play eliminated.'

To that end, he even had temporary lines painted down the middle of Victoria Park for certain training sessions to highlight the need for a 'corridor-style' of football. His game plan required a full-back such as Charlie Dibbs, who was capable of kicking in prodigiously, and at the other end of the ground a key forward such as Gordon Coventry, who had shaken off his nervousness to become the most prolific goalkicker of his generation.

Harry Collier recalled years later: 'We were told if you had to handball to get out of trouble, then to do it, but otherwise, kick the bloody ball because you can't beat a 50-yard roost.'

From the time the rule was implemented for the 1925 VFL season until the time it was rescinded in 1939, Collingwood won six Premierships, including four in a row, and missed the finals on only one occasion.

H&A P16, W8, L8 • **Finished** 6th • **Captain** Charlie Tyson • **Coach** Jock McHale • **Leading goalkicker** Gordon Coventry (28)

1925

INTRODUCING THE COLLIERS

Collingwood's tradition of unearthing young talent from within its own municipality was the club's greatest source of strength in its first 50 years. And there has never been a better example of that than the recruitment of the Collier brothers in 1925. In the years to come, Albert and Harry Collier would become stars in their own right. Collectively, they came to epitomise the spirit that would inspire some of the club's greatest glories.

Born and raised in Collingwood, in a family of 10 children, the Colliers were one-time students at that factory for producing footballers, Victoria Park State School, across the road from Victoria Park. Harry was older by 15 months, but Albert was the first to be invited down to the club.

In Lionel Frost's book *The Immortals*, he details Albert's first night of training at Victoria Park. Coach Jock McHale asked of him: 'How old are you, laddie?' Collier replied that he was only 15, to which McHale responded: 'Oh, you're too young to be playing here, I only started [playing football] when I was 16.'

At the urging of club secretary George Connor, McHale allowed Albert to train, but gave him some advice: 'All right, sonny, you can go out on the ground, but keep away from those big fellows. You'll get killed out there.'

Albert told Richard Stremski years later that he didn't listen to McHale's warning. 'I mowed into every big and small bloke, as much as I could,' he said.

Within a matter of weeks, he had impressed enough to make his VFL debut in Round 1 of 1925. He was 68 days short of his

16th birthday, and at time was thought – erroneously, as it turned out – to have been the youngest debutant in VFL history.

Thankfully, Albert's debut match did not define the rest of his career. Nerves got to him, he tried to place-kick one of his shots for goal and ended up 'toe-ending' the ball into the man on the mark, but he did manage to score one goal. He played only four games that season, but within four years would be acknowledged as the best player in the competition.

His brother Harry had also been lucky to get his first invitation to train with Collingwood in 1925. The letter sent to him by the club had been intercepted by his cousin Harold Collier, who fronted to training bearing the invitation before the mix-up was discovered.

Harry would not play a senior game until the following year, but showed great promise with the Collingwood District (seconds) side. In fact, Harry and Albert Collier both played key roles in the District team's Grand Final victory in 1925, lining up alongside one another as forward pocket and full-forward. Other Magpies of the future to play in that seconds final were Jack Beveridge, George Clayden and Norm MacLeod.

The match against Fitzroy's seconds side took place at the MCG as a curtain-raiser to the VFL Grand Final between Collingwood and Geelong. While the seconds won the flag by 24 points, the senior Magpies lost their Premiership playoff to the Cats. A changing of the guard was about to take place.

H&A P17, W12, L5 • **Finished** 4th • **Finals** P3, W2, L1 • **Finished** 2nd • **Captain** Charlie Tyson • **Coach** Jock McHale • **Leading goalkicker** Gordon Coventry (68)

A DIRTY DAY

Collingwood had 'set their hearts on the [1926] premiership', according to the *Argus*. Having lost the previous year's Grand Final, and not having won a flag since 1919, second prize wasn't going to suffice.

The Magpies won 13 of their first 15 games for the season. They finished the regular season as minor premier, equal on points with Geelong, although a loss to the Cats in Round 16 dented their confidence to some degree.

But when Collingwood took on Melbourne in a semi-final, the Magpies were overwhelming favourites. And when they opened up a 22-point half-time lead, the game appeared to be over. Melbourne, however, made a stunning comeback to win the game by 11 points, with the *Sporting Globe* saying 'Collingwood players and supporters had to absorb the big shock … they had every reason to expect a nice, comfortable win.'

With Collingwood having the right of challenge under the finals system, the two sides would later line up for the 1926 Grand Final. Magpie fans were confident of a very different result this time around, even though important players Charlie Dibbs and George Clayden could not play due to injury and suspension, respectively. There were even rumours that champion goalkicker Dick Lee, who had retired at the end of 1922, would be a shock inclusion after kicking seven of eight goals in a goalkicking competition during a club picnic at Mornington. That never happened, but still the Magpies believed their hard edge would overcome the flair of Melbourne.

The *Sporting Globe* detailed its prediction: 'Collingwood, though beaten by the Fuchsias in the semi-final, are all alert for their sixth premiership. Their last pennant carries the date 1919. It is now time for another, say the Magpies ... Melbourne will make the pace ... but if it comes to a hard, close finish, another premiership pennant will fly above the Magpie nest at Victoria Park.'

It would prove to be anything but a 'hard, close finish'. Melbourne kicked four goals to one with the breeze in the first term, and that set the scene for a dirty day for the team in black and white.

'We couldn't do anything right,' Syd Coventry said. 'Charlie Tyson, our skipper, won the toss and kicked against the wind. That was the start. We were on the wrong leg all day and Melbourne kept us there.'

There were mistakes aplenty, not just from Tyson, in a match that would be dissected and debated for years to come. Albert Collier was given conflicting advice on how to match up on Bob Johnson. Jack Beveridge was moved out of his usual spot in the centre and shifted to the half-forward flank, leaving Ivor Warne-Smith with too much freedom. And Syd Coventry was taken out of the ruck in the second half.

Tyson's form, too, was questioned, though many years later it would be revealed he had suffered a concussion a fortnight earlier, which may have impacted on his performance that day.

Collingwood cut the deficit back to nine points by half-time, but Melbourne conjured a seven-goal third term, killing off the Magpies' hopes. The margin blew out to an embarrassing 57 points by the final bell – the highest losing Grand Final margin to that time. A season that promised so much had delivered only disappointment.

The bitter recriminations wouldn't take long to emerge.

H&A P18, W15, L3 • **Finished 1st** • **Finals** P2, L2 • **Finished 2nd** • **Captain** Charlie Tyson • **Coach** Jock McHale • **Leading goalkicker** Gordon Coventry (83)

1927

DIVISIONS, DEPARTURE AND A NEW DAWN

It's been said that the darkest hour comes before the dawn, and that sums up where Collingwood was on the eve of the 1927 season. The Magpies had been runners-up in the previous two Grand Finals, and faced the prospect of a mini-revolt from its members at a heated annual meeting at the Collingwood Town Hall in March 1927.

Veteran *Herald* journalist Tom Kelynack, who wrote under the pen name 'Kickero', noted how some supporters 'tore up their [membership] tickets ... I have never seen such disappointment at the loss of the [1926] Premiership as was shown by their barrackers when Melbourne whipped them in the fight for last year's flag. There were many who had not recovered from the shock.'

Then, just five days out from the first match of 1927, the club's captain, Charlie Tyson, was sacked – as a leader and as a player. The timing gave rise to unfounded and almost certainly untrue allegations that he had 'played dead' in the 1926 Grand Final loss.

Tyson protested his innocence: 'A man is only an individual and it does not pay to have a body of officials against you.' Later, he wrote a letter to the *Herald* stating that he would sue anyone who kept the whispering campaign alive: 'Allegations, which it is unnecessary for me to say are quite without foundation, are now being circulated that I have received sums of money to induce me not to do my best for Collingwood in last year's final.'

The truth was Tyson, at 29, had outlived his usefulness. Collingwood believed it had a more inspiring leader waiting in the wings: Syd Coventry.

Collingwood was one of the best teams early in 1927. In a

late-season break due to a state match, the Magpies took their entire playing list – minus the Coventry brothers, who had been selected for Victoria – on a trip to Western Australia.

This included two 'friendly' matches, but the off-field experiences, which included a ride on a motor launch down the Swan River, dinner and smoke nights, a night at the Gloucester Park trots and a motor trip into the Perth Hills, helped to build the camaraderie of the team that would become known as 'the Machine'. Many years later, members of that team would say the experience forged the bonds that made this team one of the greatest of all time.

When the team returned home, Jock McHale spoke passionately about the tour: 'I had heard it was the golden west and I was not disappointed ... it was the finest trip I have been on in my long experience.'

The Magpies won through to the 1927 Grand Final against Richmond. The match was almost cancelled, such was the deluge of rain that broke Victoria's drought that week. The Tigers led by two points at the first change, even though no goals came in the opening term. Gordon Coventry booted the only two goals of the second quarter to push Collingwood out to a 14-point half-time lead. Incredibly, the Magpies would not kick another goal for the rest of the game. But the Tigers didn't register a goal until the final term, and Collingwood held on for a 12-point win.

The Magpies had won the Premiership, and the man who had replaced Tyson as skipper, Syd Coventry, was the hero of the season, winning not only Collingwood's first Brownlow Medal but also the inaugural Copeland Trophy.

H&A P18, W15, L3 • **Finished** 1st • **Finals** P2, W2 • **Finished Premier** • **Captain** Syd Coventry • **Coach** Jock McHale • **Leading goalkicker** Gordon Coventry (97) • **Copeland Trophy** Syd Coventry

---

1928

A STRIKE AVERTED

The Collingwood Machine faced many hurdles during its sustained run of success, but it was a threatened players' strike during the 1928 season that tested the harmony of the group more than anything else.

The proposed strike came after the club announced it would cut the players' wages from £3 back to £2 10s, citing the worsening economic situation for the belt-tightening. The information was relayed to the players just before they ran out for their Round 12 clash with Geelong at Victoria Park. The Magpies lost by 11 points, but this was likely due to injuries to four players rather than to angst associated with the wage cut. Yet the pay dispute threatened to drive a wedge between the committee and the players, and – worse still – to create divisions among the playing group.

The issue came to a head on the Tuesday night after the Geelong loss. A fiery players' meeting took place, with varying viewpoints being expressed. Veteran Ernie Wilson put forward a motion stating the players should refuse to play for £2 10s. It was seconded by young star Albert Collier, who had turned 19 just the day before. George Clayden would later say in *Kill for Collingwood* that the majority of the team had agreed with 'the tenor of the motion', while Percy Bowyer said the more experienced players seemed to be more militant than those who were younger.

At the start of the meeting, Syd Coventry seemed prepared to accept a majority verdict. But as the debate rolled on, the captain stepped forward to drag the team back from the brink of an unprecedented strike. He told his teammates that the ramifications of striking would tarnish what they had already achieved – the 1927 Premiership – and what they all knew they could still achieve. He convinced them to grin and bear the pay cut, and to get back to the thing they did best: play football.

Bowyer recalled: 'He [Coventry] was our captain, and after all was said and done, you have to be sensible about things.'

Five successive wins followed before a final-round loss to Carlton, which added further controversy, with allegations – never proven – that two Collingwood players had accepted £50 to play poorly. Syd Coventry was not one of them, knocking back an offer for the cash, though he later joked that he might as well have accepted it, such was his poor form.

A draw with Melbourne in the semi-final – the first ever draw in a final – followed, but Collingwood narrowly won the replay, and then comfortably defeated Richmond to win the 1928 Grand Final by 33 points.

In the moments before the start of that Premiership playoff, Syd Coventry – who had averted the strike months earlier – said to his sibling Gordon: 'A lot depends on you today.' The challenge was accepted, and Gordon finished the game with nine of the club's 13 goals – a record that would not be equalled for another 61 years, and has never been bettered. Back-to-back flags meant that the aborted strike was a distant memory, thanks to Syd Coventry's leadership and Gordon Coventry's goalkicking.

H&A P18, W15, L3 • **Finished** 1st • **Finals** P3, W2, D1 • **Finished Premier** • **Captain** Syd Coventry • **Coach** Jock McHale • **Leading goalkicker** Gordon Coventry (89) • **Copeland Trophy** Harry Collier

---

1929
JUST ONE BLEMISH

Collingwood was far from sated after its 1927 and '28 Premierships. The club made no secret that a third successive Premiership in 1929 was not simply an aim, but an expectation. There was to be no resting on laurels, no sense of satisfaction, until another flag was secured.

That mindset of success drove the players, the coach and, indeed, the club through what would become Collingwood's most complete season. It would be the first and only time a team won every home-and-away match. Collingwood's average winning margin in its 18 regular-season games was 43 points.

In a glittering year, the Magpies became the first team to kick 2000 points in a season, and the first to win 20 consecutive games (including the semi-final and Grand Final of 1928). Albert Collier, 20, won the Brownlow Medal in his fifth season. Gordon Coventry became the first player to smash through the 100-goal barrier.

That lust for records started from the opening game of the season. In a home match against Richmond, the Magpies opened the new Ryder Stand, unveiled the 1928 pennant and proceeded to kick 13 consecutive goals in the first three terms. A miss from Harold Chesswas in the final quarter brought some mirth from the crowd.

Such was Collingwood's dominance that Syd Coventry felt the standard of VFL football had fallen. 'I thought the game had slipped, as we were beating everybody,' he said. Some fans in the outer even offered a sweepstake over when the Magpies would finally lose a game. It was shelved because no one dared to believe they would.

Then, just as the flag seemed a formality, Collingwood 'met its Waterloo' in a game that one newspaper declared was 'the most extraordinary upset in the history of football'. Richmond smashed Collingwood by 62 points in their first finals meeting; the *Herald* summed up the shock by saying, 'Eighteen spanners were thrown into the works, and the Machine was smashed to smithereens.'

It was an apt description. Key players Syd Coventry and George Clayden were flattened in the first five minutes of the match, with the *Australasian*'s Jack Worrall claiming, 'The [Richmond] instruction had evidently been to bump into the opposition … in a manner that displayed a reprehensible spirit that marred the play all day.'

The chance to go through an entire season undefeated had been lost. But a third flag still beckoned.

Jock McHale had a dig at his Richmond counterpart when he said before the 1929 Grand Final that 'my instructions will be for our men to play the ball at all times – Collingwood want to win the Premiership by fair means only'. But he brought in third-game player Charlie Ahern to provide some physical protection for Syd Coventry, and he opted to use Gordon Coventry as a decoy to allow 'Tubby' Edmonds the space to kick goals.

The Magpies were oblivious to death threats sent in 11 handwritten letters to the rooms before the game. But this time the match was never in any doubt. The Machine kicked six goals to two in the opening term, setting the scene for a day in which Collingwood completely outplayed its rival to win by 29 points.

Collingwood had won its third successive Premiership in a stunning form reversal from a fortnight earlier – a fitting reward for what was almost a perfect season.

H&A P18, W18 • **Finished 1st** • **Finals** P2, W1, L1 • **Finished Premier** • **Captain** Syd Coventry • **Coach** Jock McHale • **Leading goalkicker** Gordon Coventry (124) • **Copeland Trophy** Albert Collier

---

FIRING UP FOR A 'FOUR-PEAT'

On the morning of the 1930 Grand Final, the *Sun News-Pictorial* highlighted the task that lay ahead of Collingwood – and the Machine – in taking on Geelong at the MCG. 'It is today or never to pull off the greatest record in league history, for it will probably be many years, if at all, before another team gets close to four premierships on end,' the paper forecast.

The Magpies had once more finished on top of the ladder at the end of the home-and-away season, but a finals loss to a faster and more youthful Geelong cast doubt on whether the Machine had enough left in the tank. To make matters worse, legendary coach Jock McHale was absent from the Grand Final – the only time he would miss a game in his long coaching career. He was confined to his Brunswick home with pleurisy and a heavy dose of influenza, and could only listen to the match on a wireless placed beside his bed.

The first half of the game would have made McHale feel even sicker. Collingwood had been completely outplayed during the second quarter. By the time the teams headed back into the dressing rooms for the main break, Geelong's lead was 21 points, and many in the crowd feared football's greatest run had come to an end.

No one officially coached Collingwood that day, though captain Syd Coventry dealt with the strategy on the field. At half-time it was left to long-time administrator Bob Rush to fill the breach. A passionate orator, Rush pleaded with the players to lift for their ailing coach, and for themselves. He told them McHale would know which members were letting the Machine down.

Harry Collier called this one of the most 'inspirational' speeches he had heard. 'Old Bob Rush was a great man for Collingwood,' Collier said. 'He got up and I remember him addressing the players ... you know, we respected him as much as anyone. Everyone loved Old Jock, too.'

The half-time rev-up over, the Magpies went back onto the MCG inspired to create history. Eight goals and six behinds for the third quarter was an extraordinary response, and brought about a 53-point turnaround – and a 32-point lead at the last change.

That same *Sun News-Pictorial* called it 'one of the finest performances ever seen in football ... an object lesson to every team in rising to the occasion after being apparently beaten, and by sheer grit and magnificent teamwork, sweeping down every obstacle in the way of finals success'.

After this third-term avalanche, Collingwood's remarkable fourth successive Premiership was never in question, and the final margin was 30 points. McHale listened with relief, while Rush was proud that the players had heeded his impromptu half-time words. The Machine players celebrated as a crush of well-wishers tried to gain entry to the rooms.

'We were up against the greatest odds a team could face at half-time,' Syd Coventry explained, 'and I thank the boys for the way they rose to the occasion.'

In the year in which Don Bradman changed Test cricket, one of the greatest compliments came when the *Herald* wrote that 'Collingwood are the Bradmans of football'.

H&A P18, W15, L3 • **Finished** First • **Finals** P3, W2, L1 • **Finished** Premier • **Captain** Syd Coventry • **Coach** Jock McHale • **Leading goalkicker** Gordon Coventry (118) • **Copeland Trophy** Harry Collier

---

1931

LOSING 'LEETER'

The headline in the *Sporting Globe* on the eve of the 1931 season was the same question most people in football were asking: 'Will Collingwood keep it going this season?' Coming off an unprecedented four successive Premierships, and with a team still boasting some of the greatest footballers to have played the game, only a brave person would have dismissed the Magpies' chances.

Leading football writer 'Jumbo' Sharland observed: 'Who can take the steam out of Collingwood? Their organisation and team management are peerless. And what teamwork! Every man pulls his weight and assists his teammate. So do other sides do this? Of course, they don't. That is why Collingwood is always formidable.'

But in his glowing assessment, Sharland also predicted a possible changing of the guard, following the unexpected loss of one of the Machine's most important cogs. Incredibly, 21-year-old Albert 'Leeter' Collier, champion centre half-back, had accepted a lucrative offer to become playing coach of Tasmanian club Cananore.

Collier had been working alongside his father as a painter when he received news he had won the 1929 Brownlow Medal. By 1931, however, he was like many others in the Collingwood community – out of work. Ultimately, a combination of the Great Depression and the club's egalitarian pay scale facilitated his departure. An offer of £9 per week from Cananore, as well as the promise of a job, was too good an opportunity to pass up. He had no option but to take it, and the club reluctantly granted their permission.

Collingwood's loss was Tasmanian football's gain. Collier won the Leitch Medal as the best player in the Tasmanian competition in 1931, and led his team to a Premiership. In contrast, the Magpies' reign came to a sudden end when they lost by 88 points to Carlton in the first semi-final.

As painful as the defeat was for Jock McHale, he knew there were excuses. It was said the Collingwood rooms resembled 'a casualty clearing station'. Charlie Dibbs (strained knee), Syd Coventry (thigh), Harry Collier (bruised thigh), Gordon Coventry (back), Frank Murphy (strained groin) and Harold Rumney (bruised thigh) were among the injured players.

The Machine's run was over. But the coach was confident his team could rebound, even if he knew a makeover was required. And Albert Collier had been sorely missed.

The news could have been worse. In September 1931, after the Magpies' early finals exit, a report in the *Sporting Globe* would have further alarmed their army of supporters. It read: 'According to information received from Tasmania, it is regarded as almost certain that Harry Collier, the Collingwood rover, will join his brother Albert in Hobart next year. If Harry goes to Tasmania, he will join Cananore.' Fortunately, that never happened. Harry remained with the Magpies, while Albert took his Cananore team to another Grand Final in 1932, before deciding to return to Victoria.

Fitzroy and St Kilda approached Albert Collier about a coaching role, but after a failed attempt to get him a Collingwood council job, businessman and club benefactor John Wren was able to secure him work as a painter at the Carlton & United Brewery. He wasn't going to be lost a second time.

H&A P18, W12, L6 • **Finished** 4th • **Finals** P1, L1 • **Finished** 4th • **Captain** Syd Coventry • **Coach** Jock McHale • **Leading goalkicker** Gordon Coventry (67) • **Copeland Trophy** Harold Rumney

---

1932

SACRIFICE FOR THE COMMUNITY

Collingwood footballers were heroes in their community long before the Great Depression began to bite deeply. But the club, and the men who wore the black-and-white jumper, gained an even greater significance as the suburb slid helplessly into the global economic gloom. Often, the success of the team provided a ray of illumination: 'If Collingwood were beaten,' one observer said, 'there'd be no *Sporting Globes* sold in the shops … people wouldn't eat their tea … they took defeat badly.'

Even as the club did its best to provide what relief it could to the Collingwood community – where the unemployment rate was more than 30 per cent for the eligible male population – it was still struggling financially. Ahead of the Round 5 clash with Carlton in 1932, rumours of a further pay cut for the players led to a 'heavy argument' in the rooms before the game. Players' representative Bruce Andrew was dispatched to speak with club officials Frank Wraith and Bob Rush, and he brought back the news that a reduction in wages was a necessity.

Four years earlier, a similar situation had almost caused a players' strike. The anger this time around was the same, but the Magpie players knew the show had to go on. And even if they were late out onto the field that afternoon, following much debate, they went out with the words of captain Syd Coventry ringing in their ears: 'Let's go out and kill the bastards.' The result didn't quite follow the script. Carlton won by 20 points, but for the Magpies it was the message that counted – to the point that some players, many years later, incorrectly recalled that they had won the game.

The players' attitude mirrored a move from Jock McHale, who offered to take the pay cut as well. From that day on, he insisted on being paid exactly the same as his players – a remarkable sacrifice for a man who could have commanded significantly more at almost any other team in the competition.

Sacrifice was the prevailing mood, and there were many examples of the Collingwood Football Club putting its community first. The Magpies were the first club to allow the local unemployed to attend its home matches free of charge, 'on the production of their sustenance tickets'; it wouldn't be long before the VFL as a whole followed suit.

The high demand from the sustenance workers – or the 'sussos', as they were called – meant the offer was restricted to Collingwood residents for a time, before a system was later instituted whereby they had to arrive at the game 15 minutes before the 3pm start to be eligible for entry.

The players also hosted a number of dances at the Collingwood Town Hall to help raise much-needed relief funds, and they staged athletic carnivals and goalkicking competitions. The club even played a match against a Ballarat league team in 1931 in aid of the unemployed.

Through the worst of it, Collingwood never lost its engagement with or its commitment to the local community. That philanthropy would become engrained in the club's DNA, and it runs through to the present day.

H&A P18, W14, L4 • **Finished** 3rd • **Finals** P2, W1, L1 • **Finished** 3rd • **Captain** Syd Coventry • **Coach** Jock McHale • **Leading goalkicker** Gordon Coventry (82) • **Copeland Trophy** Syd Coventry

---

1933

REGAN GOES BACK

Jack Regan was being groomed as a full-back through the Collingwood seconds during the 1930 VFL season when an unexpected opportunity arose. Charlie Dibbs, the regular full-back, took the weekend off to get married, which provided Regan with the perfect chance to audition for the role for the future.

Regan had already played three senior games, either as a reserve or wing/half-back, but this was his chance to make an impression against St Kilda, and on one of the best forwards of the time, Bill Mohr. Collingwood won the game convincingly, but Regan's hopes of impressing coach Jock McHale were dashed as Mohr became the first player to kick 10 goals against Collingwood in an impressive display in a losing team. Regan did not play in the seniors again that season, but re-emerged as a forward in 1931. The following season he won a regular position as the side's centre half-forward.

On one occasion early in his career he missed a late shot at goal, which proved costly, and when he apologised to McHale after the match, folklore has it that the coach glared at him and said, 'Go and throw yourself in the bloody Yarra [River].' Still, Regan impressed enough people in 1933 to be selected – in attack – in a Victorian representative side. Critically, at stages of the interstate match he was shifted to the full-back post by the Victorian (and Richmond) coach, Percy Bentley.

This proved a significant moment for Regan, and for Collingwood, and the rest, as they say, was history. After that state match he began to spend more and more time in the key defensive post for his club. Although he battled a leg injury in 1933, which restricted him to 12 games, he spent part of the second half of the season at full-back, with veteran goalkeeper Dibbs moving across to the back pocket.

The 1933 season had been an inconsistent one for Collingwood. At no stage did the Magpies strike the right gear, as they tinkered with the team to find replacements for those who had departed. The club's annual report explained: 'The all-important policy of re-organisation and rebuilding had to be carefully and systematically handled.' But a sixth-placed finish was disappointing, making it the first time the Magpies had missed the finals since 1924.

Still, McHale could sense he was on a winner with Regan's move to defence. By the end of the following season he was one of the best defenders in the game, capable of taking on and beating champion full-forwards. In time he would almost revolutionise the role, bringing his natural flair, high-flying aerial skills and attacking style of play to a position that had long been seen as a close-checking, negative one.

In 1934, the year after his state game switch, the 22-year-old Regan was a rising star. He was runner-up in the Copeland Trophy, and his popularity was such that he won the Austral Cup, an award presented by the owner of the Austral Theatre in Northcote to the Collingwood player voted by patrons as the best or most consistent player of the season.

Regan was on his way, and by the end of his career he would become universally known as 'the prince of full-backs'.

H&A P18, W11, L7 · **Finished** 6th · **Captain** Syd Coventry · **Coach** Jock McHale · **Leading goalkicker** Gordon Coventry (108) · **Copeland Trophy** Gordon Coventry

---

1934

A BLOODY RIVALRY

There was already ill-feeling between Collingwood and Carlton leading into the Round 10 clash between the sides at Victoria Park in 1934. By the end of the match, there was almost open warfare.

The first hint of trouble came when retired Magpie Bruce Andrew suggested on radio that the Blues had tried 'shock tactics' to defeat the Magpies in the 1931 first semi-final – the match that had ended the Machine's Premiership streak. The clubs had played each other five times since, and each time it seemed as if the temperature was rising, to the point that it had to boil over at some stage. That happened on Bastille Day of 1934 – 14 July – and it brought about what one newspaper described as 'the most disgraceful scene in the history of our game'.

Each side blamed the other, though both were at fault. The first half of the contest was full of animosity, but the field umpire was mostly able to keep it in check. The score was tight – the Magpies led by 16 points at the main break – and that only increased the sense of tension, both on the field and off it. Something, it seemed, was always going to ignite an explosion.

During the third quarter, Collingwood's captain, Syd Coventry, whacked Carlton's Gordon Mackie on the neck. Mackie's retaliation was as swift as it was brutal, as he belted Coventry back. The force of the hit caused the Magpie serious facial injuries as well as severe concussion; the following day Coventry said, 'It's all a blank to me ... I got a knock, but where and how I got it, I cannot say.'

The incident sparked an all-in brawl, and Coventry's normally genial brother, Gordon, ran from one end of the ground to the other to remonstrate with Mackie. Almost all the players on the field were involved – they were 'massed in a swirling group', as one reporter said – and the police hurried onto the field to break it up.

The *Age* said the match, which Collingwood won by 30 points, was 'marred by ultra-vigorous tactics, spiteful incidents and a discredited brawl in the third quarter'. The *Sporting Globe* was more dramatic: 'Club tradition and discipline, so often boasted about, were thrown to the winds in a wild disorder ... the zephyr gradually developed, and it ... assumed proportions of a tornado.'

The controversy didn't end with the final bell. The crowd stayed on long after the end, 'alternately hooting and cheering the players as they came from the dressing-rooms'. Adding fuel to the furnace of emotion, 'the feeling between the two clubs ... was even more bitter after the game, when the umpires announced that they intended to report three Carlton players'.

Two of the three Carlton players were suspended, and the Blues demanded the VFL hold an inquiry into the matter – in particular, as to why no Collingwood players had been reported. That inquiry determined that three umpires – two boundary umpires and a goal umpire – had been negligent in not making more reports, a verdict which only increased the tension between the two clubs, now bitter rivals for the future.

Collingwood made the finals; Carlton missed out. But a three-point loss to South Melbourne in a semi-final ended the Magpies' season in Syd Coventry's final game. A new captain and perhaps a new direction were now required.

H&A P18, W13, L4, D1 • **Finished** 4th • **Finals** P1, L1 • **Finished** 4th • **Captain** Syd Coventry • **Coach** Jock McHale • **Leading goalkicker** Gordon Coventry (105) • **Copeland Trophy** Albert Collier

---

1935

PIES' LUCKY BREAK

South Melbourne goalkicking machine Bob Pratt loomed large as Collingwood's biggest threat in the lead-up to the 1935 VFL Grand Final. Pratt had kicked 20 goals in three games against the Magpies that season – four in Round 1, 10 in Round 12 and six in the second semi-final – and speculation was rife that he might lift the Swans to the flag off his own boot.

Collingwood's first-year captain, Harry Collier, certainly feared that prospect and was conscious of the importance of keeping the prolific Pratt in check. Years later, he recalled: 'I remember coming home from work and going up along Hoddle Street, and someone said to me: "How are you going, Harry?" I said: "We will win it, if there is no Pratt."' What Collier didn't know was that his team would be the beneficiary of one of the biggest pre-game sensations leading into a Premiership play-off in the history of the game.

Just hours earlier, unbeknown to the Magpie captain, Pratt had stepped off a tram along High Street, in Prahran, and been knocked off his feet by a truck carrying a load of bricks. It hit the South Melbourne star with force, and he was immediately taken home with a range of injuries, including a sprained right ankle, a lacerated leg, an injured left foot and a badly bruised finger. The incident could have been so much worse for Pratt, but it was a critical blow to South Melbourne's Premiership hopes.

There would be wild and unsubstantiated whispers that one of the leading betting syndicates might have been responsible for the accident, with Pratt saying decades later that gangster 'Squizzy' Taylor was rumoured to have been involved. Given that Taylor had been killed by 'Snowy' Cutmore in a gun duel in 1927, this theory can safely be dismissed.

Pratt had actually been run down by – of all people – a South Melbourne supporter. The truck driver, Mr C.T. Peters, was so shattered by the experience that he went around to Pratt's home that night to offer him a packet of cigarettes by way of apology. Pratt accepted his message of regret, though South fans might not have been as forgiving.

Instead of playing, Pratt was reduced to the role of 'press correspondent' for the Grand Final. The *Emerald Hill Record* reported: 'South supporters have declared "war" on all truck drivers since the injury to the champion. The hand of Fate descended very heavily on South Melbourne in robbing it of the services of its crack forward.'

In a typically hard and aggressive display, Collingwood won the game – and the 1935 Premiership – with a 20-point victory over the Pratt-less South Melbourne. The Machine had been remodelled and another flag had been the result. A late goal to Harry Collier put the issue beyond doubt, and showed why Jock McHale had been so keen to have him as the new captain.

The 1935 Premiership sparked some of the most riotous celebrations in the club's history. A piano was wheeled out into the middle of Victoria Park that night. President Harry Curtis called it 'the greatest [flag] the club has won yet'.

But for the Pratt accident, however, the result might have been different.

H&A P18, W14, L2, D2 • **Finished** 2nd • **Finals** P3, W2, L1 •
Finished Premier • **Captain** Harry Collier • **Coach** Jock McHale •
Leading goalkicker Gordon Coventry (88) • **Copeland Trophy**
Albert Collier

1936

NUTS BOILS OVER

A truck had stopped Bob Pratt from playing in the 1935 Grand Final. A year on, it would be a painful case of boils, some unwelcome attention and a rare flash of anger that cost another goalkicking machine the chance to play in the 1936 Premiership decider. Collingwood had been the beneficiary in the first instance; it would be on the receiving end in the second.

Gordon Coventry was one of the game's most scrupulously fair players. Despite the close attention he copped from rivals across almost all of his 306 games, he managed to keep his cool, no matter what transpired. But that changed in a spiteful encounter against Richmond at Punt Road Oval in Round 13, 1936. The normally unflappable Coventry clashed heatedly with his opponent, Joe Murdoch, and the ramifications put a significant question mark on Collingwood's hopes of winning back-to-back Premierships.

Coventry was reported and, sensationally, suspended for eight weeks. That ruled him out for the remainder of the season – a cruel blow for the club, and shattering for the player in what was his first offence. There had been mitigating circumstances, but for whatever reason Coventry chose not to air them at the VFL Tribunal. Instead, he told the hearing: 'Halfway through the third quarter, I went up for a mark and got a blow to the head. I do not remember what happened after that.'

What he chose not to reveal was his belief that Murdoch, who himself copped a four-game ban, had been hitting into the back of Coventry's neck, knowing he had been suffering from boils. The pain had apparently caused Coventry to strike back. That is what his teammates believed had happened, and what Coventry told the club. For his part, Murdoch denied it, and would later allege that businessman and Magpie benefactor John Wren offered to pay him if he helped to have Coventry acquitted.

The tribunal verdict rocked Collingwood. Local movie theatres put the stunning result up on their screens, more than 100 people – 'including a number of young women and youths' – waited outside League headquarters, and 'scores' of telephone complaints were made to the VFL that night and the following day.

Gordon Carlyon, who joined the club later as an administrator, said the Collingwood forward had refused to reveal the real reasons for his anger because he 'didn't believe in squealing'. He added: 'They belted him [and his boils] until he exploded, and he got eight weeks – for retaliating.'

Coventry's exclusion could have meant the end of Collingwood's Grand Final hopes for 1936. But the selection dilemma brought about an opportunity for a changing of the guard. At a selection meeting that week, coach Jock McHale exclaimed: 'We have got to get a full-forward.' Captain Harry Collier offered back: 'We've got a bloody full-forward. That was young "Toddy".'

Nineteen-year-old Ron Todd had played four senior matches the previous year, but in Coventry's absence he would give a hint to his future success, as well as prove his worth in the club's chase for the flag. Todd kicked 4.10 from 16 shots in the Grand Final – just his 16th game – to help lift Collingwood to the 1936 Premiership, beating South Melbourne – this time with Pratt – by 11 points. Within a few years, Todd would be the dominant forward in the game.

H&A P18, W15, L3 • **Finished** 2nd • **Finals** P2, W2 • **Finished** Premier • **Captain** Harry Collier • **Coach** Jock McHale • **Leading goalkicker** Gordon Coventry (60) • **Copeland Trophy** Jack Regan

---

A KID CALLED 'FOTHER'

Debut games and first seasons have always been looked upon with a sense of wonder at Collingwood, especially given the club's celebrated capacity to unveil teenagers seemingly before their time. Some have flashed like comets, only to disappear almost as fast. Others have turned their precociousness into long and successful league careers. But of all those who have represented Collingwood during their teenage years, it's a fair bet that none has been as good as early as a 16-year-old who played his first VFL game in Round 6, 1937. His name was Des Fothergill.

By the end of his first few practice matches, Fothergill was being forecast as a future star. After his first year, he would not only be the youngest player to win the Copeland Trophy – at 17 years and 77 days – but also the youngest winner of any club's best-and-fairest award. It's a record that stands to this day. And before his 21st birthday, the kid they called 'Fother' had secured three Copeland Trophies, and been acclaimed as joint winner of the 1940 Brownlow Medal. Not bad for a player the Collingwood selectors wanted to progress slowly, because coach Jock McHale believed he was 'too big in the backside'.

One of the many football graduates of Collingwood Technical School, Fothergill excelled in the schoolboy curtain-raisers played at Victoria Park, and captained the state schools' team. Then, aged 15, he played in the Collingwood District side, winning the team's best-and-fairest award in 1936. He played two senior practice matches on the one day in April 1937, and starred in both of them, but McHale did not select him until six weeks into the main season.

By that time, Fothergill's form was so good that he could not be denied any longer, as the *Argus* explained the following month: '[Fothergill's] performances have been so consistent that officials are beginning to consider including him in the senior side. He is aged only 16 years, and it was the intention of the selectors to leave him with the seconds until he had settled down.'

Fothergill was selected for the clash with Carlton in Round 6; he kicked a goal and slotted almost seamlessly into the team that had won the previous two VFL Premierships. The *Football Record* said of his first game that he 'fitted so perfectly into the famous combination, one would have thought he'd been playing for years with the sides'.

Remarkably, Fothergill was almost 19 years younger than team-mate Gordon Coventry, having been born just 30 days before the champion goalkicker's first game back in Round 15, 1920. Coventry provided another significant moment for Collingwood in the 1937 season when he became the VFL's first player to reach 300 games.

Fothergill's Copeland Trophy wasn't the only award he won in 1937. Ahead of the finals, he was also presented with a 'silver cup' from an eight-year-old admirer, the grandson of a long-time Magpie member, who made 'a remarkable speech', saying his only wish was to see the club bring home the flag.

Unfortunately, on the day of reckoning, neither the club's veteran, Coventry (on his 36th birthday, and in his final VFL game), nor its young prodigy, Fothergill, could stop Geelong from winning a match the dual Brownlow Medallist Ivor Warne-Smith called 'perhaps the greatest Grand Final in the history of the league'.

H&A P18, W13, L5 • **Finished** 3rd • **Finals** P3, W2, L1 • **Finished** 2nd • **Captain** Harry Collier • **Coach** Jock McHale • **Leading goalkicker** Gordon Coventry (72) • **Copeland Trophy** Des Fothergill

---

A TRIBUNAL 'THREE-PEAT'

Collingwood coach Jock McHale believed forces were working against his club after two significant suspensions robbed them of stars in the 1936 and 1937 seasons.

Gordon Coventry had missed out on a flag in 1936. Then Albert Collier was involved in a tribunal shock in 1937, when a complaint from North Melbourne that he had spat on a female supporter resulted in a heavy suspension, though he served his ban before the finals.

Incredibly, it happened again in 1938, and some of the protagonists claimed this one cost the Magpies the Premiership. This time, Collingwood captain Harry Collier was suspended, and the incident – which followed the club's Round 5 match against Carlton at Victoria Park – became one of the sensations of the season.

Collier was frustrated his team had squandered a 39-point half-time margin, and a 23-point lead at the last change, to go down by 16 points. Percy Taylor, of the *Age*, detailed part of what happened next: '[Carlton's Jack] Carney, the smallest player on the field, had rushed up to shake hands with his leader [Brighton Diggins]. As he was doing so, Carney was struck on the face by a Collingwood player.' Taylor chose not to name Harry Collier.

Collier recalled years later: 'At the end of the day I went down to shake Brighton Diggins' hand because they'd just knocked us off... the next minute Carney comes up alongside of me, and passed a remark. I couldn't tell you what he said – you couldn't put it in [a newspaper]. But I wasn't happy, so all I did was turn around – I didn't punch him – I sort of pushed him and said: "Don't argue."'

But it was more of a punch than a push, even though Collier was confident he'd got away with it. Carlton laid an official complaint against the Magpies' skipper, which saw the VFL refer the incident to its investigations committee. To his dismay, Collier was suspended 'for all remaining premiership matches this season'.

The anger of the club, and its fans, was such that a petition of 2500 'Collingwood members and other fair-minded football followers of the game' was presented to the VFL delegates. The proposal to accept the petition was defeated 11–10, and so the penalty stood, ruling out the inspirational captain for the rest of the season.

It was a cruel blow, one that was compounded by the knee injury Collier's brother Albert was carrying during the 1938 season. Harry's ban meant McHale was forced to abandon one of the pillars of his coaching career – never playing injured footballers in matches. Sensing Collingwood could not win the 1938 flag without at least one Collier, he insisted that Albert had to play against Carlton in the Grand Final.

Harry said years later that Albert had been reluctant, but 'Jock talked him into playing ... he didn't normally do that [play injured players], but he was desperate.'

Albert's inclusion backfired. Carlton 'took it easy on him' during the game, so that he would not be replaced by a fit replacement. But he was lame and never a factor as Carlton won the game by 15 points. Harry Collier insisted to his dying day that if he had played, the result might have been different.

H&A P18, W12, L6 • **Finished** 4th • **Finals** P3, W2, L1 • **Finished** 2nd • **Captain** Harry Collier • **Coach** Jock McHale • **Leading goalkicker** Ron Todd (120) • **Copeland Trophy** Des Fothergill

---

THE FIRST ELECTION BATTLE

By 1939, Collingwood had been in existence for nearly 50 years. There had been the usual turnover of committee members in that time, and the occasional challenge or murmuring of discontent, but nothing of any great seriousness. All that changed in 1939, however, when the Magpies became embroiled in a bitter and bloody election war that divided the club, turned friends into enemies and fundamentally altered internal dynamics for decades.

The trigger, surprisingly, was something as apparently simple as control of Collingwood's reserves team. The Collingwood District Football Club had been the club's unofficial seconds side since 1906, and more officially after the VFL's introduction of a seconds competition in 1919. But even though Collingwood supported the District side financially, it was effectively a standalone club: it had its own committee, its own way of running, a highly regarded coach in Hughie Thomas, and even its own loyalties and culture. Some seconds players in the 1920s had reportedly not wanted to be selected for the seniors if it meant missing out on a final with the District side.

By the late 1930s, some Collingwood officials felt the seconds organisation had become a little *too* independent. They were also concerned at rising operational costs, and several suspected financial irregularities. So the senior club's leaders – Frank Wraith, Harry Curtis and Bob Rush – decided it was time to haul District's committee into line. But other long-serving committeemen disagreed, and refused to sign a circular to members denouncing the management of the seconds.

For the first time, a major split emerged within the club. War hero and former player 'Doc' Seddon was one of the dissidents, and he joined forces with other disenchanted local councillors and seconds committee members to challenge for the presidency and several committee positions.

But the challenge failed spectacularly, at least partly (according to Richard Stremski's *Kill for Collingwood*) because Wraith engaged the Collier brothers to help out the incumbents through the adoption of a players' 'ticket', and also by getting a group of players to door-knock members for proxy votes. This was the first time the players had become directly involved in an election campaign – something that would come back to haunt the club in the decades ahead.

Of more immediate impact was the loss of Hughie Thomas, who had played a crucial, if largely unheralded, role in the club's success of the previous two decades. His nephew, Keith Stackpole, also left the club and joined Fitzroy, where he enjoyed a handful of outstanding seasons and played in a Premiership. And 'Doc' Seddon, a Magpie favourite, was now angry and bitter, and via his position on the local council became a thorn in the club's side.

Still, when the dust settled, Collingwood had taken control of its reserves team. But it had come at a high price.

The team limped into another Grand Final in 1939 – its fifth in succession – but was thumped by Melbourne to the tune of nearly nine goals. By the time the siren sounded it was clear to most observers that an era of Magpie supremacy had ended.

H&A P18, W15, L3 • **Finished** 2nd • **Finals** P3, W1, L2 • **Finished** 2nd • **Captain** Harry Collier • **Coach** Jock McHale • **Leading goalkicker** Ron Todd (121) • **Copeland Trophy** Marcus Whelan

---

1940

THE TODD BOMBSHELL

On paper, Collingwood's task of rebuilding after the debacle of the 1939 Grand Final looked to have a solid foundation. They had the 1939 Brownlow Medallist in Marcus Whelan, the game's best forward in Ron Todd, and the gifted Des Fothergill, who would jointly win the Brownlow in 1940. Throw in Phonse Kyne, Alby Pannam and Jack Regan and the side seemed strong.

But any optimism was shot to pieces before the start of the 1940 season, when Todd sensationally crossed to Williamstown without a clearance in a mega-money deal. Even worse, his good mate Fothergill followed him there a year later.

It's perhaps hard now to appreciate just how big these defections were at the time. Todd was 23 and had established himself as the best full-forward in the competition, following seasons of 120 and 121 goals. He was a high-flying excitement machine who, at his best, was unstoppable. If his accuracy in front of goal improved, it was surely only a matter of time until he eclipsed Bob Pratt's record of 150 goals in a season.

Todd was working for the railways at the time, and wasn't happy about what footballers were paid for their efforts. Yet Collingwood was determined to stick by its view that all its players should largely be paid the same. So when a cashed-up Williamstown came calling with a three-year contract worth £500, plus match payments that were two or three times higher than Collingwood's, Todd felt it was an offer he couldn't refuse. Collingwood wouldn't clear him, of course, but it didn't matter: Todd went anyway.

Under intense pressure from the media, fans and the Collingwood board, Todd actually tried to change his mind before the season began, and there was widespread elation – and relief – when he turned up to play in a Magpies practice match in April. But Williamstown had him stitched up tight and weren't going to let go. There were other attempts to engineer a return in the years that followed, but they all ended messily, and a truce wasn't called until many years later.

If Todd's departure was a blow that rocked Collingwood to the core – and it was – then Fothergill's a year later was the knockout punch. 'Fother' was just 20 and had already won three Copeland Trophies and a Brownlow Medal. He was, quite simply, the most freakishly talented footballer in the competition, whether playing forward or in midfield. In many ways, he was a little like Peter Daicos, both in impact and style of play. With his youth and brilliance, he was also the club's most popular and marketable player – a darling of the Magpie fans.

Collingwood had planned to build its teams for the 1940s around these two young superstars. Instead, by 1941 Jock McHale was forced to cobble together a side with neither Todd's goals nor Fothergill's wizardry, and it would be weakened further by departures due to the Second World War.

It was little wonder that 1940 was a disastrous season, with the team finishing eighth – its lowest position since the 1890s. Unfortunately, this was a taste of things to come in a decade that would provide little joy for Magpie fans.

H&A P18, W8, L10 • **Finished** 8th • **Captain** Jack Regan • **Coach** Jock McHale • **Leading goalkicker** Des Fothergill (56) • **Copeland Trophy** Des Fothergill

---

1941

THE OPENING OF THE SOCIAL CLUB

Collingwood stole a march on its rivals in April 1941 with the opening of the Collingwood Football Social Club. It took other clubs decades to get similar deals across the line, and the financial and social benefits that accrued to the Magpies in the meantime were significant.

The deal that brought Collingwood its much-sought-after liquor licence was almost a decade in the making, and a tribute to the foresight and aggressive planning of the club's leadership (plus, as it turned out, the persuasive powers of John Wren). It cemented Collingwood's role as *the* power club in football – both on and off the field.

The issue of liquor at Victoria Park had long been a vexing one. There were liquor booths at the ground from its earliest days, but when the Collingwood Council took over management of the ground in 1903 it introduced a ban on the sale of alcohol. This meant that thirsty fans had to make a mad half-time rush to nearby hotels if they wanted a drink. (The club responded by lengthening the interval and introducing half-time entertainment.)

There was much joy when Vic Park's own version of prohibition ended in 1923. But club secretary Frank Wraith had bigger plans in mind: he wanted the club to gain its own liquor licence and run a bar and social club. Liquor licences were tough to get, and usually only available when another club lost one. Frustratingly, in 1936 the club looked to have missed a golden opportunity to grab a licence due to some internal dissension.

But as the Second World War loomed, Wraith and club lawyer Jack Galbally realised that the Tivoli Club in Abbotsford – a

German club – would almost certainly lose its licence. This was Collingwood's opportunity: the club just had to make sure that the licence was transferred to it, rather than revoked.

This meant getting in early – before the Tivoli licence had been withdrawn. The Collingwood committee members' foresight and planning meant they were well ahead of their rivals also looking for a licence, and they were ready to strike as soon as it became clear that the Tivoli's licence would indeed be withdrawn.

The process was a long and complicated one, and is thoroughly detailed in Richard Stremski's *Kill for Collingwood*. The club's case was not strong, but fortunately the Magpies had friends on the council. They also had an ally in influential powerbroker John Wren, who was called in to help sway the deliberations of the licensing court.

In the end, all the backroom politicking worked and Collingwood became the licensee of the Tivoli Club in 1940. The committee transferred the licence to Victoria Park later that year and, after extensive renovations, opened the Collingwood Football Social Club in April 1941.

It had been a brilliant piece of vision and planning by Wraith and the other Collingwood leaders, and the club reaped the benefits for years to come.

There weren't as many wins on the field in this era, unfortunately, though a fifth-place finish – and a win in the VFL Lightning Premiership competition – initially suggested that the 1940 downturn might be a short-term blip. How wrong that would prove.

H&A P18, W12, L6 • **Finished** 5th • **Captain** Jack Regan • **Coach** Jock McHale • **Leading goalkicker** Alby Pannam (42) • **Copeland Trophy** Jack Murphy

---

1942

THE SECOND WORLD WAR HITS

The timing of the opening of the social club in 1941 could hardly have been any better, because if Collingwood fans and members ever needed ready access to a supply of alcohol, it was surely in 1942. This was the club's 50th anniversary but there was little to celebrate, as the Pies plummeted to their lowest finish since their very first year.

By the time the siren sounded on a wretched season, Collingwood sat in 10th place. And that was even worse than it now sounds, because there were only 11 teams in the competition that year, with Geelong not involved due to wartime travel restrictions. But there were mitigating circumstances for the Pies, who were hit badly by an event way outside their control – the Second World War.

Collingwood was one of the two teams most affected by enlistments. Just a few weeks before the start of the season, the number of players available to Collingwood selectors was so small that the club seriously considered pulling out of the competition. Only four established senior players and a handful from the reserves had turned up for the early practice matches; the *Argus* reported that 'so few players are left that the club is in dire trouble'.

The next day's reports were in some ways even more alarming, with the idea floated that Collingwood might amalgamate with the other badly affected team, Melbourne. Thankfully, that didn't happen, and both clubs determined to continue as independent entities. The Pies eventually scraped together enough fit bodies to form a senior team, but had to withdraw from the reserves competition for the year.

In those circumstances it's hardly surprising that the Magpies fared so badly on the field. Even master coach Jock McHale could do nothing to reverse the poor results: he simply didn't have the 'cattle' to turn things around. It really wasn't pretty, the low point a 138-point thumping at the hands of Richmond in Round 3. Then Hawthorn – the team that had not beaten Collingwood in 29 attempts since joining the League in 1925 – finally triumphed in Round 5 at Glenferrie Oval.

This was the ultimate humiliation, and turned out to be the only game Hawthorn would win for the year. But the Pies also only won a single game (against Melbourne) in the first 14 rounds, and coming into the final game of the year, at Victoria Park against Hawthorn, found themselves in the unfamiliar position of being threatened with the wooden spoon. Needing a win over the Mayblooms to be certain of avoiding that dubious honour, in the end Collingwood scraped home by 14 points before a poor crowd of just over 2000.

In the context of this season, any victory was important. But more significantly, in the club's broader historical context, this humble win preserved the Magpies' record of never having won the wooden spoon.

Still, no Collingwood player, official or supporter was sorry to see the end of the wretched 1942 season. Perhaps the only optimistic perspective to be found was that the next season would surely be better. And at least the club had avoided merging with Melbourne.

H&A P14, W2, L12 • **Finished** 10th • **Captain** Phonse Kyne •
Coach Jock McHale • **Leading goalkicker** Alby Pannam (37) •
Copeland Trophy Alby Pannam

MEMBERSHIP DOUBLES

Collingwood had never experienced a trough like the war-induced downturn that engulfed the club across 1942–43. In many ways the 1943 season was even more difficult than 1942 had been. There was no talk of amalgamation, at least, and the seconds were back up and running again. But up to 43 senior players found themselves doing some kind of war service, the Copeland Trophy was suspended for the year, and the club's spending on equipment and clothing was rationed to the point that it used as many footballs in the whole season as it would normally have used in a month.

'Those difficulties which faced your Committee in relation to the running of the team in 1942 were met with in an even increased measure in [1943],' noted the club's Annual Report. 'Valuable players were lost as they left for a theatre of operations or were transferred to other States, while those left on our training list were so largely engaged on war work that it was quite impossible for them to train regularly.'

Coming off the back of the club's worst ever season in 1942, and with the prospects for their team looking just as bleak for 1943, you could hardly have blamed Magpie fans for staying away in droves. But incredibly, membership more than doubled. Season ticket sales, which had been above 5000 in 1939, had dropped to just 942 in 1942. In 1943, however, they bounced back to 2126. Revenue increased from £393 to £878. It was the start of a trend that would not stop.

This was a staggering result in the circumstances. It confirmed the reputation of Collingwood fans as the most loyal in the competition, and reinforced the notion that this club, more than most, would stick together during tough times. The club said it was extremely proud of the result, and that the increased membership was 'convincing evidence that the old Collingwood spirit still lives among committee and supporters alike, all pulling together to achieve the best for Collingwood'.

That spirit alone wasn't enough to make a major difference to the results, however. It wasn't just the war, either: the loss of Fothergill and Todd, the additional defection in 1940 of brilliant defender Marcus Boyall to South Australia, and the messy retirements of club legends Albert and Harry Collier all came back to bite the club in 1942–43. The team again finished in second-last spot, but at least this time had five wins it could point to as evidence of some overall improvement, however modest.

Like everybody else, Collingwood saw hope only in the end of the war, and a return to normal football life, as the Annual Report noted: 'While hostilities continue, we cannot expect to do more than find likely youngsters of talent, do all we can with them while they are available, lose them for service to their country – and feel contented that we are doing a good job for the game and our club and certain that we shall be rewarded when the dark clouds of war have rolled into oblivion.'

They were optimistic words, but Collingwood had now missed the finals for four successive years. That had never happened before. So optimism among Magpie fans was, understandably, in very short supply.

H&A P15, W5, L10 • **Finished** 10th • **Captain** Jack Regan • **Coach** Jock McHale • **Leading goalkicker** Alby Pannam (40) • **Copeland Trophy** Not awarded

---

1944

A DOUBLE BLOW

The problems Collingwood faced in 1944 were similar to those it had experienced in the previous three seasons: a struggle for players, a lack of continuity and teamwork, poor resources. But by the end of the year, such problems had paled into insignificance.

The war was far from over, but the tide appeared to be turning against Japan and Germany. Many Collingwood players and past players were still serving the Allies at home and abroad. Leading into the 1944 season, one positive amid the gloom was the fact that no Collingwood player had yet made the ultimate sacrifice. That changed in the second half of the year, however, when two men to have worn the Collingwood jumper were killed in separate incidents in New Guinea.

The first was Norman Oliver, who had been a defender of considerable promise. He had played 13 games in 1940–41 before enlisting in the army, and later transferring to the RAAF to become a flight officer. At the age of 21 Oliver was killed when the Kittyhawk he was flying crashed on a beach near Madang, on 27 June 1944, three days after his old side lost to Carlton in a Round 8 game. His plane was believed to have run out of fuel. At the club's next match, against Geelong at Victoria Park, a few days after his passing, flags were flown at half-mast in his honour as the crowd stood silent.

Almost five months later, on 15 November, the Magpies lost another former player, 36-year-old Norm Le Brun, in fierce fighting. Le Brun had long since left Victoria Park by this point. His time at the club had been fleeting, and he'd spent most of it as the second rover to the great Harry Collier, playing 19 games in 1933–34. Le Brun would have the distinction of being one of only 24 players to have represented four different league clubs – he played for South Melbourne, Essendon, Collingwood and Carlton – but he certainly left an impression among his Magpie mates.

According to the book *To the Green Field Beyond*, by Shaun O'Leary, Le Brun was the first Australian soldier to die in what became known as the Aitape–Wewak campaign, which at the time was seen as a 'mopping-up exercise' to purge the Japanese from New Guinea.

O'Leary wrote that Le Brun was killed by a rifleman concealed among the roots of a large tree. The country was too steep and the jungle too thick for the patrol to bring his body back, but it was later recovered and he was eventually laid to rest in the Lae War Cemetery – which was also Oliver's final resting place.

Collingwood mourned the death of both men. In the face of such loss, the team's 10th-place finish seemed almost irrelevant. The club appeared to sense that too, and took an unexpectedly positive tone when summing up the year, paying tribute to the 'interest, sportsmanship and enthusiasm of the players – a well behaved band of trained athletic young men developing not only as fine Australian footballers but also as better citizens and Australians … Your club has never been richer in club spirit and good fellowship than it is today.'

H&A P18, W7, L11 • **Finished** 10th • **Captain** Pat Fricker • **Coach** Jock McHale • **Leading goalkickers** Lou Richards & Bob Galbally (26) • **Copeland Trophy** Not awarded

---

1945

'FOTHER' COMES BACK

During the dark days of 1942–43, the club held out hope that brighter times would return once the war had ended. The young players given premature exposure to VFL football, combined with those due to return from active service, would ensure the club once again fielded a 'formidable' team. Many might have dismissed such claims as early attempts at 'PR spin'. But then, just as the war was coming to its end early in the 1945 season, Des Fothergill came home to Victoria Park.

The return of the 1940 Brownlow Medal winner gave everyone at Collingwood an immediate lift. Even though hopes for the impact he might have were tempered by the knowledge that he'd injured a knee while on service – he'd also lost some of his mobility and was a few pounds heavier – the powerful symbolism of 'Fother' once again pulling on the Collingwood jumper was undeniable.

So imagine the buzz around Victoria Park when Fothergill not only played in the opening round of 1945, against North Melbourne, but also kicked five goals to spearhead the Magpies to a 21-point win. These were the first of 62 goals the diminished Fothergill managed for the year – an extraordinary return. It was a glorious homecoming, and also a signal that the lows of the war years were now in the past.

Astute Magpie fans would have felt encouraged by more than just Fothergill. Making their debuts against North that afternoon were Bill Twomey Jnr, Neil Mann and Len Fitzgerald – two men who would later captain the club, and a third who might have done so had he not flown the coop to South Australia.

Suddenly, Collingwood's playing list looked solid. In addition to Fothergill and the debutants, Alby Pannam and Charlie Utting were still going strong, while a young rover called Lou Richards, Pannam's nephew, was emerging as a real talent. This mix of senior players and brilliant youngsters melded together beautifully and the Pies found themselves back in the top four after a few rounds of the season. They stayed there until the end of the year, finishing in second place, just one game behind South Melbourne and two games clear of third.

It was an amazing turnaround from the previous few seasons. But Lady Luck did not smile on the Pies in September. They lost three key players through injury on the eve of the finals, including skipper Alby Pannam, then went down narrowly to South in the second semi-final.

But the real heartbreak came in the preliminary final against Carlton, in what is still regarded as one of the most violent finals in VFL history. Collingwood led by 34 points early in the last quarter but lost their way – and the lead – as Carlton turned the game ultra-physical and the Pies could not cope. The Blues piled on the last seven goals of the game to win by 10 points.

It was a disappointing end to a season that had – unexpectedly – promised much. But only the most hardhearted supporters would not have been inspired by the club's rise from 10th to second, and by the emergence of what looked to be an exciting list. Just as the club had predicted years before, the war was over, and Collingwood was back.

H&A P20, W15, L5 • **Finished** 2nd • **Finals** P2, L2 • **Finished** 3rd • **Captain** Alby Pannam • **Coach** Jock McHale • **Leading goalkicker** Des Fothergill (62) • **Copeland Trophy** Not awarded

---

1946
BOB ROSE MAKES HIS DEBUT

The shoots of recovery so evident in 1945 had taken hold by 1946, as Collingwood once again finished the season near the top of the ladder. But in a year filled with exciting performances, it was a relatively unremarkable one in the Pies' Round 17 game, against Footscray at Victoria Park, that would have the biggest impact on the club's fortunes over the next 50 years.

That was the day a kid from Nyah West by the name of Bob Rose made his debut for the Collingwood Football Club. The young rover/centreman had just turned 18 and had been starring with the seconds, having originally come to Melbourne to pursue his love of boxing.

His debut game was entirely forgettable – in fact, he didn't get his first kick until the third quarter. But the selectors kept faith, and the following week, again at Victoria Park but this time against Geelong, young Bobby kicked three goals and looked right at home. He kept his spot for the rest of the season – including three finals – and Collingwood knew it had found a special talent.

The next nine years proved it: Rose played 152 games, kicked 211 goals, won four Copeland Trophies, was twice leading goalkicker, finished runner-up in the Brownlow Medal, made numerous Victorian appearances, and was an All-Australian and a key performer in the 1953 Premiership. Rose was a footballing wizard – fast, tough, courageous, supremely skilled, good around goals, a magnificent ball-handler and a superb user by hand or foot. He was the most inspirational footballer in the competition, and is still regarded as one of the top handful of players the Magpies have ever produced.

But while Collingwood had indeed found a special player, time would prove that the club had also found a special man – and an equally remarkable family. Three of Bob's brothers, Bill, Kevin and Ralph, followed him to Victoria Park. Kevin would go on to be a part of the famous 1958 Premiership side, and would later serve the club as president during some of its toughest times. Bob's son, Robert, also played senior football, with both Collingwood and Footscray, before he tragically became a quadriplegic in a car crash in 1974.

After leaving the game prematurely in 1955 at just 27 to take up a coaching role in the country, Bob returned to coach Collingwood between 1964 and '71, producing some brilliant teams but enduring a run of finals misfortune that would have broken a lesser man. He took on a second coaching stint in the club's hour of need in the mid-1980s, and also served on the board.

Throughout all the ups and downs of his career, Bob Rose retained a quiet dignity, grace and humility that set him apart in the football world. The Rose name today remains one of the most revered in Collingwood history – and it all started with that kickless first half against Footscray at Victoria Park in 1946.

The team he joined that day ended up in second spot on the ladder, but lost the second semi-final to the eventual premier, Essendon, after a pulsating draw at the first attempt (the Pies' wayward 13.22 costing them dearly). A loss to Melbourne in the preliminary final was crushing, but the season had proved Collingwood's resurgence in 1945 had been no fluke.

H&A P19, W13, L6 · **Finished** 2nd · **Finals** P3, L2, D1 · **Finished** 3rd · **Captain** Phonse Kyne · **Coach** Jock McHale · **Leading goalkicker** Des Fothergill (63) · **Copeland Trophy** Phonse Kyne

---

1947

A COSTLY DRAW

After successive preliminary final appearances, and with a terrific mixture of promising young talent and established stars, hopes were high at Victoria Park coming into the 1947 season – a buzz of expectation that was reflected in a record number of season tickets being sold in the lead-up.

Those expectations were heightened further in the early weeks of the year, when the team started the season with four straight wins, dispensing with Fitzroy, Hawthorn, Geelong and South Melbourne while playing a fast, high-scoring brand of football that had the critics drooling and old-timers recalling the glory days of the 1920s and '30s.

Perplexingly, the Pies then lost the next three, but rebounded to win the four after that. The see-sawing season settled down a little thereafter, and after 14 rounds the Magpies stood at 10–4, duelling for second place with Essendon, behind the eventual premier, Carlton – which Collingwood had edged out in a classic game on the King's Birthday holiday.

The key moment in the Magpies' season came at South Melbourne in Round 15, a game the Pies were expected to win comfortably. The Swans had the better of the play all day, but a late Pat Twomey goal levelled the scores with just minutes to play. Then former Collingwood rover Harry Mears bobbed up with a crucial point in the dying seconds to give South the win.

Or so everyone thought. It turned out that the scoreboard had been wrong, and Mears' point had not won the game for South but only levelled the scores. The game was drawn.

The result – whether a draw or a loss – was a major blow to the Pies, and one that had significant ramifications down the track. And the frustratingly inconsistent Pies compounded the impact the next week with a hugely disappointing loss to Melbourne at Victoria Park. A win over Footscray, followed by an embarrassing thumping at the hands of Richmond, left Collingwood needing to beat Essendon at Vic Park in the last game of the season to make the finals.

It was not to be. The Pies seemed nervous and repeatedly fluffed their lines in front of goal, at one stage kicking eight behinds in a row. Even so, they were in front deep into time-on of the final quarter, until two late Essendon goals stole the match. To rub salt into the wound, the last goal was kicked by an Essendon player sent to the forward pocket to recover from an injury.

Incredibly, after being in the top four all season, Collingwood had missed out on a finals berth in the very last minute. The draw with South Melbourne had turned the Magpies' season upside down. Not only did the 'dropped' two points cost them a finals berth, but it seemed to spark a late-season collapse: the team lost three of its four games immediately after the South result, and won only one of its last five games.

It was a shattering end to the season. Collingwood officials blamed injuries, and said they were proud of their exciting young team. The fans were hugely disappointed, and hoped the late fade-out was no more than an aberration.

H&A P19, W11, L7, D1 • **Finished** 5th • **Captain** Phonse Kyne • **Coach** Jock McHale • **Leading goalkicker** Neil Mann (48) • **Copeland Trophy** Phonse Kyne

---

1948

VIC PARK'S RECORD CROWD

A succession of decent post-war performances had positioned Collingwood firmly back in the top bracket of VFL clubs. But the late-season stumble in 1947 had crushed the hopes of many Magpie fans, and there was heightened interest in how the club as a whole would respond in 1948.

The answer was emphatic, with a record crowd of 47,224 cramming into Victoria Park for the first home game of the season, on Monday, 26 April. Yes, it was the Labour Day holiday, and yes, it was one of only two games played on the day, but this was a match against South Melbourne – not one of the Pies' traditional big-drawing rivals. Nobody was expecting that sort of crowd for the match.

Even now it is impossible to work out how more than 47,000 people actually squeezed into Vic Park that day. It remains by some distance the biggest crowd in the ground's history. But squeeze in they did, and they had a great day as the Magpies cruised home by 53 points. If ever there was a sign that Collingwood was well and truly back as a football force – both on and off the field – it came in the form of the huge crowd spilling onto the Victoria Park turf.

Collingwood's players responded with what the *Sporting Globe* described as their most brilliant display in years. South were 'torn apart, reduced to 18 floundering individuals by relentless precision'. Other newspapers agreed, with various critics pronouncing Collingwood among the flag favourites after just two rounds. Some critics even compared the 1948 unit to the mighty Machine teams of the late 1920s, so emphatic were some of its performances.

It seemed like the perfect combination: the fans and members were flocking back just as the team was playing its best football. And the record crowd proved to be just the start. Collingwood broke all sorts of attendance records during the year, and their total crowd numbers for the season, which included two finals matches, eventually totalled more than 613,000 – a remarkable number for the time. It was, the club noted in its Annual Report, 'a truly great tribute to the entertainment provided to followers of our great game by your club'.

The team maintained its blistering early form beyond the half-way mark of the season, winning 11 of its first 13 games, but once again stumbled in the latter stages, losing three on the trot and four in six weeks. That left the Pies needing to win the final game against Melbourne to secure second spot, but unfortunately they went down by five goals and finished third on the ladder. A come-from-behind win in the first semi-final over the Bulldogs was stirring, but ultimately provided scant consolation for another season of unfulfilled promise, which ended with a thumping preliminary final loss to the Demons.

Two late-season fade-outs in successive years had cruelled what looked at times to have been legitimate assaults on the VFL Premiership. It was frustrating for everyone – supporters, players and officials alike – to start like a train and surge to Premiership favouritism, only to stumble at the pointy end of the season. Some fans were starting to grow impatient.

H&A P19, W13, L6 • **Finished** 3rd • **Finals** P2, W1, L1 • **Finished** 3rd • **Captain** Phonse Kyne • **Coach** Jock McHale • **Leading goalkicker** Lou Richards (44) • **Copeland Trophy** Phonse Kyne

---

1949

SHOCK LOSS SOWS SEEDS OF DESTRUCTION

The 1949 season began with a curiosity: there were no fewer than eight sets of brothers training at Collingwood during the pre-season. This included famous siblings such as Bill, Pat and Mick Twomey, Ron and Lou Richards, and Bob and Bill Rose, but also lesser-known combinations such as George Hams and his brother Bruce, Ron and Stan Smith, Kevin and Fred Chard, Jack and Jim Neeson, and Jack and Bill Cummins. Not all of them made it to senior football, which is a pity: statisticians would have had a field day with a playing list with that many brothers on it.

That small slice of history aside, Collingwood's 1949 bore striking similarities to the two seasons that preceded it. Once again the Pies started brilliantly, going 9–2 from their first 11 games, and generally being at or near the top of the ladder throughout. They were still on top after Round 16, following a gutsy, nail-biting win over Carlton.

But then it happened again. Just as in the previous two seasons, there was a late-season stumble. This time the Magpies lost four of their last eight matches, including two of their last three, to once again finish third and miss out on the double chance.

This time at least there were mitigating circumstances: no fewer than five players had been injured in that brilliant win over Carlton. But even so, it all boiled down to the final match of the season against a St Kilda team that had won only three games for the year. Even an injury-depleted Collingwood would surely be too good for the struggling Saints, it was felt, especially with so much riding on the outcome.

But that's not how it turned out. The Pies jumped to an early three-goal lead but seemed to relax thereafter, and trailed by nine points at the final change. The Saints withstood everything Collingwood threw at them in a frantic final term and held on for a memorable win. This was too much for even the most patient Collingwood fan to tolerate. And things got uglier still the next week, when the team was embarrassed by more than 80 points by Essendon in the first semi-final.

Three seasons in a row now, the Magpies had at one time been regarded as the Premiership favourites. And in each of those seasons the team had suffered a spectacular late-season crash that caused it to slip out of the top two – or, in the case of 1947, out of the top four entirely.

In response, people began to openly speculate about the tenure of the doyen of coaches, Jock McHale. He had been in the role for a staggering 38 seasons and was now an old man (he turned 67 at the end of the year). Were his training methods up to scratch for modern football? Were the players fit enough? Was he up-to-date with the latest trends in coaching? Or had the game and its demands passed even the great McHale by?

It had now been 13 years since the last Collingwood flag. And for the first time, critics and fans alike were beginning to doubt whether the legendary McHale was the man to take them to the next one. As unthinkable as it might once have been, the whiff of revolution was in the air.

H&A P19, W13, L6 • **Finished** 3rd • **Finals** P1, L1 • **Finished** 4th • **Captain** Phonse Kyne • **Coach** Jock McHale • **Leading goalkicker** Jack Pimm (34) • **Copeland Trophy** Bob Rose

---

1950

A BLOODY COACHING MESS

Collingwood's 1949 Annual Report makes interesting reading. Alongside the usual financial and football reports is a tribute to long-serving coach Jock McHale, and a special acknowledgement of the 25 years served by 'popular' president Harry Curtis. The financial statements were overseen by treasurer Bob Rush, as they had been every year since 1908.

The report was delivered on 1 March 1950. Less than two months later, McHale, Curtis and Rush – together with secretary Frank Wraith – were all gone, victims of the bloodiest and messiest coup Collingwood has ever seen.

The catalyst was Jock McHale's surprise decision to hang up his coaching clipboard. That didn't come until April, much closer to the start of the season than anyone would have liked. But the spark that lit the fire was the board's decision on his replacement.

Just about everybody thought it would be Phonse Kyne, the popular captain and brilliant player who was nearing the end of his playing days. But the board decided, in its wisdom, to appoint a former player called Bervin Woods to the role. Woods had been coaching the seconds and had, apparently, been promised the position by some members of the committee.

When it came to the vote, the committee was split. President Curtis cast the deciding vote in Woods' favour, and all hell broke loose. There were allegations of vote-twisting and double voting, and vitriol was thrown by both sides of the table. The nastiness that pervaded the whole issue ensured both factions leaked to the press, which helped nobody.

Kyne was shattered by the decision but initially accepted it 'for the good of Collingwood'. But there was an immediate and significant surge of support for him from members and fans, which prompted him to change his mind and instead announce his retirement.

There were wild scenes at an intra-club practice match that Saturday, 15 April. Tempers ran high, abuse was hurled by fans towards those committee members who had backed Woods – the leaks having ensured that everyone knew which side the various board members were on – and a couple of nasty fist-fights were only narrowly avoided.

When Kyne himself turned up to watch the game, he was hailed as a hero and cheered wildly by thousands of fans, who chaired him from the ground on their shoulders. It was the craziest and most significant practice match in the club's history.

Woods took the only course open to him and quit the next day. Having had one coach for 38 seasons, Collingwood's next had lasted less than a week, and did not coach a VFL Premiership game.

The committee duly appointed Kyne as coach, but it was all too late. Angry fans organised a special club meeting a few weeks later, and Curtis, Wraith, Rush and the rest of Woods' backers were ousted. The club was torn apart.

In such a fervid environment, it was hardly a surprise when the team dropped out of the top four. Young star Len Fitzgerald compounded a miserable year for the club by quitting to go to Sturt, where he would win three Magarey Medals. For Collingwood, season 1950 couldn't end quickly enough.

H&A P18, W9, L9 • **Finished** 7th • **Captain** Gordon Hocking •
Coach Phonse Kyne • **Leading goalkicker** Lou Richards (35) •
Copeland Trophy Charlie Utting

1951

THE UNDER-19S

The 1950 season had been so acrimonious, and so scarring, that the club needed something to help it heal and regenerate in 1951. And what better way to do that than through youth? So it was fortunate timing, as it turned out, that the club chose 1951 as the year in which it finally launched its own under-19 team to act as Collingwood's thirds.

The VFL had actually started an official thirds competition in 1946, although only seven clubs took part that year. Collingwood was one of those that resisted, due partly to the cost and partly to the club's commitment to its own schoolboy competition. That had started in 1934, providing teams from local schools with the opportunity to strut their stuff on Victoria Park before Collingwood home games.

The schoolboy games were highly popular – much more so than the baseball matches that had previously served as curtain-raisers in those days – and also produced some extremely good footballers, including Des Fothergill, Bill Twomey and Len Fitzgerald. The club took its responsibility to the competition seriously, paying for footballs, jumpers and umpires, as well as providing trophies for the premier team and the best players.

The club's decision to field its own under-19 team in 1951 spelled the beginning of the end for the schoolboy competition, which folded a few years later. From 1951 it was the under-19s, not the schoolboys, who played the curtain-raisers at Victoria Park.

The first coach of the Collingwood thirds was former player and Second World War hero Jack Pimm. Another former player, Eric Cock, acted as team manager. The team's purpose was to provide recruits for the senior team, and a number of the first intake went on to play senior VFL football for Collingwood, including Les Smith (the winner of the thirds' inaugural best-and-fairest award), Neville Waller, Bill Jones and Laurie Rymer. In the years to come, the under-19s would provide the seniors with a steady stream of high-grade talent.

Collingwood's 'baby Magpies' finished sixth in the 12-team thirds competition in their first season, a highly creditable performance that saw the club brand its first year of operation an unqualified success.

That result added to the sense of optimism that pervaded the club in 1951. For its part, the senior team rebounded brilliantly from the horrors of 1950 to finish second on the ladder, equal on points with the seemingly unstoppable Geelong. The Magpies were the youngest team in the finals but went into September with plenty of hope. An 82-point loss to the Cats in the second semi-final was sobering, while a two-point loss to Essendon in the subsequent preliminary final was heartbreaking.

But there was little or no anger from Magpie fans at the 'straight sets' finals exit. Instead, there was relief that the club was again unified, and excitement that the team had so quickly returned to the top reaches of the ladder. There was even a Premiership to celebrate: the 1951 Lightning Premiership, played on a Wednesday in May to celebrate the 50th anniversary of Australia's Federation. As ever, the fans hoped it would be a sign of things to come.

H&A P18, W14, L4 • **Finished** 2nd • **Finals** P2, L2 • **Finished** 3rd • **Captain** Gordon Hocking • **Coach** Phonse Kyne • **Leading goalkicker** Maurie Dunstan (40) • **Copeland Trophy** Bob Rose

1952

MAGPIES TAKE FLIGHT

In 1952 the VFL broke new ground in spreading the message of Australian football by scheduling a round in which every game was played outside of Melbourne. These were not exhibition games but matches played for Premiership points. So in Round 8, while Victoria played Western Australia at the MCG, Carlton met Hawthorn in Euroa, Fitzroy and Melbourne battled it out in North Hobart, Footscray took on St Kilda in Yallourn, South Melbourne and North Melbourne clashed in Albury, and Geelong and Essendon travelled north to the Brisbane Exhibition Ground.

And Collingwood? The Pies headed back to the Sydney Cricket Ground, where they'd played their pioneering match against Fitzroy way back in 1903. This time, Richmond was their opponent, but the aim was the same: promotion of the game and the search for a wider audience.

Collingwood was vehemently opposed to the idea of playing outside Melbourne, but it had no choice in the matter. And the venture turned out to be historic for two reasons.

The first was that, while the Tigers took the train to Sydney, the Magpies boarded a plane, making this the first time they had flown interstate for a game with four points on the line. It was very much a taste of what football would become 50 years later. The different approaches of the two teams also underscored – yet again – just how far ahead of most of the competition Collingwood was. The Pies were the first club to have a liquor licence and their own social club, and their state-of-the-art training facilities and club headquarters were the envy of the rest of the competition. Despite a Premiership drought that now stretched to 16 years, Collingwood was a powerhouse football club.

The other significant thing about the game in Sydney was that Jock McHale didn't go. As far as anyone could work out, it was only the second Collingwood game Jock had missed in the best part of 50 years. He was no longer coach, of course, but he had remained chairman of selectors after quitting coaching in 1950, and still wielded enormous influence around the club. His failure to board the plane for Sydney was a signal that, at last, he was prepared to relinquish some of that influence. It was also, perhaps, a sign that old age was catching up with him.

The Sydney game was not much of a spectacle – poor weather turned it into little more than a boggy scrap. But at least the Pies won this time, unlike the encounter with Fitzroy in 1903. The four points proved valuable, continuing an early-season run of form that saw the Pies at the top of the ladder when they returned from Sydney. They would finish the year in second place, 10 points adrift of the all-conquering Geelong.

That gap was reinforced in the finals, when the Cats easily outpointed the Pies in both the semi-final and the Grand Final, by a combined total of 100 points. The gulf in class between the two teams was obvious in September; the question was whether Collingwood could close that gap and mount a serious flag challenge. Geelong seemed to be invincible at the end of 1952, in the middle of a record run of wins. But the Magpies understood better than most that success can't last forever.

H&A P19, W14, L5 • **Finished** 2nd • **Finals** P3, W1, L2 • **Finished** 2nd • **Captain** Lou Richards • **Coach** Phonse Kyne • **Leading goalkicker** Maurie Dunstan (43) • **Copeland Trophy** Bob Rose

---

1953

THE TURNING POINT

The most significant event in any Premiership-winning season is almost always the Grand Final. But not in 1953.

In this season, the turning point for Collingwood came in a visit to Kardinia Park to take on Geelong in Round 14. The Cats were sitting pretty on top of the ladder at the time and were unbeaten for the year. In fact, they'd won 23 matches in a row, and had gone 26 without defeat (including a draw). They had broken Collingwood's record of successive victories just a few weeks earlier and were unbackable favourites for the flag.

The Magpies had taken great encouragement from their defeat by Geelong at Victoria Park earlier in the year. The Pies got close that day, and even led at half-time, despite missing a handful of their best players through injury and suffering terrible inaccuracy in front of goal. They didn't end up winning but came away *believing*, rather than merely hoping, that the Cats could be beaten.

Collingwood took that confidence and immediately had a run of six successive wins. But they'd wobbled a little in the weeks leading up to the return bout at Kardinia Park, losing two in a row and narrowly avoiding a third, and were just hanging on in the top four.

But none of that seemed to matter that afternoon at Geelong, in what amounted to a changing of the guard in VFL supremacy. The Collingwood players broke with tradition by having their steak and eggs *before* they left Melbourne, rather than after their arrival in Geelong, and the change seemed to work, as the Pies stormed home in the final quarter to turn a two-point deficit into a 20-point victory, with Bob Rose, Des Healey and Thorold Merrett all starring.

The victory ended Geelong's record-breaking run. More importantly, it provided the Pies with a huge psychological boost. 'That win was a turning point,' wrote Lou Richards later. 'We felt that if we could beat them down on their own ground we could beat them any time.'

And so it proved: the Pies did not lose again for the year, and outpointed Geelong not once but twice in the finals. And they did this despite an injury list that at times defied belief, continuing profligacy in front of goal (the team only kicked more goals than behinds in five games), and an ongoing battle to develop a coherent forward structure.

That forward-line struggle saw the club blood a young key position player called Murray Weideman, and play inexperienced full-back Keith Batchelor at full-forward and an almost unknown flanker called Terry Waites at centre half-forward. Incredibly, just about every move worked. Every time a star player went down, a lesser-known backup stepped in and filled the role superbly. The end result was a Premiership that was a testament to courage, teamwork and the famed Collingwood spirit.

But the celebrations were soon tempered by sadness, with club benefactor John Wren and legendary coach Jock McHale both suffering heart attacks within days of the Grand Final. McHale, the most successful coach in VFL/AFL history, was dead just over a week later, his funeral attracting thousands of fans lining the streets. Wren, too, would be gone within a month. It was a sad end to an extraordinarily triumphant season.

H&A P18, W14, L4 • **Finished** 2nd • **Finals** P2, W2 • **Finished** Premier • **Captain** Lou Richards • **Coach** Phonse Kyne • **Leading goalkicker** Bob Rose (36) • **Copeland Trophy** Bob Rose

---

1954

THE INJURY CURSE

There is an old adage in football that injuries are no excuse. But Collingwood was hit by such an extraordinary run of accidents in 1954 that the club had no hesitation in abandoning the accepted practice and directly blaming that misfortune for the team's failure to make the finals.

And who could blame them? There were, of course, the usual minor niggles and soft-tissue injuries. But three players – Thorold Merrett, Bill Rose and Kevin Wylie – suffered broken legs. Keith Batchelor broke a bone in his foot. Captain Lou Richards broke his collarbone in a pre-season intra-club game, returned mid-season and then promptly broke his wrist. Frank Tuck battled an ongoing ankle injury, the team's best player, Bob Rose, suffered a serious groin injury, and Bill Twomey and Neville Waller had significant knee injuries. In the vital stages towards the end of the season, all of these players other than Twomey were unavailable. The team's four stars – Bob Rose, Merrett, Lou Richards and Bill Twomey – managed only 37 games between them.

The club did not mince its words, or look for other explanations, when evaluating the season. 'Season 1954 will be long remembered as the most disastrous ever experienced in the annals of the club,' its Annual Report began. 'Week after week brought serious injuries to our leading and experienced players, [and] the playing strength of the team gradually weakened, thus upsetting the balance of teamwork so necessary in league football today ... [the players'] absence had much to do with the failure of the team to gain final four honours.'

In the context of what had been the worst injury run in the club's history, the team actually did reasonably well to finish just a game and percentage outside the finals, though its ladder position fall from first to seventh made things look worse.

What made the season all the more frustrating was that it had started amid great optimism. Being the reigning premier does that, but there were other factors too. Membership had ticked over the 10,000 mark in 1953, and grew further in 1954, despite that of most other clubs dropping back because of a VFL-mandated increase in season ticket costs.

The Pies began the year with five straight victories – making a run of 14 in all across 1953–54 – before a loss to Geelong in Round 6 (the match in which Merrett broke his leg). Then the injuries began to bite, and the Pies managed only five more wins for the year. Even so, they clung on to a spot in the top two until the third-last game. The low point came when, while still on top of the ladder, they lost to bottom-placed Fitzroy. They also managed to lose to third-bottom South Melbourne after leading by 34 points. It was that kind of season – one where everything that could go wrong did go wrong

About the only thing that went right for the black-and-whites that year was Neil Mann's performance in finishing runner-up in the Brownlow Medal to Richmond's Roy Wright. He had placed third the year before (when Bob Rose had finished second), but this capped off what was his best ever season.

H&A P18, W10, L8 • **Finished** 7th • **Captain** Lou Richards • **Coach** Phonse Kyne • **Leading goalkicker** Keith Bromage (22) • **Copeland Trophy** Neil Mann

---

1955

THE HEALEY—ADAMS CLASH

It's late in the final quarter of the 1955 Grand Final. Collingwood had been within a point early in the last term, but Melbourne now leads by just over two goals. Still, the Pies feel they're a chance. Star winger Des Healey has the ball and is running at full pace along the members' wing, just as Frank 'Bluey' Adams dashes off the Demons' reserves bench. Healey is scanning the options further afield and prepares to launch Collingwood into attack when ... Crash! And the lights go out.

Adams had come from Healey's blind side and ran straight into him at pace, dipping his shoulder for maximum impact. Their heads clashed, and both players lay prostrate on the MCG turf, out cold. Teammates milled around in an ugly melee while the two injured men were stretchered off.

It was one of the most sickening collisions football had ever seen. The newspaper photograph showing both players lying on the ground, flung metres apart by the impact, remains one of the most famous in football history. Healey's nose was broken in five places and his skull fractured, and he was still suffering dizzy spells weeks later.

The immediate outcome of this horrific clash was to deprive Collingwood of any chance of making a late comeback. The Pies were reduced to 17 men, and Ian Ridley booted a steadying goal for Melbourne while Healey and Adams were still being stretchered off. They added another late major for a 28-point win. But the longer-term impact was more significant, as the incident ultimately cost Collingwood the services of the player who would, a few weeks later, be awarded the Copeland Trophy as the club's best player of the season.

Healey was only 28 and in the form of his life. He'd received a well-paid offer to coach Wodonga but hadn't yet decided what he would do. The incident with Adams, he said later, helped make up his mind, and he resolved that the Grand Final had been his final match as a player.

This compounded a bad year for departures from Victoria Park. Captain and club legend Lou Richards had struggled for form through much of 1955, and eventually pulled the pin just before the finals. Reliable back pocket George Hams had also hung up the boots earlier in the year.

But the biggest blow of all, especially in the wake of Healey's departure, came when Bob Rose decided to accept a lucrative coaching and employment offer at Wangaratta. He was just 27 and, like Healey, seemed to have plenty of good football left in him. But the club knew both players had given outstanding service, and felt honour-bound to grant them clearances.

So Collingwood said goodbye to three greats of the club in the one year – a season in which the injury curse of 1954 abated and the Pies once again returned to football's biggest stage, albeit unsuccessfully. Lou Richards left with a promise that he would always be a part of Collingwood, while Des Healey would return for a stint coaching the under-19s. And there was always a sense that Bob Rose would be back one day.

H&A P18, W14, L4 • **Finished** 2nd • **Finals** P3, W1, L2 • **Finished** 2nd • **Captains** Lou Richards & Neil Mann • **Coach** Phonse Kyne • **Leading goalkicker** Ken Smale (47) • **Copeland Trophy** Des Healey

---

1956

COLLINGWOOD TAKES CONTROL OF VIC PARK

In 1956 Collingwood showed it had recovered from the loss of Bob Rose, Des Healey and Lou Richards by producing a season that was eerily similar to the one that had preceded it. Once again the Pies finished second on the ladder to Melbourne, and once again the Demons proved too good – this time, *way* too good – in the Grand Final, which was played just before the MCG was handed over to host Australia's first Olympic Games.

It was no disgrace to be beaten by a unit as frighteningly good as Norm Smith's Melbourne, and Collingwood fans must have taken heart from their own team's continued run at or near the top of the ladder. But making it to another Grand Final was not the most significant thing that happened in 1956. Indeed, most Collingwood fans were unlikely to have been aware of the seismic shift that was taking place behind the scenes.

The issue of control of Victoria Park had been a thorn in the club's side since the 1890s. At different times the club had threatened to leave the ground due to frustration with what it perceived to be the Collingwood Council's greed, or with its levels of interference. The council, on the other hand, was periodically annoyed at what it felt were poor financial returns from a highly successful venture.

The frustrations on both sides increased after the war. In 1946 Collingwood announced plans for palatial new clubrooms and grandstand areas, but later put them on hold because of an older deal that forced it to renew its tenancy agreement with the council every seven years. No sensible business would invest that sort of money without real security of tenure, and Collingwood in those days prided itself on being a very sensible business indeed.

So the works were put on hold, and long, complex and at times heated negotiations (well detailed in Richard Stremski's *Kill for Collingwood*) between the two parties commenced. The turning point came in 1950, when Gordon Carlyon became the first full-time secretary/manager of a VFL club – yet another Collingwood first. Carlyon was a brilliant administrator, and he immediately set about securing a long-term lease that would keep Collingwood at Victoria Park.

It took years of wrangling, but the agreement was finally reached on 18 June 1956. Collingwood had won a 40-year lease at £500 per year, and in return agreed to undertake an extensive rebuilding and renovation program. There were also deals reached around expenditure and revenue sharing.

Although the club did not own Victoria Park, the long-term lease meant Collingwood became the first VFL club to manage its own ground. And as Stremski notes, this was a financial bonanza for the Pies, because ground managers received one-third of net revenue from gate receipts. Having control of the ground also gave the club the security it needed to proceed with its planned major capital works program.

Once more Collingwood had proved itself an off-field power-house, streets ahead of its rivals. The club had been professionally and aggressively run almost since birth, and its deal with the Collingwood Council suggested that wasn't going to change any time soon.

H&A P18, W13, L5 • **Finished** 2nd • **Finals** P3, W1, L2 • **Finished** 2nd • **Captain** Neil Mann • **Coach** Phonse Kyne • **Leading goalkicker** Ken Smale (33) • **Copeland Trophy** Bill Twomey

---

1957
FOOTY COMES TO TV

It is 20 April 1957, and the opening round of yet another footy season. Collingwood is locked in a tight and tense battle with Essendon at Victoria Park, with the Bombers having fought back from an early deficit to go into the final quarter just two points behind. We have a thriller on our hands.

Right then, at 4.15pm, is the moment when the magic happens – when footy changes forever. In living rooms and shop windows across Melbourne, these newfangled contraptions called television sets flicker into life. And as they do, for the first time ever, footy fans can tune in and watch the last quarter of a VFL match live on the small screen – on their *own* small screen, if they're an early adopter of the technology.

It was not due to chance that the first match to be broadcast featured Collingwood. Time and again the Pies have been the VFL's (and later the AFL's) go-to club when trying something new. And television was no different.

Channels Nine, Seven and Two (the ABC) all took part in those historic football broadcasts that April afternoon in 1957. Tony Charlton was at the helm of Channel Seven's coverage, former Test cricketer Ian Johnson called it for Nine, while Ken Dakin and Ray McDonald were at the microphones for the ABC. By a quirk of fate they all featured the same Collingwood–Essendon game because of a dispute between the VFL, the television stations and various ground managers over who deserved the biggest slice of the income. Yes, even before the first game had gone to air, there was a dispute over TV rights.

Bill Strickland, Collingwood's first great captain.

W. PROUDFOOT

Bill Proudfoot, who quit as captain in 1899.

Grand Premiership

Football Match,

Collingwood

v.

Fitzroy.

Official Programme.

Price One Penny.

Sydney Cricket Ground,

MAY 23rd, 1903.

The program from the historic match against Fitzroy in Sydney in 1903.

R. CONDON

The brilliant but combustible Dick Condon was at the heart of many big moments.

THE
MAGPIES
TEAM SONGS

COLLINGWOOD FOREVER
Magpies On Parade
Plus a Medley of
FOOTBALL
PARTY SONGS

Collingwood's club song was written in 1906 and has been popular even since.

Dick Lee's incredible mark against Carlton in 1914.

The 'good luck' horseshoe sent by 'Doc' Seddon to the football club in 1917 helped Collingwood to a flag that year, and it remains an important club artefact today.

Opposite: The iconic commemorative artwork produced to celebrate Collingwood's fourth successive Premiership in 1930.

The architects of the legendary 'Machine' teams of the late 1920s: captain Syd Coventry and coach Jock McHale.

COLLINGWOOD FOOTBALL CLUB
PREMIERS 1930

COMMEMORATIVE PICTURE
FOUR SUCCESSIVE PREMIERSHIPS 1927·1928·1929·1930

The high-flying Ron Todd shocked the club when he left to join VFA side Williamstown in 1940.

The first Social Club medallion, from 1940–41, is today a keenly sought piece of Collingwood memorabilia.

The brilliant Des Fothergill, who had won three Copelands and a Brownlow by the age of 20, was another young star whose departure rocked the Magpies.

Lou Richards riding high after the 1953 Premiership win over Geelong.

How the newspapers saw the infamous clash between Des Healey and Frank Adams in 1955.

Hats off to the Premiers! Coach Phonse Kyne, acting captain Murray Weideman and other players toast their miracle win over Melbourne in the 1958 Grand Final.

Ray Gabelich sinks what every Magpie hoped would be the winning goal in the dying minutes of the 1964 Grand Final. But it was not to be.

Peter Eakins, the high-priced WA
recruit whose arrival shook up
Collingwood's player payment system.

LEN THOMPSON
COLLINGWOOD MAGPIES

RUCK

DES TUDDENHAM

MAGPIES
H/FORWARD FLANK

HAVE FUN WITH SCANLEN'S GUM

Star players Len Thompson and Des Tuddenham went on strike during the 1970 pre-season, looking for better deals from the club.

Desolation row for Magpie players and officials as they try to come to terms with the horror-show of their 1970 fade-out.

Victoria Park in the late 1960s, with the Social Club building in all its glory and the newly constructed Sherrin Stand off to the left.

'Fabulous' Phil Carman – *sans* white boots at training – would have won a Brownlow in his first season if not for a cruel injury blow.

MAGPIES: IT'S OPEN WAR!

By PETER SIMUNOVICH

COLLINGWOOD football coach Murray Weideman last night called on the club's president, Mr Ern Clarke, to resign.

"I will not coach Collingwood again unless Ern Clarke resigns as president," Weideman said. "It's either him or me."

"I cannot work under this man any more."

Collingwood on Saturday lost its fourth game of the season and is second last on the VFL ladder with only one win.

Weideman, in an exclusive interview, said that he believed the club was being destroyed.

"I have been loyal to the club for the past 25 years and I feel I am in the position to let everyone at Collingwood know what is happening in their club," he said.

'Job on line'

"Even if I lose my job, which I'm sure I will, at least I've let the players, members and supporters know what is happening at Collingwood under their president.

* Mr Clarke

The Sun

NEWS–PICTORIAL

622,761*
Average daily sale

Big swing to Labor in NSW

SYDNEY. — The Labor Party last night appeared as on the edge of victory in the NSW state elections with a 7.8 per cent swing.
Report: P.2.

The 1976 stoush between coach Murray Weideman and president Ern Clarke made the front *and* back pages.

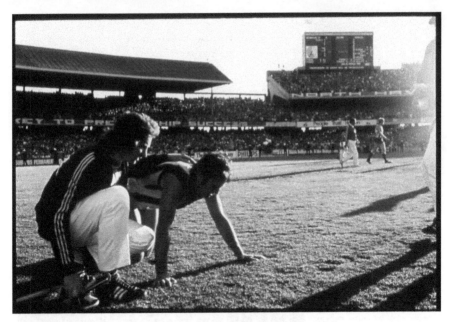

Wayne Richardson breathless and exhausted after the 1977 drawn Grand Final.

'T-Shirt Tommy' talks to his players, while a young Peter Daicos listens intently.

The 'New Magpies' came to power promising the world, but before long the club was in deep strife.

The end of the 'Colliwobbles', as Craig Kelly and Darren Millane show off the 1990 Premiership cup.

Club favourite Lou Richards acknowledges the Sherrin Stand crowd during a lap of honour before the last game at Victoria Park.

President Eddie McGuire and captain Nathan Buckley prepare to lead the players off Victoria Park for the last time, following the final game there against Brisbane in 1999.

The grainy black-and-white footage broadcast that afternoon held Melburnians spellbound. The Bombers stormed home with a six-goal-to-one final quarter, but for once the result wasn't the most important thing. For the first time, fans could see the stars in action without actually going to the game. They were also able to hear from Essendon coach Dick Reynolds straight after the siren, via an interview conducted from the roof of the Ryder Stand.

The newspapers and other media outlets were in furious agreement that the new venture had been an unqualified success. The *Sun* and the *Age*, among others, praised the 'vivid' pictures and 'astonishing' close-ups. They were stone-age by today's standards, of course, but at the time they were revolutionary.

Even for a powerful, successful and massively popular club like Collingwood, television was a game-changer. The TV stations wanted to broadcast the most popular games, which meant showing the biggest clubs. And that exposure in turn entrenched the popularity of those clubs. Collingwood and TV soon became cosy bedfellows in a mutually beneficial relationship that continues to this day, and the medium has become arguably the most powerful influence in the game.

By the end of the season, sadly, Magpie fans who'd stumped up for a TV set in 1957 might have wondered why they bothered, as their side tumbled to fifth. Even worse, they had to watch on as Melbourne cruised to a third straight flag. Collingwood's much-cherished record of four successive Premierships was under serious threat – and it looked like nothing could stop the Demons.

H&A P18, W9, L8, D1 • **Finished** 5th • **Captain** Bill Twomey • **Coach** Phonse Kyne • **Leading goalkicker** Ian Brewer (26) • **Copeland Trophy** Murray Weideman

---

1958

THE GREATEST FLAG OF ALL

Not all Premierships are equal. Every one is special, of course, but some stand out. And at Collingwood, the 1958 flag is arguably the greatest of them all.

This was a magical, against-the-odds, fairytale triumph unlike any other seen in football. The inspiration came from the 1958 team's fierce desire to protect the record of four successive Premierships won by the legendary Machine between 1927 and 1930. Collingwood cherished that record: president Syd Coventry had captained those teams, and their feats were a part of Magpie folklore. The club as a whole was dismayed at the idea that another team might match – let alone better – their mark.

But that looked almost certain to happen in 1958. That Melbourne team was one of the greatest football has ever seen. They played in seven successive Grand Finals, and finished on top in six of those seasons. They had a master coach in Norm Smith, arguably the game's best player in Ron Barassi and a host of other stars.

Collingwood was not in the same class. The Magpies finished three games behind Melbourne on the ladder, losing more matches in the season than any other Collingwood flag side, and limped into the finals by losing four out of their last six games. They also lost their captain, Frank Tuck, to injury.

By Grand Final Day it had been 10 matches since Collingwood had bested the Demons. They'd got within 11 points during the year – in a game played before a record home-and-away crowd of 99,346 – but had been thumped by more than seven goals in the second semi. The Magpies were the rankest of rank outsiders.

Everything was going to script at quarter-time, with the Demons leading by 17 points on a wet and muddy ground, despite a famously inspirational pre-match speech from Magpie coach Phonse Kyne. But then acting captain Murray Weideman and Barassi's 'shadow', Barry 'Hooker' Harrison, got together at the break and decided to throw their weight around. They did so liberally in the second quarter and the Melbourne players retaliated, losing their focus. The five-goals-to-two balance sheet of the first term was reversed, and Collingwood was back in the game.

By half-time the Pies were in front by two points, prompting Kyne to exhort his men to 'keep doing what you're doing'. Smith urged his players to focus only on the ball, but they returned to their ill-judged attempts at retribution within minutes of the restart when Collingwood's Bill Serong decked Ian Ridley. While the Demons seethed and hunted for revenge, the Pies focused on the football, piling on five goals to nil and turning for home with an unassailable 33-point lead.

The eventual 18-point victory was widely considered a footballing miracle. The newspapers branded it the biggest upset in finals history – and they were right. It was hard not to think that the magic of the Machine team had somehow found its way through to a soggy MCG that day.

There are plenty who believe that Collingwood used up two or three decades' worth of Grand Final good fortune in 1958. But those problems were for the future; for now, the mighty Magpies were Premiers again – and the Machine's record was safe.

H&A P18, W12, L6 • **Finished** 2nd • **Finals** P3, W2, L1 • **Finished** Premier • **Captain** Frank Tuck • **Coach** Phonse Kyne • **Leading goalkicker** Ian Brewer (73) • **Copeland Trophy** Thorold Merrett

---

THE NEW SOCIAL CLUB OPENS

The Magpies were flying high as the 1959 season kicked off. Not only were they the reigning premier, but they were also into the final stages of construction on what would be the most opulent social club facilities in football. Other clubs looked on with envy as Collingwood went from strength to strength. And while the '58 Premiership was obviously the club's crowning glory, the opening of a new social club building was no mere sideshow.

For this had been the best part of 20 years in the making. The visionary approach which had seen the club win a liquor licence and open its own social club back in 1941 had created a momentum that hadn't stopped in the years since. Demand for places in the social club was so high that a waiting list had to be introduced, and that in turn meant the club desperately needed new facilities to accommodate extra members – and so generate more money, of course.

The second phase of the masterplan was securing control of Victoria Park in 1956. As promised, an extensive program of works began almost as soon as the club formally took control of the ground in April 1957. This included the construction of a long brick wall along Lulie Street, building of new and larger toilet blocks, new entrances to the ground, 5000 feet of concrete terracing in the outer and general renovations to the grandstands. The ground itself was reseeded and top-dressed.

But it was the new social club building that was the jewel in the crown. Funded in part by the issuing of club debentures that were massively oversubscribed – they had been issued just after the

1958 Premiership – the magnificent three-storey building contained offices, committee rooms, a Hall of Fame, a bar and billiards room, a kitchen, a dining room overlooking the ground, a dance floor (the 1960s dinner dances were legendary), and access to sloping open terraces that could accommodate more than 1000 members. The highlight for many was the huge Magpie emblem on the outside of the building.

Opened by no less a personage than Victoria's governor, Sir Dallas Brooks, the clubrooms were easily the best in the competition – and remained that way for a long time. But this was no vanity project; indeed, the clubrooms quickly became a Collingwood cash cow. Profits boomed, not just improving the club's bottom line but also contributing directly to the building of the Rush and Sherrin grandstands.

The palatial new facilities and swelling coffers confirmed Collingwood as a seemingly unstoppable force – off the field at least. On the field, the emotional triumph of 1958 seemed to drain the life out of the players, who started the season by unfurling the flag at Victoria Park and were promptly trounced by South Melbourne. Four more successive defeats followed: the term 'Premiership hangover' might well have been invented to describe the Magpies' start to the 1959 season.

The players recovered their mojo well enough to win the last 10 games of the year and finish third, but were dumped out of the finals by Essendon in the first week. At least the members had a brilliant new facility in which to drown their sorrows.

H&A P18, W12, L6 • **Finished** 3rd • **Finals** P1, L1 • **Finished** 4th • **Captain** Frank Tuck • **Coach** Phonse Kyne • **Leading goalkicker** Murray Weideman (36) • **Copeland Trophy** Thorold Merrett

---

1960

THOROLD MERRETT BREAKS HIS LEG

As the 1960 season started, Collingwood's champion wingman/ rover Thorold Merrett was in a very sweet spot indeed. He'd won the past two Copeland Trophies, had played for Victoria and had just been elevated to the Magpies' vice-captaincy. The exquisitely gifted speedster with a laser-like left foot was in the form of his life. At age 26, he looked set to become one of the elite players of the competition.

He started the season with a five-goal, best-on-ground performance in Collingwood's opening game, against Fitzroy. But just seven weeks later his career was over.

Merrett had already come back from a broken leg (his left) once, suffered in 1954. But in Round 8, playing against Carlton, he broke his right leg – and this break was much more severe. He was in plaster until Christmas, and decided early in 1961 not to attempt another comeback.

As had happened with Des Healey and Bob Rose, the club had lost one of its most brilliant players at a particularly young age. And Merrett's loss hit the Pies especially hard in 1960, because they were starting a rebuild and had planned much of their new-look side around him.

The revered half-back line of Peter Lucas, Ron Kingston and Frank Tuck had all retired after the 1959 season, leaving a big hole in defence and an even bigger one in experience. A handful of others with VFL experience were also released. In all, Collingwood gave debuts to nine new players in 1960, as the selectors cast a wide net in their search for the club's next Premiership combination.

Merrett and new captain Murray Weideman – both survivors of the 1953 flag – were to spearhead this new generation.

The club showed its intent by calling the players back to training in January – far earlier than had previously been the case. It also engaged a fitness specialist to help coach Phonse Kyne by putting the players through a 'modern program of physical fitness exercises' designed to have them in top shape for Round 1. The unusually intense pre-season worked well early, with three wins from the first four games. But inconsistency plagued the campaign thereafter, so much so that almost all of the last half-dozen games became make-or-break affairs.

The Pies eventually snuck into fourth, got home narrowly against Essendon in the first semi-final and won their way through to the Grand Final with a nail-biter over Fitzroy in a preliminary final. But that game almost killed any slim chance the Pies had against the still powerful Demons: Bill Serong, who had become such an important player, busted his shoulder, while big man Brian Dorman suffered a horrific and career-ending knee injury. With those two absences compounding the impact of Merrett's loss, Collingwood never stood a chance against a Melbourne outfit that had a point to prove after their 1958 defeat.

The Pies' final score of 2.2 in the decider was an embarrassment, but the season was not. And there was a final bright light when the under-19s won their first ever flag. But while that was a good sign for the future, in the here and now it was hard to escape the view that an era was ending.

H&A P18, W11, L7 • **Finished** 4th • **Finals** P3, W2, L1 • **Finished** 2nd • **Captain** Murray Weideman • **Coach** Phonse Kyne • **Leading goalkicker** Murray Weideman (30) • **Copeland Trophy** Ray Gabelich

---

1961

COLLINGWOOD'S FIRST COTERIE

The 1961 season was in most ways a disaster for Collingwood. The signs of wear and tear that had emerged in 1960 proved to be accurate portents of what was to come, and the team tumbled down the ladder to ninth – a position it had not occupied since the dark days of the Second World War.

Fifteen new players were added to the senior list at the start of the year, and the team spent much of the season displaying the kind of inexperience and lack of cohesion you might expect after such widespread change. In the context of such a dire season, then, it's not surprising that the most significant developments at Collingwood in 1968 happened off the field.

The formation of the Floreat group was one of those things that almost passed without notice among the general Collingwood supporter base. But it was an important step into the world of backroom corporate support that is so much a part of football these days. And even though the Floreats crashed and burned within just a couple of years, they unwittingly played a key part in the 1963 elections that tore the club apart.

The original idea was simple enough: to establish a group of professionals and businessmen who might help the club, especially in recruiting players and finding jobs for them. Sometimes this meant coming up with some extra cash to help swing a deal, or lining up a job for the same purpose. There were also fundraising functions and exclusive social activities. The initial group of 12 well-heeled supporters included names like the Galballys, the Wrens and Jock McHale Jnr.

For once, this was not a case of Collingwood leading the way: Melbourne had had its own coterie group in the 1950s, and felt it had played no small part in their era of extraordinary success. A number of other clubs had followed suit, and the Pies risked being left behind if they did not. So the creation of the Floreat should have been seen as a positive development, opening up new avenues of financing and recruitment. And the early signs were encouraging, with the club's committee initially happy with the way it operated.

The Floreat quickly expanded in size and influence. But as it did, concerns began to be raised by others about the operations of this largely hidden group of wealthy powerbrokers. Tom Sherrin cannily used such fears to his advantage, and Jack Galbally found his involvement used against him to telling effect in the acrimonious 1963 club elections. The result was not just Galbally's defeat but also the end of official coterie groups at Collingwood until the mid-1970s – a move that cost the club dearly.

In other ways, however, the club continued to be at the forefront of new developments. The social club added its own kitchen and top-quality chef in order to produce bigger and better functions, and these became incredibly popular, often being booked out months in advance. And the Victoria Park surface – which had become waterlogged, boggy and sub-standard – was relaid in an innovative way. But after such a poor year on the field, club officials knew that no amount of window-dressing would save them if the team didn't start winning again. And soon.

H&A P18, W5, L12, D1 • **Finished** 9th • **Captain** Murray Weideman • **Coach** Phonse Kyne • **Leading goalkicker** Kevin Pay (31) • **Copeland Trophy** Murray Weideman

---

1962

COVENTRY'S BIG CALL

The story of Collingwood's 1962 season actually started in November of the previous year, with one of the biggest player clear-outs the club had ever seen. No fewer than 17 players who had played a senior game in 1961 were removed from the list. This included retirees such as Mick Twomey, a good number of younger players who were deemed not good enough, and also a clutch of 1958 Premiership heroes who were ruthlessly cast aside, including leading goalkicker Ian Brewer, Brian Beers, Bill Serong and 'Hooker' Harrison.

Fans and members didn't quite know what to make of such a large-scale list overhaul, and their concerns grew as many of those who had been let go enjoyed good seasons elsewhere. Serong, for example, was dumped after Collingwood's last practice match but was picked up by North Melbourne and won their best-and-fairest. Beers spent three years at Fitzroy, Brewer continued to kick goals wherever he went in a fine career that took him to both South Australia and Western Australia, and youngster Keith Burns went to VFA club Sandringham and won the Liston Trophy.

Collingwood, meanwhile, continued to struggle, rising from ninth to seventh but never really threatening a finals berth. Such a result was hardly unexpected with the club's young list – only Murray Weideman and Ken Turner had played more than 100 games – but the Magpies were not used to missing out on finals action in successive years, and fans and members started to grumble. The club's phenomenal record of success in its first 70 years had spoiled its supporters, and patience was in short supply.

Syd Coventry knew better than most how Collingwood demanded success: he had delivered much of that himself as a player and inspirational captain. He had taken over as president in the wake of the 1950 upheaval and had done a remarkably good job at reuniting what had been a bitterly divided club, thanks in no small part to the universally high regard in which he was held by all at Victoria Park.

Two Premierships had come under his watch, as well as four other Grand Final appearances, and there had been extraordinary growth both in the social club and in the development of Victoria Park. But as 1962 drew towards a close, he decided that the time was right for some new blood. Soon after the season ended he announced that he would not be seeking re-election at the annual meeting in March 1963.

Syd's fellow committee members later described his announcement as a 'severe shock'. But it turned out to be much worse than that, because the three men who most coveted his position – Jack Galbally, Tom Sherrin and John Harris – almost immediately began lobbying for the job.

Syd's announcement was intended to give the club sufficient time to organise a smooth transition from one president to the next, but actually it had the opposite effect, plunging the club into what became a virtual six-month election campaign. Combined with growing discontent at two years without finals football, that was never likely to end well.

H&A P18, W9, L9 • **Finished** 7th • **Captain** Murray Weideman •
Coach Phonse Kyne • **Leading goalkicker** Murray Weideman (48) •
Copeland Trophy Murray Weideman

1963

THE GREAT ELECTION BATTLE OF '63

Collingwood's first two significant boardroom stoushes had centred on specific areas of concern: the appointment of a new coach in 1950, and control of the seconds side in 1939. But the fight that dominated the club in 1963 began as a pure play for the top job. What had started out as a straightforward campaign for the club presidency between two or three hopefuls quickly degenerated into another of the messy boardroom battles that were becoming an all too familiar part of the Collingwood landscape. Unfortunately, this one also ended up involving the coaches and players – and nobody escaped unscathed.

The initial plan was sound: the three candidates to take over from Syd Coventry at the March election – Jack Galbally, Tom Sherrin and John 'Jiggy' Harris – agreed to accept the result of a secret ballot of the rest of the committee in January. Whoever won would be the committee's nominee, and the transition should be relatively smooth.

But, as excellently detailed in Richard Stremski's *Kill for Collingwood*, the plan fell apart a mere two weeks after Galbally had won the secret ballot, when Sherrin reneged on his commitment and decided to challenge for the top job anyway. That decision plunged the club into open warfare for the best part of two months – with ramifications that lasted for years.

Galbally and Sherrin went at each other with the kind of fervour normally found in general political elections. Sherrin presented himself as a man who lived for football and for Collingwood, while Galbally was painted as a parliamentarian with disparate interests who was part of a secret cabal for wealthy supporters, the Floreat (which Sherrin vowed to disband if he won).

Although the campaign was acrimonious, it remained a fairly standard footy club election fight until the eve of the vote, when coaches Phonse Kyne and Neil Mann issued a statement in support of Galbally. Skipper Murray Weideman and many of the players were angry that the coaches had become involved, and even angrier at what they interpreted as suggestions the players, too, were behind Galbally. So the team gathered forces behind the Sherrin ticket – even handing out how-to-vote cards on the day.

From here it didn't really matter who won: the club was in a diabolical situation, with its coaches and players on opposite sides of an election war. What was more, player involvement in club elections had effectively been normalised – a development that would haunt the club over the next 20 years.

Sherrin duly became president – the players' intervention had all but guaranteed that – but the club was torn apart. The Floreats were disbanded, and the coaches and players spent most of the year at loggerheads, with key personnel either fighting with each other or not talking. It was a horrible environment. In those circumstances the team actually didn't do too badly to finish eighth.

Kyne declared he would quit at the end of the season, and he and other Galbally supporters finally left the committee late in the year. Weideman also announced he was retiring after a wonderful career. The decks were being cleared for a fresh start in 1964, and for the biggest return of all.

H&A P18, W7, L11 • **Finished** 8th • **Captain** Murray Weideman •
Coach Phonse Kyne • **Leading goalkicker** Terry Waters (50) •
Copeland Trophy Des Tuddenham

1964

BOBBY COMES BACK

There's nothing quite like the feeling at a footy club when a favourite son returns. And that's exactly what Collingwood experienced when Bobby Rose took over as coach at Victoria Park for the 1964 season. After a 1963 campaign marked by bitterness, division and infighting, the Magpies were once again able to feel good. And they loved it.

Rose had enjoyed a highly successful coaching stint with the Wangaratta Rovers since leaving Collingwood, but Magpie fans had always hoped he would one day return to Victoria Park. And when he put his name forward as one of the vice-presidential candidates in 1963, everyone knew that day was not far away. Other VFL clubs were sniffing around, but the Pies moved quickly and lined him up to take over the role of coach from Phonse Kyne.

His impact was immediate. For starters, it was clear that Collingwood was once again a united club, both on and off the field. But the change of coach, and of coaching philosophy, also made a huge difference. Like Kyne, Rose was a traditionalist who believed in 'playing for the jumper' and the need for discipline and a team focus. It also became clear very early on that he expected each of his charges to play as he had done – at 100 per cent, full-bore, for every second of every game.

But Rose was also determined to speed up Collingwood's game. He encouraged play-on football, promoted players with pace and looked to develop those with greater skills. These qualities would shape Collingwood's game plan and style of play for the next decade.

Expectations of the side were initially low. Critics felt there were too many holes in the Magpie line-up, and only big man Paul Wadham and full-back Peter Boyne were significant new additions in 1964. This was essentially the same line-up that had failed so badly in 1963. But somehow Bob Rose transformed them into a wonderful outfit. Micky Bone and David Norman became quality rovers, Terry Waters and Des Tuddenham looked like two of the brightest young stars in the game, while Ian Graham emerged as a dangerous forward. Just as importantly, the team started to believe in itself again.

By the season's end they were second on the ladder – only half a game behind Melbourne and level on points with Essendon and Geelong. A belting in the second semi was followed by a nail-biting win over Geelong in the preliminary final, and suddenly the Pies were back in the Grand Final. It was an amazing turnaround in such a short time.

It could have been – and very nearly was – one of football's great fairytale stories. Big Ray Gabelich looked to have won the game for the Magpies when his legendary fumbling, bumbling run into an open goal put them in front with just minutes to play. But then Melbourne's back pocket player Neil Crompton – committing a football sin by following his resting rover beyond halfway – crumbed a contest and snapped the winning goal with a minute or so left.

It was a heartbreaking end to Bob Rose's debut season as coach. But Collingwood was already a different team, and a different club, just because of his very presence.

H&A P18, W13, L4, D1 • **Finished** 2nd • **Finals** P3, W1, L2 • **Finished** 2nd • **Captain** Ray Gabelich • **Coach** Bob Rose • **Leading goalkicker** Terry Waters (43) • **Copeland Trophy** Ian Graham

---

1965

THE SOMERVILLE INCIDENT

Coming into the 1965 season, the big question on the lips of every Collingwood supporter was whether or not the team could sustain its remarkable resurgence. Had the 1964 success simply been a short-term spike because the team had a new coach, or had there been a fundamental change under Bob Rose? Was it, perhaps, the start of something big?

By preliminary final day in 1965 the answers were clear: this was no flash-in-the-pan change in fortune. Bob Rose had taken a team that had missed the finals for three straight years and within eight months had turned it into a serious Premiership contender. The Pies backed up their runner-up effort in '64 with another brilliant season, again finishing second, this time just one game behind St Kilda.

The second semi-final had been a classic, with the Pies going down by a solitary point. Essendon had finished fourth, and most observers expected Collingwood to be too good for them in the preliminary final. But nine minutes into the season's penultimate game the crowd started buzzing. Players and supporters became aware that Essendon half-forward John Somerville was out cold about 40 metres behind play. Behind him stood the impassive, glowering figure of Magpie hard man Duncan Wright. The Collingwood player was the only man near Somerville, and he was making no effort to remove himself from the scene. Although TV commentator Alan 'Butch' Gale wondered aloud if Somerville might have fainted, everyone else at the ground realised what had happened.

Wright initially took a vow of silence but in later years owned up to the hit, blaming some early provocation from his opponent.

But whatever the provocation might have been, Wright's response backfired – badly, and in multiple ways.

In the short term it rallied the Bombers and seemed to demoralise his own teammates. The fans were hooting and howling – even the neutrals were incensed at what seemed to have happened – and the Collingwood players went into their shells. Essendon captain Ken Fraser urged his players to focus on the ball, but Ian 'Bluey' Shelton and others were delivering a far more retributive message. Peter McKenna, then a youngster in his first year at Collingwood, still recalls the febrile and threatening atmosphere that came over the game after Somerville went down.

The end result was that Essendon careered away and won by nine goals. Collingwood's hopes of another crack at a Premiership seemed to have hit the deck along with John Somerville.

There was a massive outcry after the game. The police interviewed Wright, but a lack of firm evidence or eyewitnesses meant he was never charged by the VFL or the police. But he paid a price, being cut from Collingwood's list during the 1966 pre-season, ostensibly for form and team balance. He never played for the club again. Des Tuddenham, for one, believed his presence could have proved the difference in 1966.

As it was, Duncan Wright's VFL career was over, as were Collingwood's 1965 Premiership hopes. And with them went the chance of a rare hat-trick, with the club's under-19s and reserves both winning flags that year.

H&A P18, W13, L5 • **Finished** 2nd • **Finals** P2, L2 • **Finished** 3rd • **Captains** Ray Gabelich & John Henderson • **Coach** Bob Rose • **Leading goalkicker** David Norman (32) • **Copeland Trophy** Trevor Steer

1966

TUDDY'S RUN

It's late in the 1966 Grand Final. St Kilda has its nose in front by a point, courtesy of Barry Breen's wobbly punt kick. The Saints are attacking again, but Terry Waters takes a magnificent mark in the back pocket, between the goal and behind posts. He makes the courageous decision to switch play and heads to the outer side of the ground, where wingman Peter Patterson is running with his St Kilda opponent. Waters' kick clears their heads, and the huge crowd audibly gasps when they see what is about to unfold.

Des Tuddenham, Collingwood's inspirational force, has run onto the bouncing ball. And in front of him is ... well, nothing. Ross Smith is chasing from the side but looks unlikely to catch him. In old-school footy parlance, 'Tuddy' has a paddock in front of him.

Then came the moment that every Collingwood fan, and Tuddy himself, later wished he could have over again. Knowing that the seconds were running out fast, Tuddenham grabbed the ball, took a stride or two to settle and then threw it onto his boot. His long punt kick made it all the way to centre half-forward, but Bob Murray marked in defence for St Kilda and famously 'hit the boundary line' as the siren blew.

What if? What if?

In hindsight, all Tuddy needed to do was run a little further. One bounce and he might have been within scoring distance; two and he definitely would have been. A point would have secured a replay, or a goal would have won it. Such are the moments in which big games of football are often decided. For the second time in three years, Collingwood lost a Grand Final by less than a goal.

It was cruel for coach Bob Rose, of course, but also for Tuddy, who had turned in one of the greatest individual games in the club's history in the second semi-final, when he kicked seven goals in his team's 10-point victory. He kicked three more in the Grand Final, but oh, what Magpie supporters would have given for just one more ...

As it was, the one-point loss inevitably soured a season in which Collingwood had finally returned to the top of the ladder for the first time since – unbelievably – 1930. To make matters worse, both the reserves and under-19s also made it through to their respective Grand Finals – and lost. The social club rooms at Victoria Park were packed as expected that Saturday night, but they were a very unhappy place to be.

But the final results shouldn't obscure the remarkable transformation Bobby Rose had brought to the football club. A senior team that had been woefully uncompetitive in 1963 had been to two Grand Finals in the three years since, and a preliminary final in the other. And the seconds and thirds had each won a flag and then been runners-up. The club, as a whole, was flying: all its teams were playing free-flowing, high-octane football and regularly competing for Premiership honours.

The only missing ingredient was a touch of good fortune in September. Lady Luck had not smiled upon the Magpies in Rose's first three years, but everyone knew that such misfortune couldn't continue forever ... Could it?

H&A P18, W15, L3 · **Finished** 1st · **Finals** P2, W1, L1 · **Finished** 2nd · **Captain** Des Tuddenham · **Coach** Bob Rose · **Leading goalkicker** Ian Graham (58) · **Copeland Trophy** Terry Waters

---

1967

COLLINGWOOD ZONES OUT

The footballing decision of 1967 that had the most far-reaching effects on the Collingwood Football Club unfortunately had very little to do with Collingwood at all. Indeed, the Magpies were implacably opposed to the VFL's major initiative of that year: the introduction of country zoning. It was a move by the VFL that would cost the club dearly for years to come.

Collingwood hated the idea of zoning. Its reputation as the biggest club in football had always been enough to attract a good portion of the best recruits, so it saw no reason to change. But other clubs and the VFL viewed things differently.

The league set up a special committee to look at the concept, and its report was delivered in 1967. It recommended that regional Victoria be divided into 12 zones, and that each club be 'given' one of those zones. Only two other clubs shared Collingwood's objections, while nine voted in favour, so the new rule was introduced.

The VFL claimed the zones were allocated by chance, being drawn out of a hat, and as luck would have it Collingwood was given the worst zone. In fact, some of the results were farcical. Only eight of 20 teams in the two main leagues given to the Pies (around the Western Border region) were actually available to them for recruiting: the others were tied to South Australia, and so players from these clubs needed clearances from the SANFL! Players from four smaller leagues were considered to have 'poor recruiting potential'. And other numbers were made up by counting under-18 and under-16 players, when clubs were prevented from recruiting players for their under-19 teams.

Collingwood officials were incensed. 'It is obvious to any sensible person that a serious mistake in the allocation of this district to any club has been made,' the club said. 'It was most unfortunate that our club was selected to have this area allocated to it: we have become severely handicapped in our recruiting efforts.'

If this really was 'the luck of the draw', then Collingwood paid dearly for a slice of misfortune. For a start, the club's country zones simply produced far fewer quality recruits than the zones of its opponents. That had an almost immediate impact on the strength and fortunes of the team.

The situation forced the club to look elsewhere for good newcomers. High-priced interstate recruits, for example, suddenly became in greater demand at Victoria Park – and that, in turn, would have consequences for the team's existing star players, and for the club as a whole.

At one stroke of the VFL's pen, Collingwood had been set back on its heels and disadvantaged compared to its opponents. It had also been thrown – perhaps unwillingly – into the murky world of aggressive recruiting and poaching. Neither of those developments served the club well.

Just as 1966 had ended with all three teams losing on Grand Final Day, 1967 finished in eerily similar circumstances when all three lost on first semi-final day. With a brave new world of country zoning about to begin, no wonder the club predicted that 1968 would be 'one of the most serious and challenging [seasons] ever experienced'.

H&A P18, W12, L6 • **Finished** 4th • **Finals** P1, L1 • **Finished** 4th • **Captain** Des Tuddenham • **Coach** Bob Rose • **Leading goalkicker** Peter McKenna (47) • **Copeland Trophy** Len Thompson

---

1968

THE SHERRIN STAND

As Collingwood faced up to the first year under the VFL's new country recruiting system, there was at least some good news closer to home: a new grandstand would finally be built at the railway end of Victoria Park.

This had been a long time coming, and just 12 months earlier the idea had looked like it might have to be shelved indefinitely. But in 1968 the go-ahead was given for what would become the final piece in the Vic Park jigsaw – a magnificent new stand to extend virtually from the social club building to the long, low grandstand protecting the outer on the ground's southern side.

That facility, the R.T. Rush Stand, had been opened in April 1966 to much fanfare, with the VFL and even Collingwood's rivals praising the club's far-sighted decision to build a grandstand for patrons in the outer. Less than a week after the Rush Stand was opened, the committee agreed to fund another modern grandstand, this one to replace the magnificent but dilapidated 1909 grandstand behind the goals at the western end of the ground.

But in 1967 the club announced it was going to defer the project. It had been blindsided when the VFL, with very little warning, proposed the virtual dismantling of the Outer Ground Levy (which the club had been relying upon for repayment of the loan for the Rush Stand). The league also changed entitlements for season tickets, leading to reduced sales, and altered the way match receipts were distributed.

Collingwood was angry on a number of fronts. Still smarting over the country recruiting zone fiasco, the Pies felt they were also being penalised by the VFL's moves to change the distribution of match receipts. They believed they were being called upon to prop up other clubs (sound familiar?), and were incensed that the changes to funding rules had not been flagged before they'd committed to the Rush Stand; if they'd known, they claimed, they might not have proceeded. The Magpies were so angry that they even took legal action against the VFL, claiming the league was acting beyond its powers, but later discontinued it.

The club's hand was forced in 1968, when it became likely that the 1909 stand would be condemned on health grounds. So a scaled-back version of the original plan for a new stand was approved, with funding coming from a mixture of more club debentures and the sale of reserved seating. What became known as the Sherrin Stand would eventually be opened in 1969, and the noise generated by the cheer squad who based themselves there seemed to be even louder in the new structure. It was the culmination of the extensive ground development program the club had undertaken since the late 1950s, making Victoria Park one of the best equipped and most modern grounds in the league.

None of this helped the team much in 1968, however, and Bobby Rose's Pies tumbled down the ladder to finish seventh. Excuses were at a premium for what the club described as 'one of the most disappointing seasons ever experienced': nobody had expected the team to miss the finals. With Collingwood at war with the VFL, worried about money and pessimistic about its recruiting prospects, Victoria Park was not a happy place to be.

H&A P20, W9, L11 • **Finished** 7th • **Captain** Des Tuddenham •
Coach Bob Rose • **Leading goalkicker** Peter McKenna (64) •
Copeland Trophy Len Thompson

1969

COLLINGWOOD BREAKS OUT THE CHEQUEBOOK

Whatever was ailing Collingwood in 1968 seemed to have disappeared by the time the 1969 season rolled around. The team played some breathtaking football at times in this season, and ended it on top of the ladder.

Rarely has a Magpie outfit played better than the '69 version did against the reigning premier, Carlton, at Princes Park in Round 4. A scarcely believable 12-goal third term was the highlight of a 64-point shellacking, and John Greening reminded everyone of his precocious talents with a stunning seven-goal display. (This was the infamous game where there were so many brawls that the reported players got off on a technicality – the umpires took too long to lodge the reports!)

But it wasn't just Greening who was flying. Mop-topped full-forward Peter McKenna kicked 98 goals for the year, including a memorable haul of 16.4 against South Melbourne. Len Thompson dominated the rucks, while Barry Price, the Richardsons and inspirational skipper Des Tuddenham were brilliant in the middle. This was a formidable Magpie outfit.

Yet somehow the team managed to lose both its finals matches. Everyone at Victoria Park was shell-shocked. While no team is ever guaranteed a flag, most observers expected the Pies to at least make the Grand Final. Their failure to do so sparked a chain of events that had lasting consequences.

The Australian National Football Carnival had been held in Adelaide in June. Peter Eakins, a blond-haired key defender from Subiaco, had been named in the All-Australian team, and jointly won the Tassie Medal as the best player at the carnival.

Collingwood wanted him – badly. The club's diabolical straight-sets exit from the finals further fuelled its desperation, as did its already dark view of the recruits likely to emerge from its country zones. So the Pies broke the bank for Eakins. They paid him a huge signing-on fee and an extremely generous annual salary in order to lure him across from Western Australia.

In theory, this was laudable – aggressive recruiting had often been lacking at Collingwood. But in this case, and with the benefit of hindsight, the Magpies chose the wrong guy, and ended up massively overpaying for someone who never made much of an impact in the VFL.

But the really heavy cost was the damage done to club harmony. Existing stars heard rumours about what Eakins was supposedly earning, and wanted something similar – or more – themselves. These rumblings of discontent reached their low point in the 1970 pre-season, when Tuddenham and Thompson went on strike for a few weeks over their demands for more money.

The club duly changed its payment structure for all players, and Thommo and Tuddy came back to the fold before the 1970 season started. But Eakins' recruitment had thrown Collingwood into the new world of professional football, which nobody at the club found particularly appealing. His failure to succeed perhaps made the Pies wary of paying big bucks to other recruits – and there is certainly a long list of stars who 'nearly' became Magpies in the 1970s.

Still, as the 1960s ended, most Magpie fans were just wondering when their perplexing finals jinx would end.

H&A P20, W15, L5 • **Finished** 1st • **Finals** P2, L2 • **Finished** 3rd • **Captain** Des Tuddenham • **Coach** Bob Rose • **Leading goalkicker** Peter McKenna (98) • **Copeland Trophy** Barry Price

---

1970

DISASTER

If they could magically change one event in Collingwood's history, hundreds of thousands of Magpie fans would no doubt choose the 1970 Grand Final.

It wasn't just that the Pies lost a Grand Final. It wasn't just that it was a game that looked unloseable. It wasn't even that it was against Carlton. It was all of those things, of course, but losing the 1970 Grand Final after being 44 points up at half-time scarred the club for at least 20 years, shattered one of the best teams Collingwood has ever put on the park and almost certainly cost the Pies chances at other flags too. It was, in almost every sense, a seismic event in the history of the Collingwood Football Club.

Funnily enough, the early signs in 1970 weren't encouraging. Skipper Des Tuddenham and star ruckman Len Thompson went on strike in the pre-season while arguing for more money, and when they returned after three weeks Tuddy was stripped of the captaincy. But once the matches began (22 of them in all, meaning that each team played the others twice), none of that seemed to matter. The Magpies started like a train and never slowed down. All the signs of brilliance that had been there in 1969 were back – only perhaps even better.

High points were many, but one of the best came against St Kilda in Round 10, when the Pies came back from a staggering 52 points down to win by seven. Round 19 provided another, as the rampaging Woods kept Carlton to just two goals for the entire game, allowing Peter McKenna to become the first Collingwood player since 1939 to kick 100 goals in a season; he would finish the year with a staggering 143 goals. Victoria Park went berserk.

This was footy at its best. The team played scintillating, free-flowing football that made them a delight to watch. Tuddy, Thommo, McKenna, Price, Greening, Waters and the Richardson brothers were all bona fide stars. Former Magpie champ Thorold Merrett once said this was the best Collingwood team he'd ever seen – and he played in two that had won Premierships. The Magpies of 1970 were *that* good.

They won a remarkable second semi-final over Carlton by 10 points, and the two teams met again a fortnight later. The story of that Grand Final is almost too well known to bear repeating: Collingwood completely dominated the first half, and its 44-point half-time lead could easily have been 60 or 70 if not for poor kicking. But the Blues brought on Ted Hopkins, who kicked four, McKenna was concussed in a collision with Tuddy, leaving the champion full-forward dazed and less effective, and the former skipper hobbled with a corked thigh, and Carlton came from the clouds to win by 10 points.

The result crushed everybody at the football club. Indeed, it is arguable that the club as a whole didn't recover until 1990. If Collingwood had won that day in 1970, Bob Rose would have stayed on as coach, the team would have stayed together and there would have been no talk of 'Colliwobbles' or finals hoodoos. The modern history of the Collingwood Football Club would likely have been completely different. And there would almost certainly have been more Premierships.

Instead, all that's left is to ponder, 'What if?'

H&A P22, W18, L4 • **Finished** 1st • **Finals** P2, W1, L1 • **Finished** 2nd • **Captain** Terry Waters • **Coach** Bob Rose • **Leading goalkicker** Peter McKenna (143) • **Copeland Trophy** Peter McKenna

---

1971

ROSE AND TUDDY CALL IT QUITS

Just about every Collingwood player who played under Bob Rose has since recalled how much they loved him – not just as a coach, but also as a good and decent man. Many are still haunted by the feeling that they let him down. Rose was equally strong in his love for his players, and for the football club. Even so, by the end of 1971 it was clear that Bob Rose and Collingwood would have to part ways.

The catalyst was yet another near miss of a season – the club's sixth in eight years – and yet another inexplicable implosion that left everyone shaking their heads and wondering exactly what had happened.

The moment that set the scene for 1971 came when the committee rejected Rose's pleas for Des Tuddenham to regain the captaincy. Tuddy was easily the best leader at the club, but the committee couldn't forgive him for going on strike the previous year, and so Terry Waters was again given the nod as skipper. Tuddy was furious and initially refused to play. Eventually, he relented and once again pulled on the jumper, but it was an open secret in football that he had been all but promised a clearance at the end of the year.

Once again, Collingwood's pre-season had been derailed by internal dissent and player militancy. And once again, it seemed to have almost no effect when the season started. The Pies were unbeaten through the first seven rounds, and after 17 rounds had lost only three games. They were well clear in second spot, and equal Premiership favourites with Hawthorn.

Then it all fell apart. The Pies lost four of their last five games, and just sneaked into fourth. To complete the humiliation, the last of those losses came to Carlton at Victoria Park in an eerie repeat of the 1970 Grand Final: Collingwood led by 42 points at half-time, only to lose by 19. With the wounds of 1970 still so fresh, it was the cruellest of results.

To make matters worse, the captaincy had become a major issue. Waters had battled for form and confidence through much of the year – which was hardly surprising given he knew his own coach wanted someone else as captain. His struggles were brought into even starker relief when Tuddenham, who had been in great form, was named captain of Victoria in June. Waters eventually resigned the leadership in August and handed the reins to Wayne Richardson, and didn't play again after being dragged from VFL Park in Round 19.

Almost inevitably, the Pies capitulated against Richmond in the sudden-death first semi-final. Waters then publicly vented his anger, attacking the club for undermining him and calling for big changes, including replacing the coach. Rose duly quit soon afterwards, saying he needed a break from football (though he ended up at Footscray).

Tuddy left too, for Essendon, and Waters himself lasted only a handful of games in 1972. The rollercoaster ride of the past eight years had taken its toll on everyone at Collingwood, and it was time for a change.

H&A P22, W14, L7, D1 • **Finished** 4th • **Finals** P1, L1 • **Finished** 4th • **Captains** Terry Waters & Wayne Richardson • **Coach** Bob Rose • **Leading goalkicker** Peter McKenna (134) • **Copeland Trophy** Wayne Richardson

---

1972

THE GREENING INCIDENT

Coming into the Round 14 clash with St Kilda at Moorabbin in 1972, John Greening seemed to be on the verge of superstardom. The 21-year-old from Tasmania had been in scintillating form for the Magpies, either ruck-roving or in the centre, and was leading many media awards. His mixture of speed, skills and athleticism was proving irresistible, and he had become a true star of the competition.

But just two minutes into that game against St Kilda, Greening lay unconscious on the Moorabbin turf, the victim of a brutal behind-the-play blow that shocked the football world. The incident all but ended the career of one of the most exciting players ever to pull on a Collingwood guernsey.

He'd taken the first mark of the game and kicked the ball towards the goal square. But just as everyone – including the TV cameras – was looking at the goalmouth scramble, Greening hit the deck and lay there, motionless.

Greening's injuries were probably the most serious ever suffered by a Collingwood footballer during a game. He was in a coma for 24 hours, and it was days before he regained consciousness. At one stage doctors even feared for his life. He was expected to be permanently disabled but, incredibly, recovered well enough to play some VFL football again within a couple of years. But he was never the same footballer as he'd been before the incident.

The perpetrator, Jim O'Dea, was suspended for 10 weeks by the VFL tribunal. A writ for alleged assault was filed in the Supreme Court but later withdrawn. Yet the incident remained a nasty blot on the game; some fans were so sickened that they never went to another match. Relations between Collingwood and St Kilda plummeted, and many Magpies have never forgiven the Saints.

Worst of all, of course, the incident cost Greening the best years of his football life, and Collingwood the services of a player who might have gone on to be one of the greats. Bob Rose said Greening was the best young player he had seen; Peter McKenna said he was the most talented and exciting he'd ever played with. And he still had 10 years, probably more, in front of him when his career was cruelly cut short. It's impossible not to think that Greening would have made a major difference to Collingwood's fortunes in the decade that followed.

The incident soured what had always shaped as a difficult year. President Tom Sherrin had been widely criticised over his handling of the Rose, Tuddenham and Waters situation in 1971, and was challenged once again by the Galbally forces. That challenge failed, and Rose's deputy, the respected former captain Neil Mann, was appointed to take over as coach.

The team responded well to Mann's coaching. Len Thompson would go on to win the Brownlow (Greening finished seventh, despite missing nine games), Peter McKenna topped the VFL goalkicking table with 130 goals, and the team finished third in what had become a final five. But losses to Richmond and St Kilda saw the Pies tumble out of the finals with barely a whimper. It was a disappointing end to what will always be remembered as a black season.

H&A P22, W14, L7, D1 • **Finished** 3rd • **Finals** P2, L2 • **Finished** 4th • **Captain** Wayne Richardson • **Coach** Neil Mann • **Leading goalkicker** Peter McKenna (130) • **Copeland Trophy** Len Thompson

---

1973

ANOTHER FADE-OUT

At half-time in the 1973 preliminary final, Collingwood supporters had every reason to believe that their team was heading to a Grand Final. They had just witnessed the Magpies turn in a exhilarating half of creative, free-flowing football that had blown Richmond away. Coach Neil Mann's decision to start Len Thompson at centre half-forward and relief ruckman Graeme Jenkin in the ruck had caught the Tigers by surprise, and the Pies' fleet-footed midfield had run them off their feet. By the long break, Thommo had kicked four and the lead had blown out to six goals – and even that margin probably flattered the Tigers.

That first-half performance was entirely in keeping with the football the Magpies had played throughout the season. They had won 14 of their first 15 matches, and ended up losing only three games for the entire home-and-away season to finish two games clear on top of the ladder. A final-quarter fade-out against Carlton – of course – in the second semi-final had brought a first finals loss, but the first half of the preliminary final seemed to have confirmed that the Neil Mann–led Magpies were made of sterner stuff than their predecessors.

Unfortunately, the second half confirmed the exact opposite. Star Richmond centre half-forward Royce Hart, who had injury concerns, had been named on the bench because of doubts over his ability to play a full game. But with the game seemingly gone and nothing to lose, the Tigers threw him on for the second half.

Hart's mere appearance on the field galvanised the Tiger crowd, and his teammates lifted almost immediately. When he goaled from distance on the run during the third quarter, you could almost feel the confidence drain from the Collingwood players, and the nerves set in. Richmond hauled in most of the first-half lead in the third term, and went on to win by seven points.

The loss, from yet another seemingly unassailable position, was devastating. It confirmed that whatever problems there were with this group hadn't been fixed by the change of coach, or by the normal comings and goings of players. Collingwood's inability to close out big games, especially finals, had now become the equivalent of a golfer with the yips: this was a psychological problem within the playing group, or perhaps even the entire club. The Colliwobbles, for many, had become real.

The preliminary final defeat made it six losses from Collingwood's last six finals matches. The fans were starting to lose faith: it was one thing to dominate in the home-and-away season, but ultimately pointless if you couldn't seal the deal in September. The club pointed to injuries, and even a lack of depth, but the explanations sounded increasingly like excuses. The pressure was building, and was likely to get even more intense in the 1974 campaign, unless there was a major change in fortunes.

And while all this was going on, Peter Eakins, the controversial recruit who had unwittingly changed the entire player payment structure when he arrived in 1970, was quietly cleared to return to Subiaco. Collingwood's first foray into high-priced interstate recruiting had been a costly, and failed, experiment.

H&A P22, W19, L3 • **Finished** 1st • **Finals** P2, L2 • **Finished** 3rd • **Captain** Wayne Richardson • **Coach** Neil Mann • **Leading goalkicker** Peter McKenna (86) • **Copeland Trophy** Len Thompson

---

1974

THE ERN AND WEED SHOW COMES TO TOWN

Collingwood endured yet another groundhog day in 1974. After 17 rounds the Pies were on top of the ladder, having lost only three games. Five weeks later they had lost a further four and slipped to fourth spot.

Even that all-too-familiar fade-out might not have proved disastrous if the team had been able to defeat ninth-placed South Melbourne in the final game of the year – a result that would have secured the Pies third place and the double chance. But South won by seven points and Collingwood ended the season playing like a team that expected to lose. For fans, it was horrible to watch.

Remarkably, the Pies turned it around to win their first final since 1970, beating Footscray in the elimination final, only to be thumped by Hawthorn the following week. The 1974 campaign was over.

So, too, was Neil Mann's coaching career. And Tom Sherrin's presidency. The pressure that had been building at Victoria Park since 1969, and especially since the messy end to 1971, had captured two more victims.

Mann quit almost as soon as the season ended, realising he wasn't going to be able to take this playing group any further. By that time, Sherrin had already announced he would not be recontesting the presidency at the December election: he, like many at Collingwood, had been worn down by all the drama and near misses.

The choice of replacements for Mann and Sherrin was telling, and both were in place before 1974 ended. The club decided it had 'to produce more vigor in its efforts on the field' and, when recruiting, should 'look for players who can use the hip and shoulder as well as skill'. Someone at Vic Park had obviously decided the team was a bit on the soft side.

So they brought back the most famous Magpie enforcer of all, Murray Weideman, as the new coach. He'd had a good record coaching with West Adelaide in the SANFL and seemed a reasonable compromise between outsider and club legend. He became the club's first full-time coach.

Sherrin made the appointment before he relinquished his role, and justified not leaving the decision to the new president by saying the new coach needed to start work before Christmas. In hindsight, that was a bad move.

Unlike previous presidential changes, this one involved very little acrimony; that would come later. Frank Galbally couldn't be convinced to stand, so in the end the battle came down to one between traditionalists, who backed Neil Mann, and a new broom of professionalism and modernisation, fronted by a young and little-known businessman called Ern Clarke. To members deeply frustrated by the repeated failures of the past decade, the pitch to break with tradition and try something new was instantly appealing. Clarke and his running mates won the election comfortably.

By the end of 1974, the club had been so reduced that it could only hail the fact that 'we proved that Collingwood can win a finals match'. Now all eyes turned to 1975, to see if a new president and a new coach could return the club to the point where such 'achievements' were considered a given.

H&A P22, W15, L7 • **Finished** 4th • **Finals** P2, W1, L1 • **Finished** 4th • **Captain** Wayne Richardson • **Coach** Neil Mann • **Leading goalkicker** Peter McKenna (69) • **Copeland Trophy** Wayne Richardson

---

1975

CARMAN'S BAD BREAK

In addition to a new coach and a new president, Collingwood found itself a new superstar in 1975.

Phil Carman had been a long time coming to Victoria Park. Collingwood had been aware of him since the mid-1960s, and he had been talked about as the 'next big thing' to come out of South Australia as far back as 1970. But every time he seemed to be on the point of donning the black-and-white jumper, something would get in the way. There were clearance wrangles, disputes between the Pies and his SANFL club, Norwood, and offers and counter-offers.

In many ways, this continual game of 'will he? won't he?' massively heightened the sense of expectation around Carman. So when he did – finally – land at Victoria Park for the 1975 season, it created a huge buzz of excitement. But that was nothing compared to the excitement generated when the crowds actually got to see him play. For once, here was an interstate player who lived up to the hype.

Carman was brilliant in 1975, and took the competition by storm. He played just 15 games for the year but still won the Copeland Trophy, and was named in the Victorian interstate side after just 10 games. He kicked a staggering 11 goals in a game against St Kilda at Moorabbin, and captivated the football world with his rare mix of athleticism, power and freakish skills. He even introduced the VFL to his ground-breakingly lairy white boots.

Collingwood won six of Carman's first 10 games to be comfortably in the upper reaches of the ladder, but the turning point of the season came when he played for the Vics against Western Australia – and broke his foot.

The impact on Collingwood's season was huge, and immediate. In the eight weeks he missed, the Pies dropped from third to seventh. When he returned, they won the remaining four games of the regular season to sneak into fifth spot – from where they would be dumped out of the finals in the first week. In his first year, Carman had already become the most important player in the Magpie line-up.

But the longer-term impact of the injury was also significant. Had it not happened, Carman would almost certainly have won the 1975 Brownlow Medal. Instead, he finished three votes behind Footscray's Gary Dempsey, despite missing those eight games. Carman himself would later say that the rest of his career might well have been different if he'd gone on to win the medal – that it might somehow have validated him as a footballer. As it was, he missed out, and Phil Carman's career story became a tangled mixture of controversy and 'what might have been'. He never again got close to the giddy heights of 1975, although he was never far from the headlines.

The season ended with an agonising loss to Richmond in the elimination final. Even so, Magpie fans must have been thinking that – with Carman added to their core of established stars, together with emerging young talent such as Bill Picken, Peter Moore, Rene Kink and Ray Shaw – they finally had a combination that could take them a lot further than fifth. As it turned out, they couldn't have been more wrong.

H&A P22, W13, L9 • **Finished** 5th • **Finals** P1, L1 • **Finished** 5th • **Captain** Wayne Richardson • **Coach** Murray Weideman • **Leading goalkicker** Phil Carman (41) • **Copeland Trophy** Phil Carman

---

1976

THE FIRST WOODEN SPOON

Until 1976, Collingwood had never finished bottom of the VFL ladder. The Pies' only flirtation with the wooden spoon came in their very first year, 1892, when they finished equal last in the VFA with Williamstown. But in 1976 that claim to fame disappeared. The entire season was a disaster, from start to finish. The president and coach were at war, the coach lost the players, and the players seemed to be fighting harder with each other than with their opponents. Season 1976 was, in many ways, the year when Collingwood hit rock bottom.

The problems began before the season had even started, when former skipper Des Tuddenham was controversially enticed back from Essendon to resume the captaincy. There was far from universal support for the move, and unfortunately the doubters were proved correct: Tuddy wasn't the same player he had been, and his appointment as captain also disenfranchised the existing captain, Wayne Richardson.

Tuddy's return on a lucrative contract once again raised the issue of player payments, and there were rumblings of discontent among many in the playing group. There were more than rumblings directed towards Phil Carman, one of the highest paid players but also one of the most undisciplined and temperamental. He ran his own race, sometimes kept his own training schedule and occasionally even had a drink before training. He later admitted he completely lost focus that year as the club imploded around him.

Two weeks into the season, with the Pies 0–2, Wayne Richardson and his brother Max were controversially dropped. Wayne complained bitterly to the newspapers about a supposed vendetta against him, then criticised both the coach and the president – an outburst that unsurprisingly earned him a four-week suspension. Max, in turn, refused to turn up for the reserves game.

The club was falling apart. Chaos ruled: there was no discipline, no control, and everyone seemed to be fighting. And there could be no leadership from the top, as coach Weideman and president Clarke were themselves fighting out an increasingly bitter feud in public.

Clarke's presidency had begun with a blaze of activity in 1975, but his energy, drive and 'damn the tradition' approach alienated as many people as it won over – maybe more. He was soon at loggerheads with the coach, who felt he was too interventionist in football matters, and as 1975 unfolded it became obvious that this was a relationship likely to end in tears. Early in May 1976, that's exactly what happened, with Weideman publicly announcing that he would quit if Clarke didn't. The two eventually papered over the cracks in order to provide the newspapers with a front-page photo, but Clarke resigned several weeks later anyway to protect the club from further turmoil, citing his business commitments as the main reason.

In the face of such chaos, the surprise is not that the team finished bottom but that they somehow managed to win six games along the way. By the end of the season, with Clarke already gone, the club's last-place finish would cost Weideman his job too. It also prompted the club – for the first time – to look outside Victoria Park for its next coach. And that proved to be a game-changer.

H&A P22, W6, L16 • **Finished** 12th • **Captain** Des Tuddenham • **Coach** Murray Weideman • **Leading goalkicker** Phil Carman (38) • **Copeland Trophy** Robert Hyde

---

1977

T-SHIRT TOMMY ARRIVES

If you had told any Collingwood fan at the end of 1976, after the Magpies had just finished bottom of the ladder for the first time in their history, that their team would be playing off in the Grand Final 12 months later, they would have thought you crazy. And rightly so. But that's exactly what happened. And that stunning resurgence was largely due to one man: Tommy Hafey.

Hafey was a legend at Richmond. He was appointed coach there in 1966, when the Tigers were at a low point, and promptly turned them into a machine that delivered four Premierships in seven years. But Hafey's methods – which largely revolved around intensive physical preparation and a long-kicking game plan – seemed to have a use-by date, and the Richmond powerbrokers sacked him after the Tigers finished seventh in 1976.

Collingwood, having dispensed with Murray Weideman, finally decided to try an outsider as coach. And in Hafey they were fortunate enough to have available one of the best coaches going around.

He transformed the club almost instantly. Players who felt that discipline and hard work had been lacking in 1976 soon discovered it was a new story under Hafey – and they loved it. The hard yards at training ensured they became fitter than ever, and Hafey's simple, long-kicking, play-on football suited the emerging crop of Magpie youngsters and re-energised the experienced core.

Plus there was the fact that Hafey was one of the nicest guys in football. Earnest, honest, teetotalling and T-shirt wearing, the players at Punt Road had loved him, and he formed a similar bond with those at Victoria Park. The fans also adored him.

Initially, it didn't look like 'T-shirt Tommy' had much to work with – just the 1976 list, plus a few new recruits in Stan Magro, Kevin Worthington and Ricky Barham. But Magro and Worthington transformed the backline, and the brilliant, super-quick Barham was a revelation on the wing. Together with a much improved and more consistent year from Phil Carman, and with Peter Moore emerging as a gun goalkicker, the Pies were unrecognisable from the rabble of '76. By season's end they had become the first team in VFL history to rise from last to first in one year. Eighteen wins and four losses. It was extraordinary.

Collingwood held off second-placed Hawthorn in the second semi-final by just two points, but lost Carman in a devastating blow after he was rubbed out for two matches – which turned out to be two Grand Finals – for thumping Michael Tuck right in front of an umpire. Even so, everything seemed to be going to plan at three-quarter-time of the Grand Final (the first such game to be broadcast live on TV), with Collingwood leading by 27 points. But North flew home, and it took a Ross 'Twiggy' Dunne mark and goal in the dying seconds for Collingwood to draw the game and force a replay. The second game was a high-scoring affair but the Pies were never really in it – rumours of over-training in the lead-up to the match persist to this day. They went down by 27 points in a game memorable only for Phil Manassa's long running goal late in the last quarter.

Still, it had been a remarkable resurgence that nobody could have seen coming. And Tom Hafey, so long a Tiger, was now a certified hero of the black-and-white army.

H&A P22, W18, L4 • **Finished** 1st • **Finals** P3, W1, D1, L1 • **Finished** 2nd • **Captain** Max Richardson • **Coach** Tom Hafey • **Leading goalkicker** Peter Moore (76) • **Copeland Trophy** Len Thompson

---

1978

THE CLEAR-OUT

Many people expected Collingwood to experience a significant return to earth in 1978 – almost as if they couldn't believe the dramatic 12th-to-first rise of the previous 12 months. But the Pies were having none of it. Yes, they lost a couple more games, but they still finished third on the ladder, just a game behind eventual Grand Finalists North Melbourne and Hawthorn.

The finals ran largely true to ladder form: a thumping at the hands of Hawthorn, a thrilling victory over Carlton in the first semi-final, and a gutsy but ultimately failed showing against North in the preliminary final. But that 12-point loss to the Kangaroos ended up being much more significant than most people realised at the time. It prompted a massive clear-out of players, and a recruiting program that not only gave the team its identity for the next few years but also sowed the seeds for the eventual demise of both coach Tom Hafey and the man who had replaced Ern Clarke as president, John Hickey.

Soon after the loss to North Melbourne, Hafey and his match committee decided it was time to jettison some dead wood and rejuvenate the playing list. No fewer than 16 players were moved on, including some very big names. Wayne Richardson retired, while brother Max was sent to Fitzroy. Twiggy Dunne, who had retired earlier in the year then come back, this time retired for good, as did wingman Alan Atkinson. Captain Len Thompson – who had won a record fifth Copeland just 12 months earlier – was also pushed out of the club (first to Fitzroy and then South Melbourne), very much against his wishes.

But the biggest name to be shown the door was 'Fabulous' Phil Carman. Such a move would have seemed inconceivable three years earlier, but yet another inconsistent, frustrating season from the mercurial Carman made his departure entirely understandable. He went to Melbourne, along with talented players John Dellamarta and Wayne Gordon.

The clear-out left some major holes in the Magpies' line-up. A solidly built kid called Tony Shaw had debuted in '78, and fellow youngsters Peter Daicos and Denis Banks would join him in the seniors in 1979. But the team was now desperately short on experience, so the club went hunting for recruits from other clubs.

And it was here that the Pies experienced decidedly mixed results. It is now well known that the club approached a number of star players in that period – most famously Bernie Quinlan – and for a variety of reasons failed to land many of them. Those big names who did make their way to Victoria Park were too often injured or past their best, or both.

Instead the numbers were made up by a ragtag mix of cast-offs and second-chancers, whose appearance on the Collingwood team list didn't exactly set supporters' pulses racing. Craig Davis and Ray Byrne, both from Carlton, turned out to be excellent buys, but others who joined in the wake of the 1978 exodus, such as Geoff Austen, David Young, Russell Ohlsen, Stephen Roach and Michael Woolnough, were pedestrian at best.

Magpie fans didn't know it at the time, but they were witnessing the birth of 'Hafey's Heroes'.

H&A P22, W15, L7 • **Finished** 3rd • **Finals** P3, W1, L2 • **Finished** 3rd • **Captain** Len Thompson • **Coach** Tom Hafey • **Leading goalkicker** Peter Moore (57) • **Copeland Trophy** Ray Shaw & Bill Picken

1979

IN HARMES' WAY

Ask any Collingwood supporter to nominate the defining moment of the 1979 season and it's odds on they'll splutter the name Wayne Harmes and then add – bitterly – a mumbled, disgusted reference to a boundary umpire.

This season boiled down to one moment. Eighteen minutes into the last quarter of a low-scoring Grand Final on a wet and muddy MCG, Carlton was leading Collingwood by four points. But the Pies had kicked the last two goals and were coming fast. Harmes gathered the ball between wing and half-forward and set his sights on goal. But the ball slewed off the side of his boot, went high and headed towards the boundary line in the forward pocket.

As most spectators' thoughts turned to the throw-in to come, Harmes reappeared as if from nowhere, having frenetically chased down his own kick. He dived and punched the ball from the boundary line into the goal square, where Ken Sheldon was waiting to kick the sealer. The Blues hung on to win by five points.

Debate has raged ever since over whether the ball was inside or outside the boundary line when Harmes punched it back. Collingwood fans are convinced not just that he was over the line, but that he was some distance back among the seats of the members' stand.

Once again, Collingwood had lost a Grand Final. Once again, it had been to Carlton. And once again, they seemed to have been the victims of a cruel stroke of misfortune. This one confirmed the almost self-fulfilling belief that a jinx truly existed. From Crompton and Breen to Hopkins and Hart and Baker, the Magpies now had Harmes and that bloody boundary umpire.

In truth, Collingwood had done well to get that close to Carlton on the final day of the season. The Blues were clearly the best team in the competition that year, having finished four games clear of the third-placed Pies.

Collingwood's uninspiring summer of recruiting had left it with a line-up that wasn't the most skilled the club has ever put on the park. There was talent, sure – Peter Moore moved into the ruck and won the Brownlow, the gifted Peter Daicos debuted on a day when the Pies kicked their highest ever score – 31.21 (207) against St Kilda – and Ricky Barham and Bill Picken were high-quality players.

But mainly what this team had was heart and hard work and team spirit. Had it not been for the non-call on Harmes, it could have been one of the great fairytale football stories – this gutsy team of underdogs finally ending one of football's biggest jinxes. But it was not to be.

Unfortunately, the loss, and the manner of it, took the gloss off the other big event of 1979 – Collingwood's first Premiership since 1958. Sure, it was only the night competition, but the Pies' 28-point victory over Hawthorn at Waverley Park in July, achieved on the back of outstanding performances from Moore and full-forward turned full-back Peter McCormack, was celebrated enthusiastically just the same. Many fans believed at the time that it might signal an end to Collingwood's Grand Final hoodoo. But Wayne Harmes put paid to that theory, just two months later.

H&A P22, W15, L7 • **Finished** 3rd • **Finals** P4, W2, L2 • **Finished** 2nd • **Captain** Ray Shaw • **Coach** Tom Hafey • **Leading goalkicker** Craig Davis (88) • **Copeland Trophy** Peter Moore

1980
RECRUITING FAILURES

Collingwood had finished top of the home-and-away ladder in 1977, third in 1978 and third again in 1979. On paper that reads well – a solid, consistent base of high-quality play that ensured the team was always in contention.

But anyone who had watched the Pies in '78 and '79, in particular, knew that the list was short on quality. And as the break leading into the 1980 season continued, it became clear that running Carlton so close in 1979 had had an unexpectedly negative consequence: the club seemed to have decided it was closer to Premiership success than many external observers judged.

How else could you explain a summer recruiting program that netted the club ... well, not much. One-time St Kilda star Allan Davis, well past his best, arrived, as did Jon Hummel from South Melbourne and Ian Low from Footscray. They played just 17 games between them, and all were gone within a year. The only other additions to Collingwood's 1979 list were the usual youngsters, none of whom enjoyed long careers. So any improvement was going to have to come from within.

To nobody's surprise, except perhaps those who had overseen that summer's recruiting 'drive', that didn't happen. Instead, the Pies went slightly backwards during the year, winning one less game and finishing fifth. The 'highlight' of the year was being robbed of a second successive night Premiership when umpires didn't hear the siren that rang with Collingwood in front. Instead, Kerry Good's post-siren mark was allowed to stand, he kicked truly and the Pies lost yet another Grand Final in impossibly cruel circumstances.

Still, all that was forgotten come September, as Tom Hafey's men embarked on an improbable charge to become the first team ever to win a flag from fifth spot on the ladder. That charge started with an eight-point elimination final win against North, followed by a comprehensive and thoroughly enjoyable 50-point victory over Carlton in the first semi-final. A nail-biting four-point thriller over Geelong in the preliminary final came next.

Against the odds, 'Hafey's Heroes' were in the Grand Final. Along the way they'd won countless accolades for their fighting qualities and incredible spirit. Hard as it is to believe, even some neutrals wanted them to win. The film of David Williamson's play *The Club* had opened during the finals, only adding to the buzz around the Magpies.

Unfortunately, Richmond wasn't buying in to the fairytale, and the Tigers demolished the Pies by a then Grand Final record margin of 81 points. The unprecedented scale of the loss brought the focus squarely on the club's recruiting. In the end, the general view was that Collingwood 'had done well to get there'. That was rapidly becoming the unofficial motto of the Hafey era: it had been true in 1979 and was true again in 1980.

As it turned out, the club had tried to recruit some bigger names – first after the 1978 overhaul and again after 1979 – but had failed. The supporters loved their team of battlers, and they loved Hafey: the spirit at Collingwood had rarely been better. But spirit could only take this group so far. The question was how far – and whether that point had already been reached.

H&A P22, W14, L7, D1 • **Finished** 5th • **Finals** P4, W3, L1 • **Finished** 2nd • **Captain** Ray Shaw • **Coach** Tom Hafey • **Leading goalkicker** Craig Davis (52) • **Copeland Trophy** Peter Moore

---

1981

HAFEY LOSES THE PLAYERS

The 1981 first semi-final was one of the most thrilling finals matches Collingwood has ever been involved in. The high-scoring, seesawing contest with Fitzroy eventually fell the Pies' way by a single point after a late, late snap from Ross Brewer in the dying minutes.

It was a hugely important win for the Magpies. After finishing in second place, equal on points with Carlton, they had lost the qualifying final to Geelong. The nail-biting win over the Roys kept the Pies' season alive.

But the win came at a massive cost. Peter Moore, who had been appointed captain at the start of the year and was arguably the team's best player, tore his hamstring during the game. So when the Pies narrowly defeated Geelong in the preliminary final, the focus shifted to whether or not Moore would be fit to play in the Grand Final.

Collingwood's list was stronger in 1981 – the addition of Mark Williams, Michael Taylor, Graeme Allan and Warwick Irwin ensured that. But it still wasn't strong enough to withstand the loss of their inspirational and brilliant ruckman/forward. Two weeks is not normally enough time to recover from a decent 'hammy', but the pressure on Moore to play was enormous, and he and the club eventually decided it was worth the risk.

It wasn't. A clearly lame Moore battled manfully but was only a shadow of his usual self. Even so, Collingwood was well placed late in the third quarter of the Grand Final, 21 points up after five successive goals. But Carlton grabbed the last two of the term to deflate the Pies' momentum, and ended up winning comfortably by 20 points.

If Moore tearing his hammy was the pivotal moment pre-match, there was another, perhaps even more telling one immediately afterwards. Coach Tom Hafey lost his players.

Hafey was so gutted by yet another lost Grand Final that he wouldn't address the club's post-match function that evening. The next day on TV he looked shattered, and seemed to have no answers. But then a newspaper journalist with close connections to Hafey ran a story naming a number of players who, the journalist felt, had repeatedly let Collingwood down in big matches – stars such as Kink, Ray Shaw, Ricky Barham and even Moore himself.

The players blamed Hafey for leaking his views to the press, and felt he was publicly 'throwing them under the bus' for the losses. Many had already started to tire of Hafey's methods anyway: the relentless training, the strict discipline, the 'sameness' of his routines. All that was bearable when there was a special bond between coach and players, and when the team was on the rise. But Hafey's post-game criticisms fractured that bond irrevocably.

The 1981 Grand Final loss was the proverbial final straw. The team had gone too close, too often, and this loss – and Hafey's response to it – prompted anger and bitterness, whereas before there had been pride and disappointment.

Hafey could see what was happening and offered his resignation to the board, but just three days after the game the club decided to keep him on. As it turned out, that was a massive mistake – one which virtually preordained one of the most tumultuous years in the club's history.

H&A P22, W17, L5 • **Finished** 2nd • **Finals** P4, W2, L2 • **Finished** 2nd • **Captain** Peter Moore • **Coach** Tom Hafey • **Leading goalkicker** Peter Daicos (76) • **Copeland Trophy** Mark Williams

---

1982

A SEISMIC SACKING

There was almost an air of inevitability about the Collingwood Football Club during the tumultuous 1982 season, even if few could accurately have predicted just how significant the ramifications would be.

The board had knocked back Tom Hafey's offer of resignation only days after the 1981 Grand Final loss. From that moment, he was on borrowed time. And that pressure only intensified after one of the club's worst starts to a season, culminating in a Round 10 loss to Melbourne, which left the team with only one win from its first 10 matches.

Hafey acknowledged: 'It could not have been a worse year ... everything which has happened has just been wrong.'

A petition calling on the committee to resign was being passed around; the players' confidence and commitment was at the lowest possible ebb; and speculation centred on Hafey's position.

On the Monday morning after the Melbourne game, the *Age* quoted an unnamed club senior official: 'Be prepared for interesting developments in the next 24 hours.' What followed was one of the most dramatic afternoons in the club's history. Hafey was given two options by club president John Hickey: resign or be sacked. On principle, he chose the latter.

In a four-paragraph statement, Hickey acknowledged that the club owed Hafey 'a deep debt of gratitude'. 'That he failed to win a Premiership for Collingwood will undoubtedly be recorded as one of the greatest tragedies in football history,' the president said. Hafey had lifted the club off the bottom of the ladder to Grand

Finals in 1977 (two), 1979, 1980 and 1981. In his 138 games as coach of Collingwood, the club had a 65 per cent winning record.

Even though his sacking had been forecast, it still deeply shocked many in the game. Veteran football writer Mike Sheahan would ultimately rank it as the third-most significant coach sacking in the game's history.

The dismissal created even more division within the club; and if it was meant to secure the position of Hickey and the board, history would show that it did the complete opposite.

In the same edition of the *Herald* that reported Hafey's sacking, there was talk of a board challenge, with media proprietor Ranald Macdonald mentioned as one of the likely candidates. Describing himself as 'just an enthusiastic supporter', Macdonald admitted that he might be interested in playing a more active role within the club. And indeed, as the on-field season slid further out of control, Macdonald and a group known as the 'New Magpies' – featuring high-profile businessmen and former players – emerged to take on the Hickey administration.

The seeds of revolution had been sown. In a typically bitter election campaign, which Collingwood seems to specialise in, the New Magpies promised to drag the club into the modern era, start an aggressive search for a progressive coach, and undertake the biggest recruiting drive in the club's history. Soon after the 1982 season ended – Collingwood had achieved only four wins, its lowest tally since 1942 – the New Magpies were swept to power. As the new president, Macdonald had a mandate for change the likes of which the Collingwood Football Club had never experienced before.

H&A P22, W4, L18 • **Finished** 10th • **Captain** Peter Moore • **Coaches** Tom Hafey & Mick Erwin • **Leading goalkicker** Peter Daicos (58) • **Copeland Trophy** Peter Daicos

---

1983

RECRUITING SPREE

The New Magpies didn't promise a Premiership when they took power in late 1982, but the implication – and expectation – was there. Collingwood hadn't won a flag since 1958, and the reform group's commitment to embark on one of the most aggressive and expensive recruiting campaigns in the game's history would at least give the Magpies a serious crack at attaining that elusive 14th VFL Premiership. No amount of money would be too much to attract the right players; no effort would be spared in transforming the club's playing group.

The late Jock McHale, three decades gone, might well have been spinning in his grave, given the depth of change occurring at Victoria Park, which included the altering of a line in the club's time-honoured theme song. The new board put a pen through the most lampooned line in 'Good Old Collingwood Forever', changing 'Oh, the Premiership's a cakewalk' to the less emphatic, almost bland 'There is just one team we favour'. Fans never warmed to the change to a song steeped in Collingwood tradition, which dated back to 1906 and which was almost learned as a birthright, passing down from generation to generation. It would revert to the original in time. But the angst over the theme song was a portent of the drama ahead.

Highly rated South Australian coach John Cahill was named as Collingwood's new coach for 1983, and he promised to bring a new style. But the most significant change came in the talent search the committee launched from the outset against other VFL clubs (eventually sparking a poaching war with Richmond), as well as from state leagues and anywhere they believed good talent was available.

Collingwood fans felt slighted when the club's captain, Peter Moore, accepted a lucrative deal to join Melbourne, but that only made the club more determined to seek potential stars. And the Magpies shopped with abandon, spending a fortune on Richmond pair David Cloke and Geoff Raines, Sydney's Shane Morwood, high-priced Western Australian players Mike Richardson and Gary Shaw (who was originally a Queenslander), South Australian Greg Phillips, as well as cheaper recruits such as Phillip Walsh, from Hamilton. Shaw's transfer fee alone was more than $300,000 – the price of a half-dozen houses in some suburbs at the time. But he was deemed important to the rebuilding of the club, so no expense was spared.

Having beaten the Demons – and, tellingly, Moore – in the opening round of the 1983 season, the new-look Magpies took some time to gel as a team. They missed the finals in 1983, despite winning more than half of their matches. They would perform much better in 1984, Cahill's second season as coach.

But the massive financial commitment the club made during those years would soon cause a debt crisis. And the Premiership the New Magpies had hoped for didn't materialise. Macdonald and his board had plunged the club into almost $3 million of debt within three years, pushing it to the verge of bankruptcy.

Before too long, a new mindset would be needed, as would a new wave of more affordable players mixed in with some older ones – and another new coach.

H&A P22, W12, L10 • **Finished** 6th • **Captain** Mark Williams • **Coach** John Cahill • **Leading goalkicker** Michael Richardson (49) • **Copeland Trophy** Bill Picken

---

THE ARRIVAL OF 'PANTS'

If Hawthorn had been a little more welcoming to a strongly built, strong-willed Noble Park teenager in the 1984 pre-season, the fortunes of the Collingwood Football Club might well have been very different.

The young player's name was Darren Millane. He had originally been tied to Sydney, under South Melbourne's old residential zone, and he had even played in the Swans' Little League team as a kid. St Kilda had taken an interest, but shied away when talk of a $25,000 transfer fee to the Swans was sought. Then Hawthorn offered him the chance to train with the club after he had shown considerable promise while playing for Dandenong in the VFA. But he never felt comfortable with the 'cliques' that existed at Glenferrie Oval, and he walked out after the reigning premier's final practice match in early 1984. 'I'd made such a big impression that it took three nights before they even noticed I was missing,' Millane would later recall.

He went back to Dandenong and was, for a time, the club's captain at age 18. But his continued good form meant he was invited down to Victoria Park midway through the 1984 season. Fortunately, he liked the club and its players, even if his new teammates had a concern about his fashion sense.

'He wore these long pants which had floral things or stars on them, and that's, of course, how he got his nickname,' Tony Shaw recalled. 'They were just unbelievable pants – they stood out like dog's ears – and for a young bloke to come into a club to wear things like that really stood out. It just showed that he had enormous confidence in his own ability.' Thereafter, Millane became known as 'Pants', and he fitted into his new club just as naturally as he fitted in those much-talked-about trousers.

Following a mid-season exhibition match against an ACT representative team in Canberra and just two reserves games, he graduated to the Collingwood senior side. He was just four days off his 19th birthday when he made his debut against Richmond in Round 18, and he never looked back.

In his third senior game he kicked one of the goals of the season, against Melbourne, intercepting a loose handball, tapping it over an opposition player and then driving it home for his first VFL goal. Millane kept his spot for the rest of the 1984 season, breaking into a side that was destined to play finals. Tellingly, despite playing only eight games, he was adjudged Collingwood's best first-year player.

His best performance for the year came in the 1984 preliminary final, against Essendon. He had 25 possessions as the eventual premier crushed Collingwood by 133 points – the greatest loss in a VFL/AFL final. It was a bleak afternoon for the black-and-white fans, and John Cahill's last game as coach. But at least the performance of the kid running around in the number 42 jumper, which he would make famous, gave them some solace.

Within three seasons, Millane would win a Copeland Trophy. Within six years, he would help end one of the most ridiculed droughts in football history.

H&A P22, W13, L9 • **Finished** 4th • **Finals** P3, W2, L1 • **Finished** 3rd • **Captain** Mark Williams • **Coach** John Cahill • **Leading goalkicker** Mark Williams (53) • **Copeland Trophy** Tony Shaw

---

1985

FRIDAY NIGHT LIGHTS

Revolutions, sporting or otherwise, are rarely predictable. Generally, they take most people by surprise, sometimes even those intimately involved. That was the case when the VFL chose Collingwood to take on North Melbourne in the first Friday night match under lights at the MCG to kick-start the 1985 season.

Though few people were able to comprehend it at the time, Victoria's first Friday night match, and the flow-on effects of subsequent games in the coming years, would transform the way we play, watch and attend football.

It would prove to be a watershed moment for the game, but even the secretary of the Melbourne Cricket Club at the time, Dr John Lill, wasn't so sure it would be a success. 'The lights are obviously good,' he said before the game, 'but I don't believe night football is a chance in winter, when it's cold.'

Dr Lill wasn't alone in this view. Even as 65,628 people battled queues that stretched back almost to Jolimont Station that night, with insufficient gates opened to deal with the larger-than-anticipated crowd, and a few fences torn down by irate fans, there were many who believed it may prove a one-hit wonder. Instead, it would become football's marquee night, and the Magpies were there to help make it happen.

There had been a one-off Friday night match played in Sydney two years earlier, but this Collingwood–North Melbourne 1985 encounter showed a bright new future for footy. It also heralded the return of two of the game's most revered coaches after several years out of the hot seat. Collingwood had reappointed

Bob Rose, while North Melbourne brought back three-time Hawthorn Premiership coach John Kennedy, both of them 56 years of age.

The Magpies unveiled a handful of young recruits that night, including an 18-year-old Tasmanian, James Manson, and a 21-year-old from Greensborough, Russell Dickson, who kicked four goals on debut. But the biggest addition to the Collingwood team was a powerfully built forward who was sick of not getting enough game time at Richmond. Brian Taylor, 22, was seeking a new challenge at Collingwood, and he excelled on the big stage that night in his first game in the black and white.

Taylor booted seven of Collingwood's 21 goals in the 38-point win over North Melbourne. He followed that up with further hauls of seven goals in his second and third games, against Geelong and Melbourne. His best return for the season was a bag of 12 goals against Sydney at the SCG in Round 16. By season's end, the player they called 'Barge' had scored 80 goals from his 21 games – a stunning start to his time at the club. There would be many more goals to come, and more than a bit of controversy along the way.

But there would also be frustration for Collingwood as 1985 failed to pan out the way the club had hoped. Despite the addition of Taylor in attack, the Magpies finished in seventh spot, with only 10 wins for the season. At the end of that season, the club knew it needed to seek some outside assistance. It was a bold move that even coach Bob Rose supported.

H&A P22, W10, L12 • **Finished** 7th • **Captain** Mark Williams • **Coach** Bob Rose • **Leading goalkicker** Brian Taylor (80) • **Copeland Trophy** Mark Williams

---

1986

'LETHAL' TAKES OVER

Collingwood lost its president, senior coach and general manager on one tumultuous day in April 1986, but it would prove to be the catalyst required to drag the club back from the brink of extinction.

The Magpies were ailing financially, and football-wise. The club was in debt to the tune of more than $3 million, and had asked the players to take a 20 per cent pay cut to satisfy worried creditors.

Collingwood had lost its first three games of the season under Bob Rose, who was grooming the club's new assistant coach, Hawthorn great Leigh Matthews, to take over the role from him in the future. But the more alarming issue was the fact that the relentless recruiting drive had put the club in a precarious financial position. And still that elusive Premiership seemed so far away.

All these issues came to a head after the team's Round 3 loss to North Melbourne. Rose called Matthews on the Sunday morning and said he was ready to hand over the reins immediately. In keeping with his love of the club, Rose was thinking only of what was best for Collingwood. 'The last thing I wanted to do was throw in the towel,' he said. 'But someone had to make the first move to clean things up.'

When the coaching handover was announced, Matthews played down expectations: 'I make no promises whatsoever. Talk of Premierships and the [top] five are pretty much folly.'

On the same Monday, general manager Peter Bahen reluctantly resigned, and president Ranald Macdonald, who had overseen the economic mismanagement, knew he had no choice but to step down.

Macdonald accepted the responsibility for the club's predicament, but said: 'With the strength and dedication of the Magpie Army, it would be wrong to underestimate the powers of recovery of Collingwood – both as a team and as a club.'

On that point, Macdonald was right. The Magpies won their next match – the first under Matthews as coach – defeating Geelong. Caretaker president Allan McAlister, who would soon assume the role on a permanent basis, set about a cost-cutting scheme.

Years later he revealed how close Collingwood came to calamity: 'The bank decided it would have three days to think about the situation, and then let us know whether the club would continue to trade or not.' Fortunately, the Magpies were given 'one last chance'.

The two players who would not accept the 20 per cent pay cut – Geoff Raines and Mike Richardson – were cleared to Essendon, while the rest of the group got on with the business of playing. Matthews reversed the slow start to the season, overseeing 12 wins from his 19 matches as coach that season. One of the highlights was when second-year Magpie Brian Taylor booted his 100th goal of the season in the final-round win over St Kilda at Waverley.

Unfortunately, the Magpies missed the finals on percentage, though the club had success of sorts when the under-19s side – featuring a host of impressive young players, including Gavin Brown, Mick McGuane, Damian Monkhorst and Gavin Crosisca – won the Premiership.

The club had a plan for the future. It knew it had the right man as coach, and an exciting batch of young players capable of chasing senior success.

H&A P22, W12, L10 • **Finished** 6th • **Captain** Mark Williams • **Coaches** Bob Rose & Leigh Matthews • **Leading goalkicker** Brian Taylor (100) • **Copeland Trophy** Wes Fellowes

---

1987

SHAW TO THE FORE

Leigh Matthews wasn't especially convinced about Tony Shaw's worth as a player, let alone as a leader, when he first came to the Collingwood Football Club. It didn't take long for him to change that belief. Ahead of Matthews' first full season as the Magpies' coach, it was Shaw he turned to as the club's new skipper in February 1987, following the departure of Mark Williams to Brisbane.

It would prove to be one of the most astute decisions Matthews made in his time as Collingwood coach, with Shaw – who got the nod over the previous year's vice-captain, David Cloke – playing an important role in shaping the club's future.

Shaw, 26, joked after his appointment that 'I'd probably be the shortest-lived captain if we won the flag, don't worry about that ... I'd probably hang them straight up.' He was proud to have emulated his brother Ray as having been appointed the club's skipper, and he promised to give it everything he had. 'I'd say I'm an honest competitor ... anything I've done, I've had a go.'

That was precisely the reason Matthews chose Shaw. The coach had a plan to bring through a number of talented young players, as well as some interstate recruits. As things turned out, it would need all of them, for in the lead-up to the 1987 season, the Magpies appeared cursed by injury. Each practice match brought about fresh casualties, leaving the club dangerously short of players ahead of the opening round.

Shaw himself was expected to miss. He spent a week in a traction harness at his Eltham home after suffering a back issue, but in keeping with his never-say-die attitude, he convinced the medical staff he could play. He felt as if he had to, as Matthews named a new-look Collingwood side: nine players would play their first senior game for the club, including four from the under-19s' Premiership side the previous year.

Never mind that the Magpies lost their Round 1 game, against Sydney, by 91 points, or the fact that the club won only seven games for the season. Matthews' side slipped to 12th on the ladder, but that had as much to do with a lack of personnel as with performance, given the injury curse, which lasted the entire year. Collingwood used 45 players in 1987, the most it had fielded in a season since the war-interrupted year of 1943.

When Shaw's own season ended after a Round 20 knee injury, the *Herald* memorably summed up the Magpies' miserable year: 'The way things are going, coach Leigh Matthews could pick the winning numbers in mid-week Tattslotto, only to find the coupon was for Saturday.'

Through it all, president Allan McAlister pleaded with Magpie fans to understand what the club was trying to do. 'We made a conscious decision to introduce young talent,' he said. 'What we want is for these young blokes, with the help from established players and top recruits, to form a side that will stick together for the next decade and win us a Premiership.'

Shaw's leadership would play a significant role in this. He was captain for seven seasons and 123 games, with Matthews rating Shaw as 'one of football's all-time great captains … I don't think there's a captain who's had a greater influence on his team.' His reward would come in time.

H&A P22, W7, L15 • **Finished** 12th • **Captain** Tony Shaw • **Coach** Leigh Matthews • **Leading goalkicker** Brian Taylor (60) • **Copeland Trophy** Darren Millane

---

1988
MUTINY IN THE MOUNTAINS

One of the celebrated Collingwood traditions has been the use of camps, tours and training trips to varied locations to strengthen the bonds between the playing group. The most famous example was in 1927, when a group of players and officials embarked on a mid-season visit to Perth. Those who made the journey maintained until their dying days that it had been the catalyst for the string of four successive Premierships that followed, despite the fact some players weighed in a few kilograms heavier on their return.

A very different but perhaps equally important club trip took place leading into the 1988 VFL season, one that would play a significant role in the Magpies' future success.

Collingwood's 1987 season had ended poorly, after injuries and inconsistent form saw the team slump to 12th. The belief was that the young playing group needed to harden up and become more resilient. But a gruelling training camp the next pre-season in the Alpine National Park, in Victoria's High Country, became a much bigger test of character for the players than coach Leigh Matthews could ever have imagined.

The camp started with four days of exhausting activities at base camp. That led to the next phase: a three-day hike, which started with a race up Mount Margaret and ended up with the men lost in inhospitable terrain.

On the morning of the third day, one of the instructors announced to the group that they were within hours of reaching the buses, and with that knowledge the players consumed most of their remaining provisions. But an advance party returned with disturbing news:

not only were the buses not there, but the group was hopelessly lost. With limited food and fresh water, the trekkers' outlook was bleak.

It wasn't long before the players lost faith in their instructors. Some began to assume control, as others looked set to crack under the strain. As club fitness coach Mark McKeon recalled in Michael Gleeson's book *Cakewalk*, 'We eventually decided that we were going to mutiny. The guides were "out" and we were going to hike back out the same way we came in.'

Players such as Darren Millane and Shane Kerrison helped unite and inspire the group, keeping their spirits up for the challenging return trek ahead of them. After they sent out another advance party, there was relief all round when contact was made with the outside world. The 'lost' Magpies had been found before anyone knew they were missing.

The players emerged from the wilderness a different group. In a way, it was a metaphor for what was to come next.

'It was the turning point for the group, for the club,' Gavin Crosisca recalled. 'I honestly believe that was the start of that group really bonding, and having something.'

Some players fell by the wayside after the camp; others thrived long into the future. As a collective, the team became more united, resilient and resourceful, and emerged with a harder edge.

The immediate impact was that Collingwood won its first five games of the 1988 season, and the club finished the home-and-away season in second place, even if it bowed out of the finals in straight sets. But the real reward of this 'Camp from Hell' was still to come.

H&A P22, W15, L6, D1 • **Finished** 2nd • **Finals** P2, L2 • **Finished** 4th • **Captain** Tony Shaw • **Coach** Leigh Matthews • **Leading goalkicker** Brian Taylor (73) • **Copeland Trophy** Darren Millane

---

RIGHTING A BROWNLOW WRONG

Collingwood great Harry Collier's determination and sense of justice meant that he never gave up on securing the Brownlow Medal he felt was robbed from him. It was the best part of six decades since he had lost the 1930 Brownlow under controversial circumstances, but at no stage did his resolve waver. He continued lobbying for the reward that he felt should have been his more than half a lifetime before.

Collier had every reason to feel hard done by. In 1930, a year after his younger brother Albert won the Brownlow Medal, Collier finished equal with Richmond's Stan Judkins and Footscray's Allan Hopkins on four votes. (At the time, only one vote was awarded in each game, to the man the umpire judged the best and fairest player.) This was the first time there had been a Brownlow Medal tie.

Initially, the VFL was uncertain how to break the deadlock. But Richmond's VFL delegate pointed to a rule that stated: 'The player attaining the largest percentage of votes to games played [is] to receive the medal.' That was Judkins, who had played fewer games than either Collier or Hopkins, and the VFL declared him the sole winner of the award.

Adding to Collier's frustration, there was even a suggestion he should have won the award outright. One vote from the 1930 count had been deemed ineligible because it stated simply 'Collier', without differentiating between Harry and Albert. The umpire who had cast that vote was alleged to have said that he intended it to go to 'the little rover fella', which indicated Harry. If that evidence had been accepted, Collier would have won the medal outright, by one vote.

Collingwood felt an injustice had been served. And if it hadn't been for Collier's persistence and the club's lobbying of the VFL over many years, that injustice might have remained.

The momentum intensified in October 1980, when the VFL decided to alter the 'countback' rule to allow future players who finished with an equal number of votes to become joint medallists. Then in 1989 Magpies president Allan McAlister outlined to the VFL the special circumstances which supported Collier being declared a joint winner of the 1930 Brownlow Medal. If the request was agreed to, that would also mean that Hopkins, and the other men who had lost medals on the countback system in other years, would also be declared winners and receive retrospective medals.

The 81-year-old Collier was washing dishes in his West Preston home in April 1989 when he received a phone call from VFL chief Ross Oakley telling him he would finally receive his medal. 'I was pretty thrilled,' Collier said. 'It would have been more of a thrill at the time, but it was a very pleasant surprise.'

Others to be awarded retrospective Brownlow Medals were Hopkins (1930), Hawthorn's Col Austen (1949), Essendon's Bill Hutchison (1952), St Kilda's Verdun Howell (1959) and North Melbourne's Noel Teasdale (1965). Collingwood's Des Fothergill and South Melbourne's Herb Matthews, who could not be separated in their tie in 1940, had originally received only replica medals, but now were also granted new Brownlow Medals.

Collier stole the show when the VFL handed out the retrospective medals at a gala function in August 1989, showing the good humour, grace and gratitude that had been 59 years in the making.

H&A P22, W13, L9 • **Finished** 5th • **Finals** P1, L1 • **Finished** 5th • **Captain** Tony Shaw • **Coach** Leigh Matthews • **Leading goalkicker** Brian Taylor (49) • **Copeland Trophy** Gavin Brown

---

1990

FINALLY, A CAKEWALK

Collingwood's quest to end football's most lampooned Premiership drought looked in doubt during a tight and tense qualifying final against West Coast at Waverley Park in 1990. After a season that had seen Leigh Matthews' Magpies finish second at the end of the home-and-away season, it was the Eagles – in just their fourth season – who appeared ready to write another painful chapter in the long-running Colliwobbles saga.

Enter Peter Daicos, and an act of sheer genius. With the game in the balance, he accepted a Darren Millane handball deep in the left forward pocket and slotted through a miraculous right-foot banana goal. It was an extraordinary feat that helped to keep the Magpies in a game that was rapidly slipping away. Without it, the Eagles would almost certainly have won; as it was, the visitors managed to throw the football world into chaos by drawing the match with an after-the-siren behind kicked by Peter Sumich.

That tied game stalled the momentum of Premiership favourite Essendon, and Collingwood comfortably won not only the qualifying final replay, but also the second semi-final against the underdone Bombers.

Collingwood fans dared to dream that the flag hoodoo – which now stretched back 32 years – was coming to an end. Much of the inspiration came from Millane, who had fractured his right thumb late in the regular season, but had played on in extreme pain throughout the finals.

Nine of Collingwood's Grand Final 20 were aged 23 or under. Yet the club still had seasoned veterans in captain Tony Shaw, star forward Daicos, who would finish the season on 97 goals, and Denis Banks, all eager to finally taste Premiership success.

The Bombers kicked the first two goals, but the Magpies fought back to lead by three points at quarter-time. A flash of aggression turned into an explosive quarter-time melee, which saw players and even some officials involved. Gavin Brown was concussed by Terry Daniher; 'He'll be back to get you,' Matthews said to the Essendon veteran at half-time.

But Matthews' most important moment came when he gathered his players around him at quarter-time, and insisted that if they concentrated on the ball – and remained disciplined – they would win the match. Six goals to one followed in the second term, giving Collingwood a 34-point half-time lead. Brown returned in the third term, and the margin was extended to 40 points at the last change.

But the demons of the past meant that few felt truly sure that the club's elusive 14th VFL/AFL Premiership was secure until ruckman Damian Monkhorst slotted a goal at the 19-minute mark of the last term. The final margin was 48 points, and there was as much relief as elation. There were constant renditions of 'Good Old Collingwood Forever', with an emphasis on the famous line 'Oh, the Premiership's a cakewalk'.

Shaw won the Norm Smith Medal, Daicos kicked two freakish goals, and, fittingly, Millane had hold of the Sherrin when the final siren announced the end of the Colliwobbles. Just how fitting it was for Collingwood's number 42 to have the ball at that moment would become evident 12 months later.

H&A P22, W16, L6 • **Finished** 2nd • **Finals** P4, W3, D1 • **Finished** Premier • **Captain** Tony Shaw • **Coach** Leigh Matthews • **Leading goalkicker** Peter Daicos (97) • **Copeland Trophy** Tony Shaw

---

1991

MOURNING MILLANE

Collingwood's 1990 Premiership celebrations lasted for months, and the resulting hangover meant that the club was always going to struggle to chase more success the following season.

Three wins and a draw came from the first five rounds, but a string of six successive losses leading into the middle of the season cost the Magpies dearly. It mattered little that Collingwood won five of its last six games: the damage had already been done. Still there were some incredible highlights, including 13.1 kicked by Peter Daicos against Brisbane in Round 20.

The club missed the finals by half a game after failing to beat Geelong away in the final round, ending a frustrating season. Missing the finals hurt, but nothing like the pain that was to come.

In the early hours of Monday, 7 October 1991, Collingwood lost one of its favourite sons. The seemingly indestructible Darren Millane, aged only 26, had been killed in a car accident, a year and a day since he had held the ball aloft at the end of the 1990 Grand Final. The poignancy of that moment would only grow with time.

The outpouring of emotion was almost unprecedented in Australian football. Shattered supporters struggled to come to terms with the loss of their hero, gathering in a vigil at Victoria Park and inundating the club's switchboard with phone calls, to the point that the operator herself broke down in tears.

Millane's teammates were devastated. On the day of his death, he had been scheduled to meet up with the men he had shared that great bond with a year earlier, and most of the team kept that appointment, turning the occasion into a wake. No 1990 Premiership reunion would ever be the same again.

His funeral would bring out more than 5000 people at the Dandenong Town Hall, as well as thousands of others who followed the emotional proceedings on loudspeakers outside the venue. Millane's revered number 42 jumper was placed on his coffin, and it was also retired from active use at Collingwood. Fathers and sons united in tears, young girls and older fans wept uncontrollably, and a moment of profound grief united a football club.

At the Copeland Trophy night later that week, the club announced that it would strike a trophy in his honour: the Darren Millane Perpetual Trophy. And at the same event captain Tony Shaw urged the club's heartbroken playing group to ensure that Millane's memory would live on in future years. 'If you don't get goose bumps on your neck when his name is mentioned, then I don't think you have got the character to be around our club,' Shaw told the gathering on one of the most emotional nights in the club's history.

Millane's brother, John, accepted the Phonse Kyne Trophy for services to the club, which had been posthumously awarded to Darren. In doing so, he said: 'If he had been here tonight, he would want you all to have a good time ... so lift your chins and make sure you get out there next year and win the flag.'

In a football sense, the club knew it had to find a way to go on, as Millane would have wanted. But the Magpies were trying to replace the irreplaceable, even though the players pledged to honour their teammate as best they could.

H&A P22, W12, L9, D1 • **Finished** 7th • **Captain** Tony Shaw • **Coach** Leigh Matthews • **Leading goalkicker** Peter Daicos (75) • **Copeland Trophy** Tony Francis

---

1992

SAINTS SINK THE CENTENARY PIES

Collingwood seemed to have everything to play for in the 1992 season. The club staged a number of celebrations to mark its centenary, and hoped it would result in another Premiership; the players were united in wanting to honour their fallen mate Darren Millane; and coach Leigh Matthews warned his men that nothing short of their absolute best would be tolerated following the disappointment of 1991.

Leading into the season, Matthews explained: 'The 1990 season ended for us about June [1991] – that was when people stopped congratulating everybody on the previous year. [The players] were trying their guts out, no doubt about it. But there is an old saying: you cannot be comfortable when they should have been uncomfortable. Hopefully, this year we are a little bit more uncomfortable.'

Even without Millane's presence, Collingwood started 1992 well, winning five of its first six games, and for much of the year loomed as one of the Premiership favourites in what was an exceptionally even season. But Carlton gate-crashed Collingwood's centenary party at the MCG in Round 8, easily accounting for the wasteful Pies, 16.9 (105) to 9.18 (72), before 83,262 fans. That match, on 7 May, came 100 years to the day since the Magpies' inaugural game in 1892, which had also ended in a loss to the Blues.

Leaving aside the pre-game fireworks, it was far from a night to remember for Magpie fans. But Matthews' team was able to regroup from that loss to finish the season with 16 wins, the same number as ladder leaders Geelong and Footscray. The Magpies' inferior percentage, however, saw them drop down to a more precarious third place.

The *Herald Sun* posed the question: 'Is the latest Collingwood unit capable of emulating the feats of the 1990 Premiership outfit? The present side appears more flexible, certainly is quicker and has displayed greater consistency throughout the season.' Even without Millane, and the retired Denis Banks, there was plenty of cause for optimism, given the club had beaten both the Cats and the Dogs during the regular season.

In most other seasons, third place would have guaranteed Collingwood a double chance. But the AFL's switch to a final six in 1991 did the Magpies no favours, throwing them into a sudden-death final against sixth-placed St Kilda at a neutral venue, Waverley Park. By contrast, West Coast, which had finished fourth, had the luxury of taking on fifth-placed Hawthorn at Subiaco.

There were injury doubts on a host of players, including Gavin Brown, Graham Wright, Tony Francis, Troy Lehmann and Peter Daicos before the game, but all played. Things looked bright when the Magpies opened a 17-point lead during the second term, but five goals to St Kilda forward Tony Lockett ultimately proved the difference. Lockett's final goal, at the 12-minute mark of the last term, pushed the difference out to 29 points. At no stage did Collingwood throw in the towel, kicking three late goals to lose by only eight points. But it was too little, too late: St Kilda had ended Collingwood's season.

Matthews refused to blame the system, even if the fans were happy to. 'We had an incredibly consistent year. We were never very good, but neither were we very bad,' he said.

The centenary Premiership dream was over.

H&A P22, W16, L6 • **Finished** 3rd • **Finals** P1, L1 • **Finished** 5th • **Captain** Tony Shaw • **Coach** Leigh Matthews • **Leading goalkicker** Peter Daicos (52) • **Copeland Trophy** Mick McGuane

---

1993

NICKY MAKES A STAND

After winning the first three games of 1993, Collingwood was described by the *Herald Sun* as 'the self-appointed defender of all football things Victorian', and the side most capable of stopping reigning premier West Coast. Victories over Footscray, Geelong and Essendon had given hope to the black-and-white faithful that Leigh Matthews' team might once more be a flag contender.

The Magpies were confident of making it four in a row at home against St Kilda, especially when star Saints forward Tony Lockett was ruled out of the game due to suspension. The fact that the Saints hadn't won at Victoria Park since 1976 also swayed tipsters significantly in Collingwood's favour.

However, this Round 4 clash did not go to script, and it would have ramifications in both the short and the long terms, for the Magpies and for the game itself.

Indigenous Saints Nicky Winmar and Gilbert McAdam were subjected to racial taunts from a section of the Collingwood crowd an hour before the game. It prompted the two Saints to make a pre-game pact to 'run amok'. Winmar had 25 disposals and kicked a goal. McAdam booted five of his club's 18 goals. The umpires adjudged Winmar as the second-best afield, while McAdam was without doubt the game's most influential player. The Saints overcame an eight-point half-time deficit to boot seven goals in the third term, and went on to win their first game at Victoria Park in almost two decades by 22 points.

But it was what Winmar did in the moments after that emotional win which started football on the road to a much-needed revolution. He went to the middle of the ground to embrace McAdam and, as he left the ground, lifted his St Kilda jumper, pointed to his skin and said, 'I'm black – and I'm proud to be black.'

The moment was captured by leading football photographer Wayne Ludbey, and it became a seminal moment not just for Australian football, but for race relations in this country. Winmar's act shone a light on racism in sport and helped to bring about overdue change on both sides of the fence.

Just days later, Australia's Minister for Immigration, Senator Nick Bolkus, addressed a United Nations conference on racism. '[Winmar's] action deserves our support, and the support of all administrators who should act aggressively to wipe out such racism,' he said. There would be challenges to face in the years ahead, but ultimately the AFL would lead the way in educating players and fans, and promoting Indigenous culture in the game.

Collingwood won its next three games after that St Kilda loss, but hopes that the Magpies would be the most likely Victorian challenger to the Eagles' throne were dashed with an inconsistent second half of the year. Despite the emergence of second-year forward Saverio Rocca – who kicked 73 goals, including two bags of 10 – the team had three losses in the last month, and finished an unsatisfactory season in eighth place.

The focus quickly shifted to the future. A youngster who had taken the competition by storm that season, playing for the Brisbane Bears, had won the AFL's inaugural Rising Star Award. The Magpies desperately wanted him, and were confident they could pull off one of the biggest recruiting coups in the club's history.

H&A P20, W11, L9 • **Finished** 8th • **Captain** Tony Shaw • **Coach** Leigh Matthews • **Leading goalkicker** Saverio Rocca (73 goals) • **Copeland Trophy** Mick McGuane

---

1994

HELLO AND GOODBYE

Collingwood's courting of the best young footballer in Australia, Nathan Buckley, finally paid off when the club secured a deal with the Brisbane Bears, gaining Buckley in exchange for Craig Starcevich and Troy Lehmann in October 1993.

The club was supremely confident the 21-year-old midfielder would be worth every bit of the investment they had made to secure him, and Buckley promised to repay the favour to the Magpies, 'because they've put a lot of work into getting me'.

The young man shone from the moment he put on a black-and-white jumper in the pre-season games of 1994. But just 24 days before the club's Round 1 clash came the news no Collingwood fan wanted to hear: Peter Daicos had been sacked by the club after 250 games and 549 goals. 'I've just had my heart torn out,' he said as he weighed up his future and considered playing elsewhere.

Collingwood fans were relieved when Daicos opted not to play on, and even more so when he came to an arrangement with the club to make a farewell lap of honour. That came ahead of the Pies' Round 2 game, against Carlton, in front of 85,063 fans, and the champion goalkicker went around the ground with his 20-month-old daughter, Madison, who was wearing a little number 35 jumper. The Collingwood cheersquad summed up the affection fans felt for him on the game-day banner, which read: 'Peter Daicos – Thanks for the magic memories'.

It was a memorable day, and not just for a send-off of one of the club's greatest players. At the 22-minute mark of the second term, Mick McGuane took off with the ball in the centre square.

He darted left and took four bounces before straightening up, and then he took two more bounces, side-stepped Michael Sexton, had his seventh and final bounce, and kicked one of the most thrilling goals in the club's history.

Buckley's first year at Collingwood saw the club sneak into the final eight on percentage, albeit with a road trip to Subiaco to take on the minor premier, West Coast, in a final. It was an onerous task. When the Eagles pushed out to a 24-point three-quarter-time lead, few would have expected the Magpies to show the sort of resistance they did on that September afternoon. Collingwood doubled its goal count in the final term, kicking six goals to two, and were going forward in the dying seconds when McGuane dropped a mark just before the siren sounded. West Coast had won by only two points.

It was Tony Shaw's 313th and last game for Collingwood. Sadly, he played little part, having torn a calf muscle in the first quarter. 'It's very hard sitting on your bum like that when one of the best efforts in finals history is taking place,' Shaw said after the game. 'It was a shame to finish on a note like that.'

In a changing of the Collingwood guard, Buckley was along-side a tearful Shaw as he left the field for the last time. The young star would tie with first-year captain Gavin Brown for that year's Copeland Trophy. More individual success would follow for Buckley, but the question was whether the team could achieve the same.

H&A P22, W12, L10 • **Finished** 8th • **Finals** P1, L1 • **Finished** 8th • **Captain** Gavin Brown • **Coach** Leigh Matthews • **Leading goalkicker** Saverio Rocca (49) • **Copeland Trophy** Gavin Brown & Nathan Buckley

---

THE ANZAC PLAN

The link between football and Anzac Day had already been well established when Kevin Sheedy hatched a plan with Graeme Allan for an Essendon–Collingwood blockbuster that is now a permanent part of the AFL fixture.

There had been no VFL football played on Australia's most sacred day from the time of the Gallipoli landings until an act of parliament passed in 1959, which allowed two matches to be played on 25 April 1960. Neither involved Collingwood. But in time the Magpies came to play on a sporadic basis on Anzac Day, with the most significant game coming in 1977, when the club's new coach, Tom Hafey, took on his former side, Richmond, for the first time. That match attracted 92,436 fans to the MCG, and Sheedy, then a Tigers defender, never forgot the occasion.

In late 1994 Sheedy found himself daydreaming of his playing days, recalling the theatre of that match. He immediately got on the phone to Allan, who was Collingwood's football manager, and the pair devised the idea of staging an annual Magpies–Bombers clash on Anzac Day, in conjunction with the RSL. Sheedy and Allan, along with club presidents Allan McAlister and David Shaw, met for discussions with Victorian RSL chief Bruce Ruxton, a passionate Magpie fan.

When the AFL announced the game as part of its 1995 fixture, the *Herald Sun*'s Mike Sheahan called it 'an appropriate attraction'. It would be all that, and more, thanks to a remarkable crowd and an extraordinary game.

In the hours after the emotional Anzac Day dawn service, and the march of veterans through the streets of Melbourne, football fans flocked to the MCG in far bigger numbers than anyone had envisaged. A crowd of 94,823 – the second-highest in home-and-away history, and 965 more than the previous year's Grand Final – came through the turnstiles. It's likely another 10,000 or more were either turned away at the gates or gave up hope of gaining admission.

The occasion deserved a classic encounter, and that's what it got. Collingwood had lost its first three games of the 1995 season, but you would hardly have known it as the Magpies took the game up to the Bombers.

Essendon held sway by three points at the first change, then by 16 points at the main break. The Magpies grasped back the lead and took a 14-point advantage into the last quarter, even opening up a margin of almost four goals. But the Bombers stormed home.

Saverio Rocca booted 9.2, and with the scores deadlocked in the dying seconds, Nathan Buckley chose to kick towards the powerful forward rather than taking a few extra steps and shooting for goal himself. Rocca couldn't mark, and the siren sounded. The match had ended in a draw, almost a fitting result.

Sheahan admitted after the game that 'it doesn't come any better than what Collingwood and Essendon gave us ... two hours of pulsating theatre ... We had a drama without a climax, but it would have been selfish in the extreme to claim to have been cheated.'

There would be controversy in the days after the match, when Michael Long accused Damian Monkhorst of making a racist comment during the game – which became a further catalyst for change in the AFL.

H&A P22, W8, L12, D2 • **Finished** 10th • **Captain** Gavin Brown • **Coach** Leigh Matthews • **Leading goalkicker** Saverio Rocca (93) • **Copeland Trophy** Saverio Rocca

---

1996

BUCKS STAYS LOYAL

A small section of the Collingwood crowd started to jeer the club's best player, Nathan Buckley, at one point of the 1996 season. It wasn't for his performance; Buckley was well on the way to winning his second Copeland Trophy. It was about a perception, one that the Collingwood star was eager to dispel.

The jeers were coming because some Magpie fans feared that Buckley would accept a lucrative offer to join the AFL's next club-in-waiting, Port Adelaide, when it came into the competition in 1997. Buckley was out of contract. It was true he had played for SANFL side Port Adelaide before commencing his AFL career, and some fans feared he was a football mercenary chasing the best deal.

The year 1996 was one of change for Collingwood. Leigh Matthews had been replaced as coach after the 1995 season by club great Tony Shaw, while Kevin Rose had taken on the presidency after Allan McAlister's exit.

Throughout the AFL's centenary season, Port Adelaide was preparing candidates for its inaugural year of competition in 1997, and Buckley was at the top of its wish list. The Magpies knew they would be in for a battle, with Kevin Rose warning: 'If Port Adelaide is going to get Nathan Buckley, they're going to have to fight very, very hard.'

Buckley admitted at the time that Port Adelaide had approached his manager, Geof Motley, but he stressed that no decision had been made. 'Port Adelaide has approached [Motley] and so has Collingwood,' he said. 'I've no idea whether they were just contacts or offers. "Mots" said when the time is right he will speak to me and we'd work something out.'

Buckley spoke openly about how he was feeling and the pressure he was under. 'Football is a business these days, but still you don't leave a place if everything is the way you want it,' he said. 'It's only when things aren't the way you want them that you're forced to look elsewhere. The thing that is really getting on my nerves is that many Collingwood people think I'm going to go, and I don't know where that's come from but it may be a reaction to how I got to Collingwood.'

The fans, or the club, shouldn't have been so concerned. Buckley shunned the Port Adelaide offer, accepting a slightly less lucrative one from the Magpies. The signing of the three-year deal in 1996 would prove to be a hugely significant moment.

'I hope a few people sit back and think differently now,' he said after agreeing to stay. 'The public perceived I might be a football mercenary. They knew I came from Port Adelaide and that I had the opportunity to go back. And I suspect they assumed I left Brisbane without batting an eyelid, and might do the same thing at Collingwood. People obviously thought I would move on again for the money, without any remorse. I made the move from Brisbane to play for Collingwood, and people should have recognised my intent then. They never should have queried my desire and determination to play for the Pies.'

The Magpies may have finished 11th in Shaw's first season as coach, but the club had secured the most important asset it had, ensuring that Collingwood would remain Buckley's football home.

H&A P22, W9, L13 • **Finished** 11th • **Captain** Gavin Brown • **Coach** Tony Shaw • **Leading Goalkicker** Saverio Rocca (66) • **Copeland Trophy** Nathan Buckley

---

1997

SNUB SPARKS PIES INTO ACTION

An affront and an outrage – that's how former Magpies president Allan McAlister described the 1996 decision by a panel of past players and experts to choose a VFL/AFL Team of the Century that lacked a single Collingwood representative.

The AFL had embraced its past in the 1996 centenary season, creating an Australian football hall of fame and setting about the task of choosing a greatest ever side.

Collingwood had several worthy candidates for the Team of the Century. To that time, no one had kicked as many goals as Gordon Coventry (1299). Bob Rose was regarded as one of the best players of all time. No one but Syd Coventry had captained four Premierships in succession. And Jock McHale, who had coached longer than anyone and for more Premierships, had to be in serious consideration to be the coach of the side.

But the Magpie most people believed was a lock for the VFL/AFL Team of the Century was Jack Regan, described as 'the prince of full-backs' through his outstanding career in the 1930s and '40s. Journalist Jon Anderson spoke for many when he declared, 'Full back would seem to be the sole property of Jack Regan.'

When the team was announced, not only was Regan overlooked in favour of Carlton's Stephen Silvagni, but there were no Collingwood players selected in the side at all. Nor was McHale the coach; he was overlooked in favour of Melbourne's Norm Smith. The Magpies fumed at the slight, even if they did not publicly criticise the players selected. It was left to McAlister to fire back at the AFL and the selectors for the massive snub. 'It's extraordinary, having won 14 flags and appeared in Grand Finals almost twice as many times as any other club, that we've been overlooked,' he railed.

One of the selectors, Allen Aylett, recalled the panel's thinking some years later. 'Regan was considered a dead cert to be picked, but he didn't get support from the older people,' he said. 'We took notice of them because they saw him play.'

Collingwood decided the only course of action open to it was to select its own Team of the Century. In doing so, it put in place a template for the rest of the competition, and in time almost every rival club chose Teams of the Century too.

The Magpies chose their greatest side in 1997, with Kevin Rose, club stalwarts Ron Richards and Jock McHale Jnr, *Herald Sun* journalist Trevor Grant and Channel Nine's Eddie McGuire serving as the selectors. There would even be controversy surrounding this team, too, due to the omission of star forward Ron Todd, who had quit the club at the peak of his powers to accept a lucrative deal with Williamstown. McHale Jnr had been close friends with Todd, but couldn't support any decision to have him in the team because of his fractured relationship with McHale Snr.

McGuire later said that the AFL Team of the Century snub in 1996 had been difficult to understand, but that the Magpies no longer cared what the AFL did. 'The most dominant team of the century didn't receive one player,' McGuire said. 'So, to be honest, like most things at Collingwood, we prefer the AFL to just leave us alone and they can get on with their own business.'

H&A P22, W10, L12 • **Finished** 10th • **Captain** Gavin Brown • **Coach** Tony Shaw • **Leading goalkicker** Saverio Rocca (76) • **Copeland Trophy** Gavin Brown

---

1998

PRESIDENT ED

It was a moment that almost summed up Collingwood's miserable 1998 season, but it would at least spark a bloodless revolution that would shake the foundations of the most famous football club in the country. In the last quarter of the club's big loss to Carlton in Round 21, an unidentified Magpies supporter could simply watch no more. As he stormed out of the MCG, he yelled, loud enough for all to hear, 'Get fucked, Collingwood!'

Eddie McGuire heard the remark from a nearby radio commentary box, but he couldn't blame the frustrated fan. 'I felt exactly the same as he did,' McGuire would say later. 'I could feel the despondency. We always used to have bragging rights ... the biggest crowds, most Premierships and most members. [But] you felt excluded. There were so many factions in the place. And, meanwhile, the other clubs were going past us in a hurry.'

Instead of storming out, as the fan did, McGuire resolved to do something about the fading club. Collingwood had played without passion that day, and he knew that to do so against Carlton was unacceptable. The team was an unmitigated mess on the field, and the club was just as bad off it. McGuire wanted to fix it.

Collingwood would win only seven games in the 1998 season. The playing list was extremely poor, there were leaks from within the club about coach Tony Shaw's tenure, and financially the club was in grave trouble. McGuire met with the president, Kevin Rose, and together they worked towards a peaceful transition. McGuire sought to retain three of the current board – Rose included – and recruit four new board candidates. The Channel

Nine personality himself assumed the presidency on the night of his 34th birthday, when more than 1000 members approved changes to the club's articles of association to allow the new ticket to assume control.

The new president had ambitious plans. 'Tonight is a moment of truth in shaping Collingwood's future in the 21st century,' he said. 'What I can promise you from the bottom of my heart is that every decision made by the Collingwood Football Club will be made for the benefit of the club, and nothing else. We will work as hard and as passionately and intelligently as possible to make Collingwood the number one club in the AFL.'

Immediately, the new board cut costs of about $750,000, and found new, lucrative sponsorship deals that would turn around the club's finances – and its future. McGuire opened doors to the business world, and even though some suggested he had a conflict of interests due to his media work, the new president was on the way to making Collingwood relevant once more. Significantly, he embarked on a campaign to find the right long-term coach to take the Magpies into the new millennium, and the club also chased good young talent that would make the team competitive again.

It was always going to take time. McGuire knew that. He also understood it wouldn't be easy, and that the external critics would come for him if it failed. But at least there was a plan in place, and the driven, passionate and well-connected Collingwood president was determined to make it happen.

H&A P22, W7, L15 • **Finished** 14th • **Captain** Gavin Brown • **Coach** Tony Shaw • **Leading goalkicker** Saverio Rocca (68) • **Copeland Trophy** Nathan Buckley

---

1999
FAREWELL VIC PARK

As much as Collingwood hated to acknowledge it, Victoria Park had been living on borrowed time through the last decade of the 20th century.

The start of the 1990s had seen the Magpies finally celebrate their 14th Premiership at the ground – a remarkable night, during which more than 20,000 fans toasted something many of them thought they may never live to see.

But the AFL's ground rationalisation program meant that fewer and fewer games were being played at Victoria Park, and it was clear that Collingwood's famous home ground would cease to be a venue for senior football. 'Victoria Park is the last of the suburban venues and while we respect, very much, its history and tradition as Collingwood's home, the ground simply cannot accommodate all of the people who want to see the club play,' AFL chief executive Wayne Jackson explained. The competition had outgrown suburban grounds, and Collingwood's drawing power meant it, too, had outgrown the ground it had called home since 1892.

The league ruled that the club could host two farewell games in the 1999 season. Collingwood hoped to play teams from the 'big three' – Carlton, Essendon and Richmond – in these final games, but the AFL overruled it: the matches would be played against West Coast, in April, and the Brisbane Lions, in August.

The penultimate match, against the Eagles, almost never happened. Rain swept through Melbourne that week, and West Coast unsuccessfully lobbied the AFL to move it. But the game went ahead anyway, and Collingwood lost by six goals.

Then on 28 August 1999 – 39,193 days since the club's first game at the ground, in May 1892 – Victoria Park hosted its 910th and final match involving Collingwood's senior team for Premiership points. The game was also Tony Shaw's final one as coach, bringing an end to four frustrating seasons, and closing out a 1999 season that brought an unwanted wooden spoon. The opposition at least had a link to Fitzroy, the Magpies' first bitter rival, since Brisbane had merged with a reluctant Fitzroy three years earlier.

Collingwood champions of the past were driven around the ground in golf buggies, while others took part in re-enactments on the ground of famous moments in the club's history. The game was a sellout, with fans desperate to be there one last time. It was shown live on television, as was Shaw's pre-game address in the rooms, which was also displayed on huge screens erected around the ground.

Shaw urged his players to evoke the spirit of Collingwood champions of the past, but to also think of the future, even though he wouldn't be a part of it. 'Just go out there and know that there are 30,000 people out there who would love to be in your position today,' he said. The massive banner – eight metres by 40 metres – summed up the mood: 'Victoria Park 1892–1999, thanks for the memories.'

But the day itself didn't provide too many good memories, as the young Magpies were no match for the seasoned Lions. Brisbane turned the final match at Victoria Park into a solemn affair, winning by 42 points.

Even though Collingwood had lost, the club's theme song blasted over the loud speakers. The fans farewelled the ground in great voice – 'as all barrackers should'.

H&A P22, W4, L18 · **Finished** 16th · **Captain** Nathan Buckley · **Coach** Tony Shaw · **Leading goalkicker** Saverio Rocca (33) · **Copeland Trophy** Nathan Buckley

---

2000

MALTHOUSE'S MAGPIES

Eddie McGuire promised nothing but the best for Collingwood as he looked to drag the ailing club into the new millennium. So much of that rested on who, as the new coach, would oversee a program that could transform the Magpies from wooden-spooners to Premiership contenders once more.

Dual West Coast Premiership coach Mick Malthouse was McGuire's target, and fortuitously he was keen to head back to Victoria after 10 successful seasons with the Eagles. The pair met over breakfast for a preliminary chat during the 1999 season, and the persuasiveness of the president was enough to convince Malthouse that it was a worthwhile challenge.

There was a touch of romance attached. Malthouse had been a Collingwood supporter when growing up in Ballarat, and was excited by the prospect of helping to turn the club's fortunes around.

The worst-kept secret in football was revealed in September 1999, but not in the usual manner. In keeping with the club's change of direction, the announcement of the new coach was done with a touch of marketing: smoke machines created the mood, satin sheets slipped away to reveal a black Volvo ... and Mick Malthouse in the driver's seat.

Malthouse didn't promise miracles, but he explained how he was going to help take Collingwood into the modern age. 'I live for these moments ... I'm desperate to get my teeth into it,' he said in his first press conference as coach. 'If I haven't got a challenge in life ... that's not for me. I'll do what I have to do to enhance Collingwood's prospects on and off the field.'

The new coach even talked about how he – and McGuire – planned for Collingwood to become Australian football's version of Manchester United. It was a big call, even at a club with big dreams.

Malthouse coached Collingwood for the first time in the last match of the outgoing millennium – a pre-season game against Carlton on 31 December 1999. But it was what his Magpies were able to do at the start of the 2000 season that surprised the football world. Armed with the club's number one draft selection of 1999, Josh Fraser, and a reworked playing list, the club won the first five games of its season. Wins over Hawthorn, Adelaide, Carlton, Sydney and the Western Bulldogs put the team equal top with Essendon.

Malthouse was determined to restore confidence to the club in a football sense. He gave the players a structure and system they were comfortable with, and began to assess the list with an eye on the future.

The Magpies could not sustain their early-season run in 2000, and a reality check came in Round 6 against the reigning premier, the Kangaroos. The season would yield only two more wins, for a total of seven, and the team finished in 15th place.

But those five unbeaten weeks at the start of 2000, along with what the new coach had already brought to the table, gave fans a taste of what was to come. There was a new verve about the club off the field, and Malthouse turned his attention to crafting a list that could be competitive again.

H&A P22, W7, L15 • **Finished** 15th • **Captain** Nathan Buckley • **Coach** Mick Malthouse • **Leading goalkicker** Anthony Rocca (33) • **Copeland Trophy** Nathan Buckley

---

2001

TRADING PLACES

It wasn't just about changing the coach; so much of Collingwood's focus heading into the early 2000s was about developing the playing list in order to make it competitive as quickly as possible. On that measure, the club's canny recruiting and trading in the 2000 off-season, leading into the 2001 season, would prove significant in Mick Malthouse's plan for the future.

Gavin Brown and Gavin Crosisca retired after great careers, while Paul Williams was traded to Sydney. In all, 15 players from the 2000 playing list had left the club by the next pre-season. That meant Malthouse, in a little over a year, had turned over 27 players since arriving at Victoria Park.

As the eyes of the world were on Sydney ahead of the Games of the XXVII Olympiad, Collingwood pulled off what at the time looked like a routine trade deal involving two players from Fremantle. One of the players who transferred to Collingwood would become one of the most reliable defenders in the competition; the other would become a capable forward much loved by the Magpie faithful.

James Clement was the defender. By the end of his career with the Magpies, he would be a dual Copeland Trophy winner. The forward was Brodie Holland, who gave great service to the club, on and off the field. Malthouse had watched Clement as a junior, before he was picked up by the Dockers, and he had a bit of time for Holland as well. The pair would prove to be bargain pick-ups, and the trades didn't end there.

Brisbane's Jarrod Molloy moved to Collingwood and had an instant impact in 2001, finishing second to Paul Licuria in the

Copeland Trophy, while Geelong's Carl Steinfort and Eagle Chad Rintoul also became Magpies.

There were important additions on draft day, too. Collingwood used its number three selection on a talented kid from Port Adelaide. His name was Alan Didak, and he would prove to be one of the club's stars in the future. Jason Cloke became the first of three brothers to be picked up under the father–son rule; Ryan Lonie established himself in the side from the outset; and Malthouse pounced on sacked Saint Shane Wakelin.

It was a significant makeover of the squad, and when Collingwood fielded its Round 1 side against Hawthorn, there were five players representing the club for the first time. More would follow. The transformation of the list brought an instant spike in performance, particularly because some of the new faces were seasoned players who could provide toughness and experience to the team.

Malthouse's Magpies were on their way. They would win 11 of their 22 games for the 2001 season, missing the finals by one game.

A final-round win over the Kangaroos – by 48 points – at Manuka Oval in Canberra highlighted the promise that Collingwood was starting to show. Fifteen of the 22 players who represented the Magpies that day were under 25. The list had the right profile, and the potential was obvious after the club had spent a number of years in the wilderness.

Surely a finals series was beckoning for this revamped team.

H&A P22, W11, L11 • **Finished** 9th • **Captain** Nathan Buckley • **Coach** Mick Malthouse • **Leading goalkicker** Chris Tarrant (53) • **Copeland Trophy** Paul Licuria

---

2002
THE GOAL THAT WASN'T

Anthony Rocca was 'certain' he had kicked his fifth goal of the game – a long 45-metre bomb – as Collingwood's giant-killing run appeared set to continue in the 2002 Grand Final.

Just three weeks earlier, the Magpies – minus Nathan Buckley – had knocked off minor premier Port Adelaide in the qualifying final to throw open the entire finals series. In that 13-point victory in Adelaide, Ben Johnson had helped save the game with a desperate tackle on Peter Burgoyne in the goal square during a frantic last quarter. That win gave Collingwood the week off, and Malthouse's team comfortably accounted for Adelaide in a preliminary final, which set up a battle with Brisbane for the 2002 flag.

Few gave the young Magpies a chance. But in a tight and tense Premiership playoff, it seemed as if one of the great Grand Final upsets was in the offing.

Rocca, who already had four goals to his name, had that fateful shot at goal seven minutes into the final term. He could barely believe it when goal umpire Craig Clark signalled a behind. Rocca said later that he was sure the kick was 'in by about two feet'. He wasn't the only one who believed two flags should have gone up instead of one. Nathan Buckley, on his way to winning a Norm Smith Medal, backed Rocca's assessment: 'You can't be more definite than "certain", can you?' Paul Licuria was the same.

But it wasn't just Magpies players. Brisbane's Marcus Ashcroft would say, in the days after, 'I was there in the goal square and I said to the goal umpire, "That's a point," and I didn't think it was going to be given a point, but it was. I thought it was a goal too.'

Defender Chris Johnson took a contrary view. 'It was always a point; it went right over the goalpost,' he argued. 'If it had been any lower, it would have hit the goalpost smack in the middle.'

Former Magpie Mal Michael wasn't sure, but he knew the importance of the moment. 'I actually thought the goal umpire was going to give it a goal ... it could have turned the game,' he reflected.

Unfortunately for Rocca, and for Collingwood, the momentum swung the other way. Instead of giving the Magpies a flying start in the final term, the door was left ajar for the Lions. And when Jason Akermanis snapped a goal late in the game, Brisbane secured its second successive Premiership with a nine-point win over a gallant Collingwood.

The Pies had come so close. Just how shattered they were was evident when Mick Malthouse and Paul Licuria embraced on the ground, tears flowing from both of them.

The Rocca 'goal that wasn't', as Collingwood fans still call it, was a big discussion point, and remains so. In the days after the Grand Final, AFL umpiring director Jeff Gieschen ruled that the goal umpire had made the correct decision, even if others swore that it was a goal.

Malthouse referred to the decision at the Copeland Trophy night, soon after. 'Let's not turn it into another Wayne Harmes,' the coach said. He knew the club needed to focus on making amends in 2003.

H&A P22, W13, L9 • **Finished** 4th • **Finals** P3, W2, L1 • **Finished** 2nd • **Captain** Nathan Buckley • **Coach** Mick Malthouse • **Leading goalkickers** Anthony Rocca & Chris Tarrant (38) • **Copeland Trophy** Paul Licuria

---

2003

THE ROCCA SUSPENSION

Anthony Rocca's 'goal that wasn't' cost Collingwood the vital momentum it needed in the 2002 Grand Final, and his absence in the corresponding game a year later hurt just as much.

Collingwood had finished second on the ladder in the 2003 home-and-away season, and loomed as a serious chance to make amends for their 2002 near miss. When the Magpies defeated Brisbane by 15 points in the qualifying final at the MCG, and when minor premier the Power stumbled to the Swans, Mick Malthouse's team was installed as flag favourite. Collingwood enhanced its flag prospects with a 44-point win over Port Adelaide in a preliminary final, just a few hours before Brisbane stormed over the top of Sydney to set up another Lions–Magpies Grand Final.

While the Lions had to deal with some injuries to key players, the Magpies had something just as significant on their minds: Rocca had been reported for allegedly striking Port Adelaide's Brendon Lade.

A year earlier, the Magpies had lost Jason Cloke for the Grand Final due to suspension. But the likely loss of Rocca, one of the club's best and most physical players, threatened to be a much bigger blow. Within minutes of the preliminary final finishing, club officials were busy hatching a plan to try to get Rocca off. He was consoled in the rooms, as were his parents, Mick and Anna.

Grand Final week started well for Collingwood when Nathan Buckley tied with Adam Goodes and Mark Ricciuto to win the

Brownlow Medal. But the feared body blow came when the AFL Tribunal banned Rocca for two matches.

The Magpies appealed the decision, and called on the services of two former players from rival clubs who had missed Premierships due to suspension, Peter Schwab and Neville Crowe. Both men spoke passionately. The club also flew Lade himself to Melbourne, and the Power ruckman tried to argue that Rocca hadn't hit him in the head, but the shoulder. The appeals panel disregarded Lade's comments, believing he was trying too hard to help Rocca play in the Grand Final.

In the end, heartbreakingly for Rocca, the original decision stood. His ban meant he would miss the 2003 Grand Final.

Malthouse claimed that Rocca had been handed 'a life sentence'. 'The consequences are great,' he said. 'Are they greater than the crime? That's something that has got to be worked out.'

As the club consoled the big forward, the coach acknowledged his team had to find a way to physically challenge the Lions without him. 'I think, generally, most sides fear Anthony,' Malthouse said. 'He's a power forward ... We have to make sure we put the best side on the track that can cause most disruption to Brisbane.'

That task was too great. As Rocca watched on disconsolately from the stands, the Lions overwhelmed the Magpies, physically and psychologically, to win a third straight Premiership, this time by 50 points. If it had hurt to get so close the previous year, now it only seemed worse to be so far away on football's biggest stage.

H&A P22, W15, L7 • **Finished** 2nd • **Finals** P3, W2, L1 • **Finished** 2nd • **Captain** Nathan Buckley • **Coach** Mick Malthouse • **Leading goalkicker** Chris Tarrant (54) • **Copeland Trophy** Nathan Buckley

---

2004

A NEW HOME

Victoria Park had been Collingwood's home base for more than a century, and its atmosphere, history, character and charm had made it a unique place for players and spectators alike. But by the end of the 20th century, even its most passionate fans conceded that it no longer met the standards required for professional football

When the Magpies played their last AFL game there, in 1999, ambitious plans were already afoot for the club to move to Olympic Park, where a state-of-the-art training and administration base was being envisaged. Those plans came to fruition in mid-2004, when Collingwood moved into the $17 million facility, which had once hosted the swimming and aquatic events at the 1956 Melbourne Olympics. Club president Eddie McGuire explained his vision for the club's new home. 'Kids who grow up in the outer suburbs will have a place, a destination to aspire to,' he said.

On the field, the wounds from the previous year's Grand Final loss were still fresh, and the Magpies lost seven of their first eight games in 2004, putting the club on the back foot throughout the season.

Coach Mick Malthouse was certain that the August 2004 move to the facility – originally named the Lexus Centre – would provide the club's players with advantages in the future. 'I have no doubt that in the long term the shift will be fantastic for Collingwood,' he said. 'Victoria Park is full of history and fond memories, and from a purely nostalgic viewpoint, many will miss the old battle-ground. But the new digs are magnificent, and a tribute to president Eddie McGuire.'

The new facilities, just a couple of torpedo punts from the MCG, included an indoor training space, a 25-metre four-lane pool, plunge and ice pools, a world-class gymnasium, a running track, a theatre and recreation lounge. The launch of the Lexus Centre took place in late July. Tickets to the event took the form of passports, a sign that the new facility was almost a world away from what the players and the club had been used to.

Nathan Buckley was impressed. 'When I first walked into Vic Park late in 1993 it definitely was not the most up-to-date venue,' he said. 'But I was struck by the sense of tradition that oozed out of every corner. Victoria Park was home, but [we] are seeing the next era of the club.

'Yes, the facilities are state-of-the-art. Yes, they at least match those of any other professional organisations in the land, and yes, they will provide [us with] the opportunity to gain a preparatory edge on the opposition. But the heart of a club lies in its supporters, not in its location. Victoria Park memories will not be forgotten. As a team we look to move forward and create our own history at the new venue, [which will be] a successful one if we are prepared to pay the price.'

In 2004 the price was too high. The Magpies finished 13th, but they had a new home, and at least Port Adelaide had stopped Brisbane's quest for four consecutive flags. And there was now a belief that the new venue would help the Pies in their own pursuit of Premierships.

H&A P22, W8, L14 • **Finished** 13th • **Captain** Nathan Buckley •
Coach Mick Malthouse • **Leading goalkicker** Chris Tarrant (36) •
Copeland Trophy James Clement

2005

TWO LIKELY LADS

There wasn't a lot to cheer about in Collingwood's 2005 season. But as bleak as some of the times were, and as frustrating as the injury toll and inconsistent form was, there was at least a silver lining delivered at the end of the year. It came in the form of two teenagers from country Victoria who would go on to play significant roles in Collingwood's quest for Premiership success.

Just as the Magpies had in 2004, the club lost seven of its first eight games in 2005, and other than a string of three consecutive wins during the middle of the season, it was a very forgettable year. The more the season wore on, the less competitive Collingwood became, as the club was forced to put many of its best players in for surgery well before the end of the season. Eight successive losses closed out the season as the club finished second-last to Carlton, with only five wins across 22 games.

But what this meant was that Collingwood was armed with two picks in the top five of the 2005 National Draft. The club leaders were determined to ensure that the choices they made with picks two and five would help set the club up for a successful future. President Eddie McGuire call 2005 draft day 'a bit like Christmas', and the wish list came out exactly how the club had hoped.

Collingwood overlooked highly rated youngster Xavier Ellis for his Gippsland Power teammate, Drouin's Dale Thomas at pick two. 'We just decided that Thomas fitted our requirements a little better,' McGuire said of the 18-year-old.

And with pick five, the Magpies were just as excited to get their hands on a 17-year-old from Sale who had walked out on a two-year basketball scholarship at Canberra's Australian Institute of Sport to chase an AFL career. His name was Scott Pendlebury. The young midfielder was undoubtedly being modest when he said, 'I was expecting to go between 15 and 30 probably, and then to be called out five was a big thrill.'

Collingwood also selected Danny Stanley (pick 21), Ryan Cook (23) and Jack Anthony (37) in the draft, but the focus was on Thomas and Pendlebury, who it was hoped would become cornerstones of the club in the future.

'We needed some midfield brilliance and some strength, and we've been able to get all of that,' McGuire said. 'We've got a good bunch of kids now. We're very keen that we'll have a good season next year.'

Coach Mick Malthouse admitted on draft day that it had been a significant one for the club. But he also insisted he would not rush Thomas or Pendlebury in 2006, if they were not ready. Both of them were. Thomas was in the team for Round 1, and played 16 games in his debut year. Pendlebury overcame a pre-season interrupted by glandular fever to make his debut in Round 10, and represented the club in nine games across the remainder of 2006.

Within four years, the two young stars were a key part of Collingwood's push for a Premiership. Not long after that, Pendlebury would become a leader of the club.

H&A P22, W5, L17 • **Finished** 15th • **Captain** Nathan Buckley • **Coach** Mick Malthouse • **Leading goalkicker** Chris Tarrant (36) • **Copeland Trophy** James Clement

---

2006
THE FAILED MEDICAL

Collingwood's 2006 season had only been over for a month when the club made a pitch to one of the competition's most exciting but as yet unfulfilled players, Geelong's Steve Johnson.

The Magpies had made the finals for the first time since 2003, only to fall short against the Western Bulldogs in an elimination final. Not much went right on the day, from the moment that Brodie Holland cannoned into Brett Montgomery, an incident that would cost him the first six weeks of the 2007 season. The final margin ended up being 41 points, and the club knew change was required if it wanted to progress further next year.

Johnson was 23, and attainable. The Cats knew how mercurial he was, but was prepared to put him on the trade table for the right offer, given the concerns it had over both his body and a few off-field misdemeanours. Collingwood and Essendon led the race for his services in a frantic trade period, in which the Magpies were also trying to find a new home for All-Australian forward Chris Tarrant, who needed a fresh start elsewhere.

The Magpies were prepared to give up pick 28, and possibly more, to secure Johnson, who had grown up as a Magpies supporter and whose style bore some similarities to that of his childhood hero, Peter Daicos. Then, just as Pies fans were warming to the idea of seeing the highly skilled forward in black and white, the club pulled out of the potential trade without providing a reason for its decision.

The Cats were convinced that a medical report on both Johnson's ankles and one of his knees had not been 'flattering', and that this was the reason the Magpies turned their back on a deal to secure him.

Collingwood switched its attention to another forward opportunist in Fremantle's Paul Medhurst, and the club was finally able to secure a trade: Tarrant would head to the Dockers in exchange for Medhurst and pick eight in the National Draft. The Magpies would use that selection on a young defender, Ben Reid, who in time would play a significant role in the club's success.

The question marks on Johnson's durability meant other suitors, such as Essendon and Port Adelaide, also lost interest in him. He had not played more than 15 games in a season to that stage. So he remained with the Cats – and the rest is history.

In the years ahead, Johnson would dispel any doubts about the state of his ankles and knees, or about his character off the field. And he would take particular relish in playing Collingwood, especially in finals. One of those games would come the following year in a preliminary final, just a week before he won a Norm Smith Medal.

Then, in 2011, Johnson overcame a knee injury to take on the Magpies in the Grand Final. He kicked four goals for the game, including the crucial first major of the final term, which helped set the scene for Geelong's runaway 38-point win. Johnson's performance left some wondering just how different it could have been had he not been there, or better still been in black and white.

Tarrant, too, would take part in that 2011 Premiership playoff, after a return to the club where he truly belonged.

H&A P22, W14, L8 • **Finished** 5th • **Finals** P1, L1 • **Finished** 7th • **Captain** Nathan Buckley • **Coach** Mick Malthouse • **Leading goalkicker** Anthony Rocca (55) • **Copeland Trophy** Alan Didak

2007

EXTRA TIME

Collingwood's exciting 2007 season appeared to be over. It was the middle stages of the third quarter of the semi-final clash with West Coast at Subiaco, and the home side was out to a near four-goal lead. The Magpies had been brave, but the reigning premier looked set to record a big win.

However, the team that Collingwood had progressively been building not only had talent and class; it was building a resilience that it could call upon when times were tough. The Pies staged a stirring comeback against the Eagles, and when Alan Didak regained the lead midway through the last quarter, this semi-final became a war of attrition that neither team was prepared to concede.

West Coast wrested the lead back, but with less than four minutes left, Paul Medhurst found a loose Dale Thomas, and the young Magpie in his second season kicked truly. Two West Coast behinds followed, and scores were level. Both teams slugged it out for the pulsating final 103 seconds before the final siren sounded and Dennis Cometti announced: 'We're going to overtime.' For only the second time in AFL history, extra time would decide a final.

After a stunning 10-minute period – each side had five minutes kicking to either end – Collingwood's courageous and almost improbable run in the finals rolled on. Extra-time goals to Chris Bryan, Dane Swan and Scott Pendlebury had given the Magpies a clear advantage, and so the club advanced to a preliminary final against Geelong.

Coach Mick Malthouse declared: 'I look at [this] group and think the sky's the limit. I'm not saying they will go out there and walk over Geelong because that won't happen, [but] we'll go out there and give a good account of ourselves.'

The belief in the group was strong. It had been the product of several seasons of hard work, good drafting and a mindset that this team was on a journey towards somewhere special. A bonus was that Nathan Buckley got through a fourth successive game with his troublesome hamstring still intact.

Didak best summed up the club's mentality after the game. 'We came over as underdogs,' he said. 'No one gave us a chance and we got up and won.'

A week later, the Magpies again went in as underdogs, this time against Geelong, but the belief in the group never wavered. In a close encounter, the Cats opened up a three-goal lead during the final quarter, before the Magpies conjured one last big effort. And when Medhurst cut the deficit back to less than a goal in the dying moments, Collingwood still looked a chance. But with the Magpies in attack, the final siren sounded, leaving them five points short.

Buckley had finished the game – his 280th and last AFL match – on the bench with another hamstring injury. He couldn't have played, had the Magpies made the Grand Final.

Geelong won its first Premiership in 44 years the following week, by a record margin. But as disappointed as the Magpies were, they had few regrets. They had given their all, and the spirit within the group made them feel their flag dream was closer than ever.

H&A P22, W13, L9 • **Finished** 6th • **Finals** P3, W2, L1 • **Finished** 4th • **Captain** Nathan Buckley • **Coach** Mick Malthouse • **Leading goalkicker** Anthony Rocca (54) • **Copeland Trophy** Travis Cloke

---

2008

BANS FOR SHAW AND DIDAK

Collingwood had something of a tradition of losing key players for finals campaigns, but nothing quite like what happened late in the 2008 season.

In the club's long history, stars such as Gordon Coventry, Harry Collier, Phil Carman and Anthony Rocca had all been suspended by the tribunal for on-field incidents and missed key games. But an off-field incident, and what took place after it, cost two Magpies players the chance to play in the last four games of the 2008 home-and-away season – and in the finals. This time, it was the club itself that imposed the penalty.

The players, Heath Shaw and Alan Didak, had been drinking at a hotel two days after the team's Round 18 loss to Hawthorn. The night turned messy when Shaw crashed his ute into two parked cars on the way home, and it got worse when he registered 0.144 upon being breath-tested.

In an effort to protect Didak, who had previously been in trouble with the club, Shaw told Collingwood president Eddie McGuire and chief executive Gary Pert that a mate had been with him in the car, rather than Didak. The club took Shaw at his word, and he stood by his account through an awkward press conference. But when several eyewitnesses came forward to insist they had seen Didak in the car, a serious drink-driving charge had generated a separate issue: Shaw had lied to protect Didak, but in doing so had broken the trust the football club had put in him.

At another hastily arranged press conference, Pert spoke to the media. 'When you have two of your key players looking the president, the coach and their own teammates in the eye and actually lying to them, it really destroys the essence of the club,' he said. 'It was decided by the leadership group that these two players actually don't deserve to wear the Collingwood jumper, and that's why they're not playing for the rest of the season.'

Without Shaw and Didak, the Magpies took on St Kilda the following week, and surprised everyone by coming away with a morale-boosting win. But no one truly believed that the team could win the flag without one of its best rebounding defenders and one of its most important forward-midfielders.

Collingwood finished the home-and-away season in eighth place, and had the tough task of taking on Adelaide at AAMI Stadium in the first week of the finals. But the Magpies produced a stunning victory, overcoming a four-goal deficit in the second quarter to triumph by 31 points, in what cheersquad leader 'Joffa' Corfe called 'one of the most famous victories of the Collingwood Football Club when you consider everything it's been through in the last few months'.

Club great Peter Daicos said the club should reconsider the season-ending bans for Shaw and Didak, saying: 'These players may not ever get a chance to play in a preliminary final or a Grand Final again.' But Collingwood stood firm, saying that preserving the club's culture was the most important thing.

The Pies' finals run came to an end a week later against St Kilda, with a 24-point semi-final loss, as Shaw and Didak watched haplessly from the stands.

H&A P22, W12, L10 • **Finished** 8th • **Finals** P2, W1, L1 • **Finished** 6th • **Captain** Scott Burns • **Coach** Mick Malthouse • **Leading goalkicker** Paul Medhurst (50) • **Copeland Trophy** Dane Swan

---

2009
THE COACHING SUCCESSION

It's fair to say no off-field moment in the modern history of the Collingwood Football Club has had as much impact as the coaching succession plan devised and agreed to during the 2009 season.

Mick Malthouse was in his 10th season coaching the club. For all that he had done in shaping the direction of the club, he was – at that stage – yet to add to the two Premierships he had won as coach of West Coast. Nathan Buckley, the club's most famous player of the modern age, was courting coaching offers from rival clubs, having spent two seasons coaching with the AIS–AFL Academy. The club was in a dilemma. It still wanted Malthouse, at least for the time being, and yet it could ill afford to lose one of its favourite sons. President Eddie McGuire began to hatch a plan.

McGuire and chief executive Gary Pert worked with Malthouse and Buckley to see if there was any common ground, and if the club could have its cake and eat it too. The deal that followed was finalised at a Saturday morning meeting between the parties at McGuire's Jolimont offices, over toasted sandwiches and fruit washed down by coffee and tea.

The unprecedented coaching arrangement for the future – which the *Herald Sun* called 'the Deal of the Century' – was announced in July 2009, as the club was chasing another finals berth. At the press conference Malthouse looked a little ill-at-ease, but he had signed off on the plan whereby he would continue to coach Collingwood for 2010 and 2011, before becoming 'director of coaching'. Buckley was to operate as one of Malthouse's assistant coaches, before assuming the senior role in 2012.

McGuire was confident he had been able to achieve what many thought was impossible, given the ambition of both the incumbent senior coach and the man about to launch his own coaching career. The president said it was only at that breakfast meeting that he was sure what the club had planned could actually be delivered.

'Going in, I was very confident,' McGuire said, 'but to use my analogy, everyone was at the altar and the priest says, "If there is anybody here with anything to say, say it now or forever hold your peace." We were there, and we all knew that if there were any reservations whatsoever, then this would end the "I said, you said, he said, I thought" ... Everyone spoke openly and at the end of it, we all walked away with big smiles and everyone shaking hands.'

Collingwood put the coaching transition to one side for the rest of that 2009 season, and the Magpies finished fourth on the ladder. The club's season looked over when St Kilda proved too strong in the qualifying final, and when Adelaide led by six goals to one at quarter-time of the semi-final. The Crows were up by 26 points at half-time in the semi-final, but somehow the Magpies turned the game around. Down by a point with a minute to play, the Pies got the ball into the arms of young forward Jack Anthony. He held his nerve, kicked truly and kept his club's season alive. But the opposition was too strong in the preliminary final, as Collingwood went down to the eventual premier, Geelong, by 73 points.

The coaching succession plan was ready to be enacted. And 2010 loomed as a real chance for this team to make a name for itself.

H&A P22, W15, L7 • **Finished** 4th • **Finals** P3, W1, L2 • **Finished** 4th • **Captain** Nick Maxwell • **Coach** Mick Malthouse • **Leading goalkicker** Jack Anthony (50) • **Copeland Trophy** Dane Swan

---

2010
SMOTHER OF THE MILLENNIUM

It was a moment forever etched in Grand Final history, an act of desperation against the odds that provided the spark of inspiration for Collingwood's 15th VFL/AFL Premiership.

Twenty minutes into the 2010 Grand Final replay, St Kilda captain Nick Riewoldt strolled in and seemed certain to kick his team's first goal. However, as he went to take his kick from point-blank range, a presence in black and white came from nowhere. It was Collingwood defender Heath Shaw, and his sprint from outside the goal square ended in a full-length dive, and he knocked the ball away from Riewoldt's boot.

'I thought, "You don't die wondering. I might as well have a crack at it,"' Shaw recalled.

His desperate lunge was one of the lasting images of the game. What is not recalled as frequently is the fact that Shaw's kick-in after the rushed behind resulted in a passage of play that ended with Brent Macaffer kicking a goal at the other end, helping Collingwood to a three-goal lead at quarter-time. The Magpies never looked back from that Shaw moment – which the player later called 'the smother of the millennium' – and went on to win the flag by 56 points.

In many ways, Shaw's act of sacrifice summed up Collingwood's 2010 Premiership. Collingwood had recruited Darren Jolly and Luke Ball at the start of that season, and each played an important role in the club's success. The Magpies played a brand of football that coach Mick Malthouse devised from his knowledge of the Second World War, using a box setup (a zone or press situation) as well as a swarming frontal assault.

'We built the box and it is very hard to penetrate,' Malthouse said. 'That box can get smaller, but there is always someone to step up. [Field Marshall Erwin] Rommel's front-on assault was a methodology without superior numbers, but hit the opponent front-on.'

The Magpies went into the first Grand Final as clear favourites, but a dominant yet wasteful opening half wasn't enough. St Kilda turned around a four-goal half-time deficit and threatened to score an upset victory.

That theme of sacrifice had been personified by Collingwood captain Nick Maxwell in the Grand Final draw. His full-stretch dive to stop a goal from Nick Riewoldt in the frantic last term was followed by an inspirational mark, which halted a Saints' charge forward and sent the ball into the Magpies' forward line.

When Travis Cloke regained the lead for Collingwood after a smart handball from Chris Dawes, it seemed the Magpies might hold on. But a long kick from Lenny Hayes loomed for Stephen Milne, who had a break on Ben Johnson. Milne could not grasp it, though, and the ball bounced at a right angle and trickled through for a behind, tying the scores. Soon after, the final siren sounded on the third drawn Grand Final in VFL/AFL history.

Malthouse told his players they were only at half-time, with four more quarters of the Grand Final to play. And the following week, thanks to Shaw's desperate dive, and the commitment of all 22 players, Collingwood produced the perfect team performance in which individuality was shunned for egalitarianism.

The Magpies won that flag, quite literally, 'side by side'.

H&A P22, W17, L4, D1 • **Finished** 1st • **Finals** P4, W3, D1 • **Finished** Premier • **Captain** Nick Maxwell • **Coach** Mick Malthouse • **Leading goalkicker** Alan Didak (41) • **Copeland Trophy** Dane Swan

---

2011
THE MALTHOUSE INTERVIEW

By most measures, the 2011 season should be considered one of Collingwood's most successful. The club won 22 of its 25 games. Dane Swan won the Brownlow Medal. Six Magpies were named as All-Australians (Ben Reid, Leon Davis, Dale Thomas, Travis Cloke, Scott Pendlebury and Swan). Andrew Krakouer – given an AFL lifeline by the club – won the Mark of the Year. The Magpies won the NAB Challenge and were the home-and-away season's minor premier.

Collingwood won its first six games of the year by an average of 56 points, only to lose to Geelong in Round 7 after a Scott Pendlebury goal was disallowed. Some believed the flag was the Pies' for the taking. But there were a number of hurdles within and outside the club that tested it thoroughly.

Geelong loomed as a serious threat, twice beating the Magpies in the home-and-away season, including a 96-point thrashing in the final round. Heath Shaw was suspended for eight weeks and fined $20,000 for placing a $10 bet on Nick Maxwell to kick the first goal of Collingwood's Round 9 clash with Adelaide, as he knew the captain would start the match in attack. Maxwell, too, was fined $10,000 (with half of it suspended) after telling his family he might be starting forward. The Magpies also had a narrow escape in their preliminary final, against Hawthorn, and Mick Malthouse let his emotions flow in the coaches' box at the end of the game.

However, the most contentious moment of 2011 came months earlier – on a Thursday night in mid-July – when Malthouse gave a controversial interview on *The Footy Show*, which highlighted clear divisions within the club. Malthouse revealed he was no certainty to take on the director of coaching role in 2012, when Nathan Buckley was due to become the senior coach.

'I can't categorically say [I'll stay],' Malthouse told the live television audience. 'I don't want to be at a football club where I'm going to be paid well to do a job that is insignificant and doesn't help the club going forward.' He admitted several players had questioned him about his intentions. 'Nathan is going to coach next year – do they accept it? I don't know if they accept it, but they accept the fact that Nathan will be coaching next year.'

During his explosive *Footy Show* interview, Malthouse also alluded to the fact that he had only agreed to the succession plan in 2009 because he was at a low ebb personally, due to health issues in his family. Club officials did the best they could to put out the flames that the interview fuelled.

Somehow, the Collingwood players maintained their form and focus, booking a Grand Final meeting with Geelong. They wanted to send Malthouse out with another Premiership, and for a time that looked likely. The Magpies led by three goals at the eight-minute mark of the second term. Halfway through the third term, they were still clinging on to a five-point lead.

An injury to James Podsiadly changed the structure of Geelong's attack, but it seemed to be a positive for the Cats, who took control of the game. In the end, Geelong proved too strong, kicking five goals to nil in the final term to win by 38 points.

Malthouse announced after the game that he would be leaving Collingwood. The Nathan Buckley era was about to start.

H&A P22, W20, L2 • **Finished 1st** • **Finals** P3, W2, L1 • **Finished 2nd** • **Captain** Nick Maxwell • **Coach** Mick Malthouse • **Leading goalkicker** Travis Cloke (69) • **Copeland Trophy** Scott Pendlebury

---

2012
BUCKS TAKES OVER

Nathan Buckley went into AFL coaching knowing the role would be tough, though he could hardly have envisaged just how challenging his debut season would be. The fact that Collingwood performed so well when confronted by considerable hurdles was a credit to the group, and to the coach. For the most part, the Magpies were able to respond to these challenges, and the team competed in the penultimate weekend of the season after one of the most trying weeks of many players' lives.

Buckley changed the coaching structure after replacing Mick Malthouse, but in his first extended interview he baulked at making too many changes too quickly. 'It's an honour,' he said, 'and I understand and appreciate the great responsibility that comes with it. I feel a duty to the club and the people within it to make sure I do my very best to continue what's been put in place in recent times and also way back when.'

Two losses came in the team's first three games, before a 10-game winning streak put them into contention again. But injuries were a constant concern. Four players – Andrew Krakouer, Brent Macaffer, Luke Ball and Lachlan Keeffe – had to have knee reconstructions, while a number of other players also lost considerable time to injury.

There was conjecture about Travis Cloke's contract standoff too. That wouldn't be resolved until Collingwood's season was over, with debate following as to whether it had been a distraction. And a two-week suspension to Nick Maxwell from the qualifying final loss to Hawthorn cost him a spot in a semi-final against West

Coast, which the club won, and in the preliminary final against Sydney at ANZ Stadium.

The most telling blow to Collingwood's flag hopes, however, came with the shock death of former Magpie John McCarthy, who was tragically killed while on an end-of-season trip to Las Vegas. For the Magpies who had played with McCarthy – he had been an emergency in the 2010 Grand Final team – it was devastating news. McCarthy's funeral took place the day before Collingwood's game against the Swans, and the Magpies had to endure the emotional experience before rushing to Sydney to prepare for the game.

The Swans established a lead early, which they refused to relinquish. The differences at the breaks were 20, 27 and 30 points, but Collingwood kept fighting through the adversity. Eventually, the Magpies went down by 26 points, their season over, with the Swans advancing to a Grand Final they would win a week later. Given the emotional rollercoaster Buckley's Magpies had been on, a six-day break and a welter of injuries, it had been a brave performance.

When asked if McCarthy's loss had cost the Magpies any hope of victory, Buckley said, 'No idea. What I do know is when you ask our group for something, they give everything they have got. There are always going to be thunderbolts that come at you in a season, and I thought, for the most part, that we stood up as a group united and were able to face those, in particular the last couple of weeks.

'I have got great pride in the club, [and] great pride in the playing group and the leaders within it. I have no doubt we can achieve great things in the future because of that.'

H&A P22, W16, L6 • **Finished** 4th • **Finals** P3, W1, L2 • **Finished** 4th • **Captain** Nick Maxwell • **Coach** Nathan Buckley • **Leading goalkicker** Travis Cloke (59) • **Copeland Trophy** Dayne Beams

---

A TIPPING POINT

In the week leading up to Collingwood's elimination final against Port Adelaide, defender Heath Shaw admitted that his passion for the club sometimes pushed him to the edge. His words were prophetic.

Two Shaw brain-fades in the second quarter – one of which cost the team a vital goal, and another that could have – hurt the Magpies. The incidents would have an impact on Shaw's career in the black and white, and would come to be seen as the moments in which Collingwood realised it needed to regenerate its playing list for the future.

The Magpies had been in contention throughout 2013, but seemed to lack the consistency required of a serious Premiership challenger. Nathan Buckley's team had been in the top eight for 22 of the 23 rounds. Yet at no stage did the Magpies finish a week of the home-and-away season inside the top four. Losses in two of the last three games meant any hope of securing a double chance evaporated as the club ended the regular season in sixth spot, two games ahead of their elimination final opponent, Port Adelaide.

The Magpies went into that knockout final as favourites for the MCG clash, but never appeared as united or committed as the Power. Early in the second term, Travis Boak kicked a goal to push his team out by 12 points. Immediately after, and in the same goal square in which Shaw had famously run down Nick Riewoldt in the 2010 Grand Final replay, the Collingwood defender grappled with Angus Monfries. It resulted in a free kick to Monfries and a double goal for Port Adelaide.

If that moment had infuriated the coach, another as the half-time siren sounded would have raised his blood to boiling point. Shaw had the ball and proceeded to push it towards Monfries' face in a fit of frustration. Luckily, he was given the benefit of the doubt by the umpires. In what would prove to be Shaw's last game as a Collingwood player, the Power outscored the Magpies in the second half to produce a finals shock, winning by 24 points.

In the after-match press conference, Nathan Buckley said change was needed to re-align the team, admitting that it had to look at a number of things, including its culture.

'The club has got to ask itself questions,' Buckley said. 'You've got to ask if we're making the right decisions in regard to culture and in regards to environment, personnel, game plan and coaching staff. If we have any person or anyone or have any thoughts at all that we need to cling on to what we've had, well, then, this is what lets that go, and you need to keep evolving. You need to keep getting better, you need to be hungry and hard on each other and be prepared to continually improve, whether you finish first or you finish last.'

That elimination final loss would be the tipping point for change. Heath Shaw was traded to Greater Western Sydney, with Collingwood acquiring midfielder Taylor Adams in return. Dale Thomas would accept a lucrative free agency offer to join Carlton – and his former coach Mick Malthouse. Ben Johnson retired, while Darren Jolly, Alan Didak and Andrew Krakouer were among a group of senior players not offered new contracts.

A change of direction for Collingwood was imminent.

H&A P22, W14, L8 • **Finished** 6th • **Finals** P1, L1 • **Finished** 8th • **Captain** Nick Maxwell • **Coach** Nathan Buckley • **Leading goalkicker** Travis Cloke (68) • **Copeland Trophy** Scott Pendlebury

---

2014
TRADING PLACES

Sometimes you've got to make the best of a difficult situation, and that's what Collingwood was forced to do following a disappointing 2014 season. Through the first half of the season the Magpies looked certain to play finals football. They appeared entrenched in the top four after a Round 12 win over Melbourne, but a poor second half of the season saw the club miss the finals for the first time since 2005.

Compounding the frustration, one of the Magpies' most important players, Dayne Beams, revealed he wanted to return to his home state of Queensland to be closer to his ill father. It was a bitter blow, particularly as Beams, at just 24, had already won a Premiership (2010), a Copeland Trophy (2012) and All-Australian honours (2012).

Understandably, the Magpies demanded a fair and equitable trade from the Brisbane Lions; if that wasn't possible, they would insist that Beams – still a contracted player, and a very much required one – remain in black and white. 'We understand Dayne wants to go, but it's not a fire sale for us,' the club's then football manager, Rodney Eade, declared. 'We are more than happy for Dayne to stay, as the coach is.'

But Beams refused to attend the Copeland Trophy award night to accept his third placing in the best-and-fairest award, and a trade standoff loomed. Nathan Buckley gave a rousing speech at the best-and-fairest count, and it was clear that the Beams situation was in his mind. 'Premierships sit at the top of our ambitions,' the coach said. 'Every decision the club makes, it makes with that end in mind. The last eight games of the year left a pretty bad taste in everyone's mouth. Be prepared to stay the course with us.'

The Pies gave a deadline to the Lions, but it passed without resolution. The standoff centred on the fact that Collingwood wanted a player as well as draft picks in return for Beams, but all the names the club put forward – James Aish, Sam Mayes, Jack Redden, Pearce Hanley and Dayne Zorko – were swiftly dismissed. Then, at the eleventh hour, a little-known Lion and former midfielder for the Murray Bushrangers, Jack Crisp, loomed as a possible solution – or, as some suggested, the 'steak knives' – to clinch the Beams trade.

After much discussion and debate, the Magpies were finally able to set up a suitable arrangement. One trade saw the club relinquish Heritier Lumumba for Geelong's Travis Varcoe, with former Demon Mitch Clark heading to the Cats. And in a separate deal, Beams was traded to the Lions in return for picks five and 25, as well as Crisp. Collingwood then gave up pick 25 for North Melbourne inside midfielder Levi Greenwood, before claiming the highly promising Jordan De Goey with pick five in the National Draft.

Buckley and Collingwood had stood their ground and waited for the right deal to present itself. And the coach was confident that deal had added to the club's playing stocks. 'I am very happy with how we have come out of it,' he said.

By the end of the next season, Crisp had relinquished the 'steak knives' tag and had finished third in the 2015 Copeland Trophy count – the same placing that Beams had managed 12 months earlier.

H&A P22, W11, L11 • **Finished** 11th • **Captain** Scott Pendlebury •
Coach Nathan Buckley • **Leading goalkicker** Travis Cloke (39) •
Copeland Trophy Scott Pendlebury

2015

SPOILING MICK'S PARTY

When Mick Malthouse left Collingwood after the 2011 Grand Final loss, following 12 seasons at the helm, he insisted he couldn't coach against his 'boys'. All of that changed when Malthouse was coaxed out of retirement at the end of the 2012 season, when he signed on to coach Carlton after a year out of the game.

The Blues, and Malthouse, took on the Magpies twice in 2013, and twice again in 2014, with all four matches ending in Collingwood victories. But the circumstances surrounding the Friday night clash between Malthouse and the Magpies in Round 5 of 2015 drew both extraordinary media attention and a big MCG crowd. On that night, Malthouse coached for the 715th time, breaking the long-standing record of legendary Collingwood mentor Jock McHale. For several reasons, then, it seemed fitting that the Magpies were involved.

Malthouse had earlier been asked which team he wanted to play against in his milestone game, and his immediate answer was Collingwood. It was the team he had barracked for as a kid and coached to the 2010 flag.

There had of course been animosity between the two parties over the circumstances of Malthouse's departure from the Magpies, but now president Eddie McGuire attempted to thaw out the frosty relationship. Malthouse attended the pre-game president's function, and McGuire sought him out, making a presentation to the man he had recruited to Collingwood in late 1999. The pair shook hands, and then got on with business.

'I sincerely hope that when Mick's time is finished at Carlton, he comes back to Collingwood and enjoys the legacy that exists because of his skill and hard work,' McGuire said.

Once the formalities were over – which included a special public tribute to Malthouse before the game – the Magpies set about spoiling what was supposed to be a big occasion for the Navy Blue. Four goals to one came in the first term, and by half-time the difference was out to 42 points. All hope for Carlton was extinguished by that stage, and Malthouse's big night had turned into a nightmare.

While the man himself deserved all the accolades, the team he was coaching showed little of the commitment and determination he had instilled into so many sides over the years. The game ended in a 75-point victory to Collingwood, the club's biggest win in what would otherwise prove a frustrating year.

Nathan Buckley praised Malthouse, saying he believed the record benchmark would never be broken. 'I can't see that happening,' he told the press. 'You know, the game's changed so much, I can't see anyone coaching for 30 years. He's been a survivor for a long time, Mick, and I think it is due credit to him that he's received all of those accolades during the week.'

The Pies' win that night would be one of only 10 for the season, as injuries and inconsistent form saw the club fall to 12th. But the Blues fared even worse, on their way to a wooden spoon. Less than a month after Collingwood turned party-poopers on Mick's milestone night, the new coaching games record holder would be sacked, his days as a league coach finally over.

H&A P22, W10, L12 • **Finished** 12th • **Captain** Scott Pendlebury • **Coach** Nathan Buckley • **Leading goalkicker** Jamie Elliott (35) • **Copeland Trophy** Scott Pendlebury

---

2016
A LANDMARK WOMEN'S TEAM

Collingwood has always been at the vanguard of innovation in Australian football, stretching right back to the club's earliest days in the 1890s. So it's both fitting and appropriate that in 2017, the year the Magpies will celebrate their 125th anniversary, they will also celebrate the arrival of a new Collingwood: the Collingwood women's team.

Women have always played a significant role in the success of the Collingwood Football Club, and now they'll take their place on the field in what is one of the AFL's most exciting ventures.

Collingwood confirmed early in 2016 that it would apply for one of the eight available licences to take part in the inaugural year of the AFL women's competition. Soon after, it employed the highly regarded footballer Meg Hutchins to the role of Women's Football Operations Manager, and she set to work growing the game both at Collingwood and at the grassroots level.

Good news came on 15 June 2016, when the AFL announced that Collingwood had been granted a licence to form a women's team for the 2017 competition, along with Carlton, Melbourne, the Western Bulldogs, Fremantle, Brisbane, Greater Western Sydney and Adelaide. The club's $25-million state-of-the-art facilities at The Glasshouse and the Olympic Park Oval in the sporting hub of Melbourne had clearly played a big part in the decision. But the AFL also knew that the game's most popular club simply had to be part of the new league.

Club president Eddie McGuire declared it 'a great day for our football club. It's everything that we want. We want young boys and young girls to dream of wearing the black-and-white stripes on the MCG, and from this day on, they can.'

Chief executive Gary Pert said the club had a vision of providing opportunity for both men and women to reach the pinnacle in their sport. 'Collingwood members will look back on this historic day as the day Collingwood evolved into a modern sporting club that is diverse and inclusive for the entire community,' he said.

The news that Collingwood would be fielding a women's team in 2017, as well as having its own netball team, was one of the positives from what was, overall, a disappointing year.

The season had kicked off amid much optimism following an encouraging pre-season program, but that optimism was dampened in the first minutes of the first game, when Dane Swan went down with a foot injury so severe that it not only ruled him out for the year but also ultimately forced him into retirement. It was a heartbreakingly unjust way for such a champion to leave the game.

That calamitous start set the scene for much of what was to follow, with yet another horrendous run of injuries blighting the team's chances throughout the season. But gun recruit Adam Treloar showed he was worth whatever the club had paid to bring him in, and US convert Mason Cox provided the highlight of the year with his first-kick-first-goal routine on debut in the Anzac Day match against Essendon.

Almost as soon as the season finished, eyes were being cast towards 2017. Hope, as always, springs eternal. It's what supporters have done at the end of every season since 1892. And they'll be doing it for the next 125 years too.

H&A P22, W9, L13 • **Finished** 12th • **Captain** Scott Pendlebury • **Coach** Nathan Buckley • **Leading goalkicker** Alex Fasolo (25) • **Copeland Trophy** Scott Pendlebury

---

ACKNOWLEDGEMENTS

We would like to thank our publisher, Black Inc., for embracing the concept of this book and making it come to life. Thanks to all the team there, but especially to Caitlin Yates and Julian Welch, who have been a delight to work with.

A big thank you to Chris Kearon, Margie Amarfio, Gary Pert, Steve Rielly and the rest of the gang at the Collingwood Football Club for allowing us – and this book – to be a part of the club's 125th anniversary celebrations. Following the Magpies is never dull, something that's been reinforced to us time and again since we started supporting them as young kids. The club is a big part of our lives, and while we hope that the next wave of success is just around the corner, we'll be there for the ride however long it takes and whatever happens along the way.

And finally, a massive thank you to our wives, Belinda and Christine, who provide so much love and support through all our projects, and to our children: Isabel, Will, Lachlan, Elise and Charlotte. Thanks for putting up with us, especially during those times when our focus is elsewhere. We couldn't have done it without you.

Michael Roberts &
Glenn McFarlane

MICHAEL ROBERTS is a journalist and author who has written or edited more than a dozen books, most on Australian football. He is the official historian for the Collingwood Football Club, president of the Australian Football Heritage Group and co-owner of media and content company Media Giants. He always wanted to play for the Magpies but strict VFL zoning rules and a lack of talent made it impossible. He still has his childhood Collingwood jumper and autographed copy of Peter McKenna's *My World of Football*. Michael's wife, Belinda, is also a Magpie, and they're still hoping to convert their children, Isabel and Will.

GLENN McFARLANE has long been a passionate fan of the Magpies, having been 'brainwashed' by his mother at an early age. Glenn represented Collingwood in underage football and cricket teams, but his passion was always sports journalism. The Magpies won the flag in his first year of covering football in 1990. He was sports editor of the *Sunday Herald Sun* for 11 years and is now a senior sports reporter for the *Herald Sun*. Glenn is married to Christine and has three children, Lachlan, Elise and Charlotte.

Lightning Source UK Ltd.
Milton Keynes UK
UKHW021135020119
334642UK00001B/32/P

9 781863 958905